Spark GraphX
in Action

MICHAEL S. MALAK
ROBIN EAST

MANNING
SHELTER ISLAND

For online information and ordering of this and other Manning books, please visit www.manning.com. The publisher offers discounts on this book when ordered in quantity. For more information, please contact

> Special Sales Department
> Manning Publications Co.
> 20 Baldwin Road
> PO Box 761
> Shelter Island, NY 11964
> Email: orders@manning.com

Manning Publications Co.
20 Baldwin Road
PO Box 761
Shelter Island, NY 11964

Development editor:	Marina Michaels
Technical development editors:	Michael Roberts and John Guthrie
Copyeditor:	Corbin Collins
Proofreader:	Melody Dolab
Technical proofreader:	Antonio Magnaghi
Typesetter:	Dottie Marsico
Cover designer:	Marija Tudor

ISBN 9781617292521
Printed in the United States of America
1 2 3 4 5 6 7 8 9 10 – EBM – 21 20 19 18 17 16

brief contents

contents

preface

What can graphs—the things with edges and vertices, not the things with axes and tick marks—do and how can they be used with Spark? These are the questions we try to answer in this book.

Frequently it is said, "Graphs can do anything," or at least, "There are a bunch of different things you can do with graphs." That says nothing, of course, so in this book we show a number of specific, real-life ways you can apply graphs and talk about how to implement such solutions in Spark GraphX.

A lot of technology buzzwords are applicable to this book: Big Data, Hadoop, Spark, graphs, machine learning, Scala, and functional programming. We break it all down for you. Even though we end up in some fairly advanced areas, we don't assume anything more than an ability to program in some language such as Java.

This chart from Google Trends shows the relative interest in these buzzwords through early 2016:

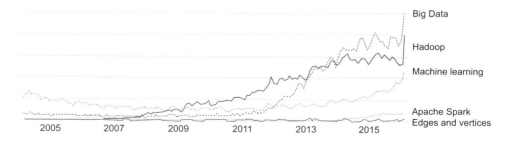

Note that for the generic terms *spark* and *graphs* we had to substitute the overly specific *Apache Spark* and *edges and vertices,* but the trends can still be seen. A couple of these technologies, machine learning and graphs, have long histories within academic computer science and are attracting new interest in the commercial realm as the availability of Big Data is now mainstreaming these technologies. If you studied these technologies in school as theory, the world is ready now for you to put them into practice.

A lot of companies, including the ones we work for and have worked for in the past, have put Spark—though not necessarily GraphX—into production. This makes it more than just a little convenient when embarking on prototyping graph solutions to try GraphX first. If you have a Spark cluster already, or if you decide to spin up a Spark cluster in the cloud, such as with Databricks or Amazon, you can get started with graphs without having to set up a new graph-specific cluster or technology, and you can use your Spark skills in the GraphX API. As more and more applications of graphs hit the newsstands—from rooting out terrorist networks on Twitter to fraud detection in credit card transaction data—GraphX becomes an easy platform choice for trying them out.

In this book, we simultaneously take on two ambitious goals: to cover everything possible about Spark GraphX, and to assume little to no expertise about any of the technologies represented by the aforementioned buzzwords. The biggest challenge was the hefty amount of prerequisites to get into GraphX—specifically, Spark, Scala, and graphs. Other challenges were the extensive GraphX API and the many different ways graphs can be used. The result is an *In Action* book that differs a bit from others: it takes a while to get started, with the first five chapters laying the groundwork, and there are a number of interesting examples rather than one that gradually gets built up over the course of the book. In books about other technologies the reader might come with a problem to solve; this book attempts to demystify graphs by showing precisely what problems graphs can solve. And it does so without assuming a lot of background knowledge and experience.

acknowledgments

We would like to acknowledge the many, many people at Manning Publications who helped usher this book into being. In particular, three individuals helped us immeasurably in transforming, and in many cases, redirecting our writing to produce the much better result you are reading now. Marina Michaels, our development editor from the beginning, tirelessly marked up our chapters with great technical questions despite being brand new to both Spark and graphs. Michael Roberts, our technical development editor for most of the process, was equally as profuse as Marina with his suggestions, but also brought technical expertise to the task. Antonio Magnaghi, our technical proofreader, went above and beyond by proofing not just the source code, but by effectively providing an extra technical development editor pass over the text of the whole book.

We would also like to thank the many reviewers who read early drafts of the book and provided helpful suggestions, including Andy Petrella, Brent Foust, Charles Feduke, Gaurav Bhardwaj, Jason Kolter, Justin Fister, Michael Bright, Paul-Michael Sorhaindo, Rodrigo Abreu, Romi Kuntsman, Sumit Pal, and Vincent Liard.

Michael Malak thanks his wife and children for their patience during the long months of preparing this manuscript.

Robin East thanks his wife Jane and their two boys. They put up with his strange writing hours and habit of disappearing upstairs at odd times.

about this book

With *Spark GraphX in Action* we hope to bring down to earth the sometimes esoteric topic of graphs, while explaining how to use them from the in-memory distributed computing framework that has gained the most mindshare, Apache Spark.

Who should read this book

We assume the reader has no previous knowledge of Spark, Scala, and graphs, but we move so quickly through the material that previous exposure to at least one of these would be helpful. We attempt to be particularly gentle with our use of Scala. We provide a brief introduction to Scala in chapter 3 and Scala tips throughout the book whenever a new Scala concept is introduced (these are listed in appendix D). In fact, we have recommended this book as a concise introduction to Scala, pointing to chapter 3, the Scala tips, and appendix D.

In addition, we completely avoid the mathematical proofs that are common in college courses in graph theory. Our focus is on graph algorithms and applications, and sometimes we pull in graph structure terminology as needed.

We target version Spark/GraphX 1.6 in this book.

The intended reader is someone who has a lot of development experience in some programming language such as Java, but graphs lend themselves so naturally to illustrations that non-developers will be able to glean ideas about what graphs can be used for.

How this book is organized

This book is divided into three parts. Part 1 consists of three chapters that cover the prerequisites to using Spark GraphX. The four chapters in part 2 cover standard and expected ways to use GraphX, and the three chapters in part 3 are on advanced topics.

We also could have divided the book into two parts, with the first five chapters covering the prerequisites and basic GraphX API, and the last five chapters covering ways to apply GraphX.

Here's a run-down of the ten chapters:

- Chapter 1 sets the stage with what Big Data, Spark, and graphs are, and how Spark GraphX fits into a processing data flow. Chapter 1 is a mini-book unto itself—not in length, but in its breadth of overview.
- Chapter 2 is a very brief, hands-on demonstration of using GraphX—no experience required.
- Chapter 3 covers the prerequisites of Spark, Scala, and graphs.
- Chapter 4 discusses how to do basic Spark GraphX operations and presents the two main methods of implementing custom GraphX algorithms: Map/Reduce and Pregel.
- Chapter 5 illustrates how to use the numerous algorithms built into GraphX.
- Chapter 6 is where something outside the API is finally covered. Here we take some of the classic mid-20th century graph algorithms and show how they can be implemented in GraphX.
- Chapter 7 is a lengthy and ambitious chapter on machine learning. Normally this would require a book unto itself, but here we cover machine learning without assuming any prior knowledge or experience and quickly ramp up to advanced examples of supervised, unsupervised, and semi-supervised learning.
- Chapter 8 shows how some operations can be done in GraphX that one might assume would come built into a graph-processing package: reading RDF files, merging graphs, finding graph isomorphisms, and computing the global clustering coefficient.
- Chapter 9 shows how to monitor performance and see what your GraphX application is doing. It then shows how to do performance tuning through techniques like caching, checkpointing, and serializer tuning.
- Chapter 10 describes how to use languages other than Scala with GraphX (but strongly advises against it) and also discusses how to use tools that complement GraphX. It demonstrates Apache Zeppelin notebook software with GraphX to provide visualization of graphs inline with an interactive notebook shell. The third-party tool Spark JobServer can be used to convert GraphX from a mere batch graph processing system to an online database of sorts. Finally,

GraphFrames is a library on GitHub (developed by some of the developers of GraphX) that uses Spark SQL DataFrames rather than RDDs to provide a convenient and high-performing way to query graphs.

We also include four appendixes in the book. Appendix A addresses installing Spark and appendix B gives a brief overview of Gephi visualization software. In appendix C you'll find a number of online resources for additional information about GraphX and where to go to keep up with latest developments. Finally, appendix D lists the Scala tips given throughout the book.

Anyone new to Spark, Scala, or graphs should progress through the first five chapters linearly. After that, you can pick and choose topics from the last five chapters.

Anyone who is expert in Spark, Scala, and graphs but new to GraphX can skip chapter 3 and probably also chapter 5.

About the code

The source code for this book is available for download from manning.com at https://www.manning.com/books/spark-graphx-in-action.

For the most part, the code presented in this book and available for download is intended to be used with the interactive Spark shell. Thus, the .scala extension is technically a misnomer, as these files can't be compiled with the scalac compiler.

Some examples are meant to be conventionally compiled and executed, and these are always accompanied by a pom.xml for Maven or by a .sbt for sbt (Simple Build Tool).

This book contains many examples of source code, both in numbered listings and inline with normal text. In both cases, source code is formatted in a `fixed-width font like this` to separate it from ordinary text.

In many cases, the original source code has been reformatted; we've added line breaks and reworked indentation to accommodate the available page space in the book. In rare cases, even this was not enough, and listings may include line-continuation markers (➥). Additionally, comments in the source code have often been removed from the listings when the code is described in the text. Code annotations accompany many of the listings, highlighting important concepts.

The code for the examples in this book can be downloaded from the publisher's website at www.manning.com/books/spark-graphx-in-action.

Author Online

Purchase of *Spark GraphX in Action* includes free access to a private web forum run by Manning Publications where you can make comments about the book, ask technical questions, and receive help from the authors and from other users. To access the forum and subscribe to it, point your web browser to www.manning.com/books/spark-graphx-in-action. This page provides information on how to get on the forum once you are registered, what kind of help is available, and the rules of conduct on the forum.

Manning's commitment to our readers is to provide a venue where a meaningful dialog between individual readers and between readers and the authors can take place. It is not a commitment to any specific amount of participation on the part of the authors, whose contribution to the AO remains voluntary (and unpaid). We suggest you try asking the authors some challenging questions lest their interest stray!

The Author Online forum and the archives of previous discussions will be accessible from the publisher's website as long as the book is in print.

About the authors

MICHAEL MALAK has been writing software since before computers could be purchased in stores preassembled. He has been developing in Spark for two Fortune 200 companies since early 2013 and often gives presentations, especially in the Denver/Boulder region of Colorado where he lives. You can find his personal technical blog at http://technicaltidbit.com.

ROBIN EAST has worked as a consultant to large organizations for more than 15 years, delivering Big Data and content intelligence solutions in the fields of finance, government, healthcare, and utilities. He is a data scientist at Worldpay, helping them deliver their vision of putting data at the heart of everything they do. You can find his other writings on Spark, GraphX, and machine learning at https://mlspeed.wordpress.com.

about the cover illustration

The figure on the cover of *Spark GraphX in Action* is captioned "Man from Šibenik, Dalmatia, Croatia." The illustration is taken from a reproduction of an album of Croatian traditional costumes from the mid-nineteenth century by Nikola Arsenovic, published by the Ethnographic Museum in Split, Croatia, in 2003. The illustrations were obtained from a helpful librarian at the Ethnographic Museum in Split, itself situated in the Roman core of the medieval center of the town: the ruins of Emperor Diocletian's retirement palace from around AD 304. The book includes finely colored illustrations of figures from different regions of Croatia, accompanied by descriptions of the costumes and of everyday life.

Šibenik is a historic city in Croatia, located in central Dalmatia where the river Krka flows into the Adriatic Sea. Šibenik is a political, educational, industrial, and tourist center of Šibenik-Knin County and the third- largest city in the historic region of Dalmatia. It is the oldest native Croatian town on the shores of the Adriatic.

Dress codes and lifestyles have changed over the last 200 years, and the diversity by region, so rich at the time, has faded away. It's now hard to tell apart the inhabitants of different continents, let alone of different hamlets or towns separated by only a few miles. Perhaps we have traded cultural diversity for a more varied personal life—certainly for a more varied and fast-paced technological life. Manning celebrates the inventiveness and initiative of the computer business with book covers based on the rich diversity of regional life of two centuries ago, brought back to life by illustrations from old books and collections like this one.

Part 1

Spark and graphs

Graphs—the things composed of vertices and edges, not graphs from Algebra class—carry a mystique about them. They seem to be very powerful, yet what can be done with them is a bit of a mystery. Part of the problem is that the answer "graphs can do anything" says precisely nothing. Right off in chapter 1, we suggest a broad categorization of different types of graphs found in the world. In the last third of chapter 3 we illustrate graph terminology.

Apache Spark is a distributed computing system growing in popularity due to its speed. GraphX is Spark applied to graphs, and chapter 1 describes how GraphX fits into a data processing workflow. In chapter 2, you'll actually get hands on with PageRank, the algorithm that launched Google.

Chapter 3 is a crash course in the three foundational technologies required for this book: Spark, Scala, and graphs.

Two important technologies: Spark and graphs

This chapter covers

- Why Spark has become the leading Big Data processing system
- What makes graphs a unique way of modeling connected data
- How GraphX makes Spark a leading platform for graph analytics

It's well-known that we are generating more data than ever. But it's not just the individual data points that are important—it's also the connections between them. Extracting information from such connected datasets can give insights into numerous areas such as detecting fraud, collecting bioinformatics, and ranking pages on the web.

Graphs provide a powerful way to represent and exploit these connections. Graphs represent networks of data points as vertices and encode connections through edges between pairs of vertices. Graphs can be used to model such diverse areas as computer vision, natural language processing, and recommender systems.

With such a representation of connected data comes a whole raft of tools and techniques that can be used to mine the information content of the network. Among the many tools covered in this book, you'll find PageRank (for finding the most influential members of the network), topic modeling with Latent Dirichlet Allocation (LDA), and clustering coefficient to discover highly connected communities.

Unfortunately, traditional tools used for the analysis of data, such as relational databases, are not well suited to this type of problem. Table-oriented frameworks such as SQL are cumbersome when it comes to representing typical graph notions such as following a trail of connections. Furthermore, traditional methods of data processing fail to scale as the size of the data to be analyzed increases.

A solution is at hand with graph processing systems. Such systems supply data models and programming interfaces that provide a more natural way to query and analyze graph structures. Graph processing systems provide the means to create graph structures from raw data sources and apply the processing necessary to mine the information content therein.

Apache Spark is the Big Data processing alternative that has all but supplanted Hadoop, the open source data processing platform that ushered in the era of Big Data. Easily scaling to clusters of hundreds of nodes, Spark's in-memory data processing can often outperform Hadoop many times over.

GraphX is the graph processing layer on top of Spark that brings the power of Big Data processing to graphs—graphs that would be too large to fit on a single machine. People started using Spark for graphs long ago, including with the predecessor Bagel module, but with GraphX we now have a standardized way to do so, and it also provides a library of useful algorithms.

Here are some of the many reasons why you may want to use Spark GraphX:

- You already have Spark data processing pipelines and want to incorporate graph processing.
- You're curious about the power of Spark and/or GraphX.
- You're among the many for whom graph data has become important.
- Your graph data is too large to fit on a single machine.
- Either you don't need multiple applications accessing the same data store or you plan to add a REST server to Spark; for example, with the add-on originally by Ooyala called Spark Job Server.
- Either you don't need database-type transactions or you plan on using a graph database such as Neo4j or Titan in conjunction with GraphX.
- You already have a Spark cluster available to your application.
- You would like to use the concise, expressive power of Scala.

1.1   *Spark: the step beyond Hadoop MapReduce*

This section discusses Big Data in relation to Spark and graphs. Big Data is a major challenge for data science teams, in part because a single machine is unlikely to have the power and capacity to run processing at the scale required. Moreover, even systems designed for Big Data, such as Hadoop, can struggle to process graph data efficiently due to some of the properties of that data, as you'll see later in this chapter.

Apache Spark is similar to Apache Hadoop in that it stores data distributed across a cluster of servers, or *nodes*. The difference is that Apache Spark stores data in memory (RAM) whereas Hadoop stores data on disk (either a spinning hard disk drive or a solid-state drive (SSD)), as shown in figure 1.1.

> **DEFINITION** The word *node* has two distinct uses when it comes to graphs and to cluster computing. Graph data is composed of vertices and edges, and in that context *node* is a synonym for vertex. In cluster computing, the physical machines that comprise the cluster are also known as nodes. To avoid confusion, we refer to graph nodes/vertices only as *vertices*, which is also the terminology adopted by Spark GraphX. When we use the word *node* in this book, we mean strictly one physical computer participating in cluster computing.

Besides differing in where data is processed during computation (RAM versus disk), Spark's API is much easier to work with than the Hadoop Map/Reduce API. Combined

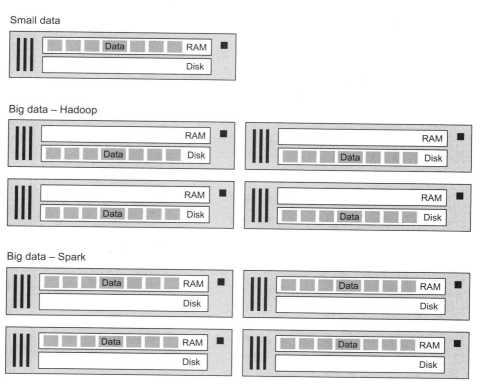

Figure 1.1   Big Data is data that is too big to fit on a single machine. Hadoop and Spark are technologies that distribute Big Data across a cluster of nodes. Spark is faster than Hadoop alone because it distributes data across the RAM in the cluster instead of the disks.

with the conciseness of Scala, the native programming language of Spark, a ratio of 100:1 for the number of Hadoop Map/Reduce Java lines of code to Spark Scala lines of code is common.

Although this book uses Scala primarily, don't worry if you don't know Scala yet. Chapter 3 provides a jumpstart into Scala, and all along the way we explain the tricks and terse, arcane syntax that are part and parcel of Scala. But deep familiarity with at least one programming language—such as Java, C++, C#, or Python—is assumed.

1.1.1   *The elusive definition of Big Data*

The idea of Big Data has gotten a lot of hype. The ideas trace back to the 2003 Google Paper on the Google File System and the 2004 Google paper on Map/Reduce, and these inspired the development of what is now Apache Hadoop.

The term *Big Data* has a lot of competing definitions, and some claim it has by now lost all meaning, but there is a simple core and crucial concept it still legitimately embodies: data that's too large to fit on a single machine.

Data sizes have exploded. Data is coming from website click streams, server logs, and sensors, to name a few sources. Some of this data is graph data, meaning it's comprised of edges and vertices, such as from collaborative websites (aka *Web 2.0* of which *social media* is a subset). Large sets of graph data are effectively crowdsourced, such as the body of interconnected knowledge contained in Wikipedia or the graph represented by Facebook friends, LinkedIn connections, or Twitter followers.

1.1.2   *Hadoop: the world before Spark*

Before we talk about Spark, let's recap how Hadoop solves the Big Data processing problem, because Spark builds on the core Hadoop concepts described in this section.

Hadoop provides a framework to implement fault-tolerant parallel processing on a cluster of machines. Hadoop provides two key capabilities:

- *HDFS*—Distributed storage
- *MapReduce*—Distributed compute

HDFS provides distributed, fault-tolerant storage. The NameNode partitions a single large file into smaller blocks. A typical block size is 64 MB or 128 MB. The blocks are scattered across the machines in the cluster. Fault-tolerance is provided by replicating each block of the file to a number of nodes (the default is three, but to make the diagram simpler, figure 1.2 shows a replication factor of two). Should a node fail, rendering all the file blocks on that machine unavailable, other nodes can transparently provide the missing blocks. This is a key idea in the architecture of Hadoop: the design accommodates machine failures as part of normal operations.

MapReduce (see figure 1.3) is the Hadoop parallel processing framework that provides parallel and distributed computation. MapReduce allows the programmer to write a single piece of code, encapsulated in *map* and *reduce* functions that are executed against the dataset residing on HDFS. To achieve *data locality*, the code is shipped (in .jar form) to the data nodes, and the Map is executed there. This avoids

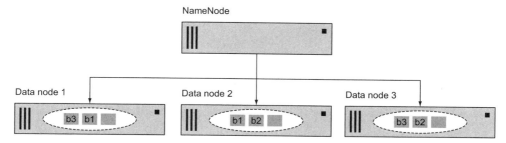

Figure 1.2   Three data blocks distributed with replication factor 2 across a Hadoop Distributed File System (HDFS)

consuming network bandwidth to ship the data around the cluster. For the Reduce summary, though, the results of the Maps are shipped to some Reduce node for the Reduce to take place there (this is called *shuffling*). Parallelism is achieved primarily during the Map, and Hadoop also provides resiliency in that if a machine or process fails, the computation can be restarted on another machine.

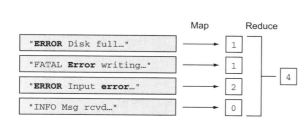

Figure 1.3   MapReduce is the processing paradigm used by both Hadoop and Spark. Shown is a MapReduce operation to count the number of times "error" appears in a server log. The Map is (normally) a one-to-one operation that produces one transformed data item for each source data item. The Reduce is a many-to-one operation that summarizes the Map outputs. Both Hadoop and Spark use the MapReduce paradigm.

The MapReduce programming framework abstracts the dataset as a stream of key-value pairs to be processed and the output written back to HDFS. It's a limited paradigm but it has been used to solve many data parallel problems by chaining together MapReduce read-process-write operations. Simple tasks, such as the word counting in figure 1.3, benefit from this approach. But iterative algorithms like machine learning suffer, which is where Spark comes in.

1.1.3   *Spark: in-memory MapReduce processing*

This section looks at an alternative distributed processing system, Spark, which builds on the foundations laid by Hadoop. In this section you'll learn about Resilient Distributed Datasets (RDDs), which have a large role to play in how Spark represents graph data.

Hadoop falls down on a couple of classes of problems:

- Interactive querying
- Iterative algorithms

Hadoop is good for running a single query on a large dataset, but in many cases, once we have an answer, we want to ask another question of the data. This is referred to as *interactive querying*. With Hadoop, this means waiting to reload the data from disk and process it again. It's not unusual to have to execute the same set of computations as a precursor to subsequent analysis.

Iterative algorithms are used in a wide array of machine learning tasks, such as Stochastic Gradient Descent, as well as graph-based algorithms like PageRank. An iterative algorithm applies a set of calculations to a dataset over and over until some criterion has been met. Implementing such algorithms in Hadoop typically requires a series of MapReduce jobs where data is loaded on each iteration. For large datasets, there could be hundreds or thousands of iterations, resulting in long runtimes.

Next you'll see how Spark solves these problems. Like Hadoop, Spark runs on a cluster of commodity hardware machines. The key abstraction in Spark is a Resilient Distributed Dataset (RDD). RDDs are created by the Spark application (residing in the Spark Driver) via a Cluster Manager, as shown in figure 1.4.

An RDD consists of distributed subsets of the data called *partitions* that can be loaded into memory on the machines across the cluster.

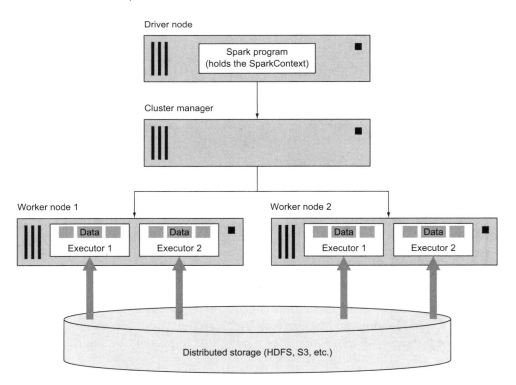

Figure 1.4   Spark provides RDDs that can be viewed as distributed in-memory arrays.

IN-MEMORY PROCESSING

Spark performs most of its operations in RAM. Because Spark is memory-based, it's more suited to processing graphs than Hadoop Map/Reduce because Map/Reduce processes data sequentially, whereas RAM is by nature random-access.

The key to Spark's usefulness in interactive querying and iterative processing is its ability to cache RDDs in memory. Caching an RDD avoids the need to reprocess the chain of parent RDDs each time a result is returned.

Naturally, this means that to take advantage of Spark's in-memory processing, the machines in the cluster must have a large amount of RAM. But if the available memory is insufficient, Spark will spill data back to disk gracefully and continue to work.

A Spark cluster needs a place to store data permanently. That place needs to be a distributed storage system, and options include HDFS, Cassandra, and Amazon's S3.

1.2 Graphs: finding meaning from relationships

Graphs can be used to represent naturally occurring connected data, such as the following:

- Social networks
- Mobile phone systems
- Web pages on the internet

Limited for decades to the realm of academia and research, graphs have over the past few years been adopted by organizations from Silicon Valley social media companies to governmental intelligence agencies seeking to find and use relationship patterns in their data. Graphs have now even entered the popular lexicon, with Facebook introducing its Graph Search, intelligence agencies publicly calling for the need to "connect the dots," and the old internet meme/game called the Six Degrees of Kevin Bacon. Even the now-universal and ubiquitous icon for *share* on social media and smartphone cameras is that of a miniature graph:

One of the most common uses for graphs today is to mine social media data, specifically to identify cliques, to recommend new connections, and to suggest products and ads. Such data can be big—more than can be stored on a single machine—which is where Spark comes in: it stores data across multiple machines participating in a cluster.

Spark is well-suited to handling graph data for another reason: it stores data in the memory (RAM) of each computer in the cluster, in contrast to Hadoop, which stores data on the disk of each computer in the cluster. Whereas Hadoop can handle sequential access of data, Spark can handle the arbitrary access order needed by a graph system, which has to traverse graphs from one vertex to the next.

GraphX is not a database. Instead, it's a graph processing system, which is useful, for example, for fielding web service queries or performing one-off, long-running standalone computations. Because GraphX isn't a database, it doesn't handle updates and deletes like Neo4j and Titan, which *are* graph databases. Apache Giraph is another example of a graph processing system, but Giraph is limited to slow Hadoop Map/Reduce. GraphX, Giraph, and GraphLab are all separate implementations of the ideas expressed in the Google Pregel paper. Such graph processing systems are optimized for running algorithms on the entire graph in a massively parallel manner, as opposed to working with small pieces of graphs like graph databases. To draw a comparison to the world of standard relational databases, graph databases like Neo4j are like OLTP (Online Transaction Processing) whereas graph processing systems like GraphX are like OLAP (Online Analytical Processing).

Graphs can store various kinds of data: geospatial, social media, paper citation networks, and, of course, web page links. A tiny social media network graph is shown in figure 1.5. "Ann," "Bill," "Charles," "Diane," and "'Went to gym this morning'" are *vertices*, and "Is-friends-with," "Wrote-status," and "Likes-status" are *edges*.

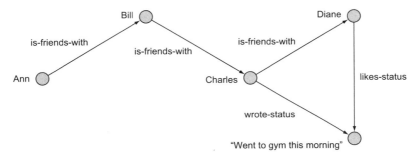

Figure 1.5   If Charles shares his status with friends of friends, determining the list of who could see his status would be cumbersome to figure out if you only had tables or arrays to work with.

1.2.1   Uses of graphs

It's well-known that we are now living in a world where we are generating more data than ever before. We are collecting more data points with richer content from an ever-expanding variety of sources.

To take advantage of this situation, organizations big and small are also putting data analysis and data mining at the heart of their operations—a move that some have dubbed the *data-driven business*. But data is not just getting bigger, it's more connected. This connectedness is what gives data its richness and provides ever greater opportunities to understand the world around us. Graphs offer a powerful way to represent and exploit these connections.

What forms does this connected data take? Start with one of the most well-known connected datasets: the World Wide Web. At a simplistic level, the web consists of billions of pages of metadata, text, images, and videos, and every page can point to one or more of the other pages using a link tag.

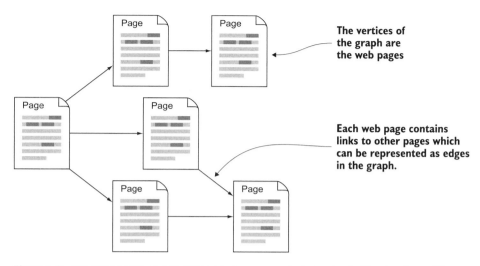

Figure 1.6   The links between web pages can be represented as a graph. The structure of the graph provides information about the relative authority, or ranking, of each page.

As figure 1.6 shows, you can represent these pages and links as a graph. You can then use the structure of the graph to provide information on the relative authority of each page. You can visualize this as each page providing a vote for each page it points to. But not all pages are equal; you might imagine that a page on a major news site has more importance than a posting by an unknown blogger. This is the problem that's solved by the PageRank algorithm, as you will see in chapter 5, and it has many more applications beyond ranking web pages.

The graphs we have looked at so far have captured links between pages; there is either a link or no link. We can make the graphs richer if we have more information about the connection. A typical example would be ratings information. When you give a 5-star rating to a movie on Netflix, not only do you create a connection between yourself and the movie, you also assign a value to that connection.

Movie ratings aren't the only value that can be applied to connections in graphs. Dollar values in the analysis of financial fraud, distances travelled between cities, and the traffic carried across a network of mobile phone stations are other examples of ways to enhance the richness of the connections represented in graphs.

Even if the connections between data points don't have a measurable value, there is still valuable information that can be captured in the graph. Take a social media site as an example. Each profile could store details of where a person went to school, and as before, this represents a connection between the person and the school. If we capture other information, such when they attended the school, that additional information can be represented in the graph. Now when we want to show friend recommendations to our user, we can make sure we don't show them the class of '96 when they are in the class of '83.

Graphs existed long before social networking. Other uses for graphs include

- Finding the shortest route in a geo-mapping app
- Recommending products, services, personal contacts, or media based on other people with similar-looking graphs
- Converting a tangle of interconnected topics into a hierarchy for organizational schemes that require a hierarchy (computer file system folders, a class syllabus, and so forth)
- Determining the most authoritative scholarly papers

1.2.2   *Types of graph data*

What kind of data can you put into a graph? The usual answer "anything" is not very helpful. Figure 1.7 shows some different types of data that can be represented by a graph:

- Network
- Tree
- RDBMS-like data
- Sparse matrix
- Kitchen sink

A *network* graph can be a road network as shown in figure 1.7, a social network, or a computer network. A tree graph has no cycles (loops). Any RDBMS can be converted into a graph format; an employee RDBMS is shown converted into a graph. But this would only be useful if some graph algorithms are needed, such as PageRank for community detection or minimum spanning tree for network planning.

As discussed in chapter 3, every graph has an associated *adjacency matrix*. This powerful concept has an important implication: that a graph is just an alternative data structure and not something magical. Some algorithms, which might otherwise have to deal with unwieldy matrices, can take advantage of the more compressed representation of a graph, especially if the alternative is a *sparse matrix*. SVD++, discussed in chapter 7, is an example of such an algorithm.

Attempts have been made to create *kitchen sink* graphs to encode all of human knowledge. The Cyc project is an example that attempts to encode all of human common sense into a graph. The YAGO (Yet Another Great Ontology) project has the slightly more modest goal of encoding an ontology (dictionary, hierarchy, and relationships) that represents everything in the world. Sometimes people think artificial intelligence will automatically result from such an ambitious graph. That doesn't happen, but such graphs are useful for assististing natural language processing projects of reasonable goals.

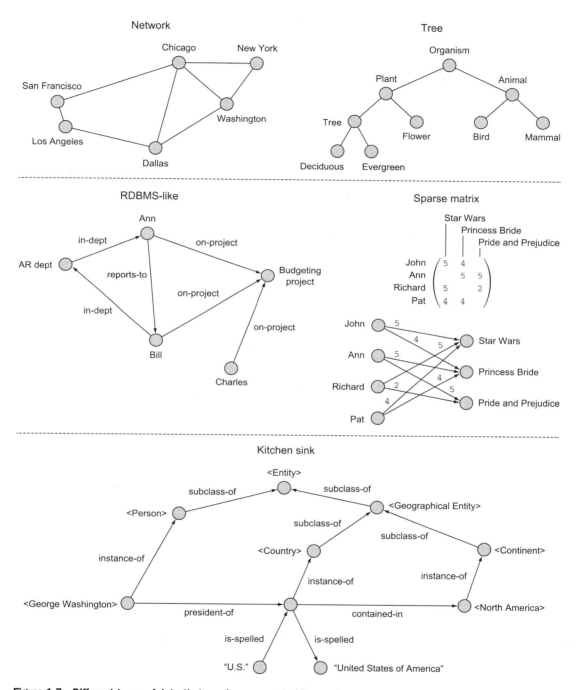

Figure 1.7   Different types of data that can be represented by graphs

1.2.3   Plain RDBMS inadequate for graphs

If you were to try to represent a graph in an RDBMS—or arrays of objects, if you're not familiar with SQL—you would probably have one table (or array) of vertices and another table of edges. The table of edges would have foreign keys (references) to the vertices table so that each edge would refer to the two vertices in connects. This is all well and good, provided you don't need to query deeply in the graph.

In the example graph in figure 1.5, suppose we want to find out who can see Charles's status "Went to gym this morning." If Charles shared it only with direct friends, then finding who can see it—who Charles' direct friends are—would be easy to do with a table structure. But suppose Charles shared his status with friends of friends; then to reach Ann would require hopping through the tables. In terms of SQL, we would have to join the edge table to itself. If we wanted the Six Degrees of Kevin Bacon, we would have to join the edge table to itself six times within the same SQL query.

What is common to problems that can be modeled as graphs is that we are focusing as much on the connections between entities as on the entities themselves. In many cases we want to traverse the connections to find things such as friends-of-friends-of-friends in social networks, cascades of retweets on Twitter, or the common component in a network of failed computers.

Furthermore, not all connections are created equal. Suppose we are analyzing surveillance data on a known criminal and his many associates and connections. We want to identify those people most likely to provide us with information, but it doesn't make sense to investigate everybody who has some connection; we want to prioritize by some sort of metric that measures the strength of the connection. One such metric could be the number of times a week that contact is made. Graphs allow us to assign a value or weight to each connection and then use that weighting in subsequent processing.

1.3   Putting them together for lightning fast graph processing: Spark GraphX

GraphX is a layer on top of Spark that provides a graph data structure composed of Spark RDDs, and it provides an API to operate on those graph data structures. GraphX comes with the standard Spark distribution, and you use it through a combination of the GraphX-specific API and the regular Spark API.

Spark originated out of AMPLab at the University of California, Berkeley in 2011 and became a top-level Apache project in 2014. Not everything from AMPLab is part of the official Apache Spark distribution. And to operate, Spark requires two major pieces shown in the bottom two gray layers of figure 1.8: distributed storage and a cluster manager. In this book, we assume HDFS for the distributed storage and not having a cluster manager, which is running Spark on a single computer; this is sometimes called *pseudo-distributed* mode for test and development.

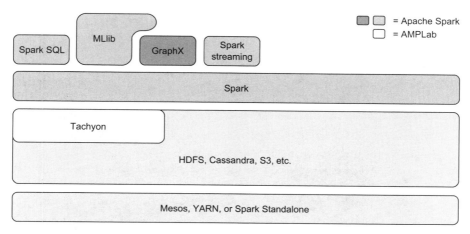

Figure 1.8   The Spark stack. Some components, including GraphX, come with Spark. Others, such as HDFS and YARN, are part of Apache Hadoop. In the last category, Tachyon comes from AMPLab at the University of California, Berkeley. Most of MLlib stands alone on top of Spark Core, but a couple of its algorithms make use of GraphX under the covers.

NOTE   Because GraphX is fully part of the base Spark package from Apache, version numbers for Spark Core and its base components, including GraphX, are synchronized.

1.3.1   Property graph: adding richness

We've seen that graphs in the real world contain valuable information beyond simply the connection between a vertex and an edge. Graphs are rich with data, and we need a way to represent this richness.

GraphX implements a notion called the *property graph*. As shown in figure 1.9, both vertices and edges can have arbitrary sets of attributes associated with them. The attribute could be something as simple as the age of a person or something as complex as an XML document, image, or video.

GraphX represents a graph using 2 RDDs, vertices and edges. Representing graphs in this way allows GraphX to deal with one of the major issues in processing large graphs: partitioning.

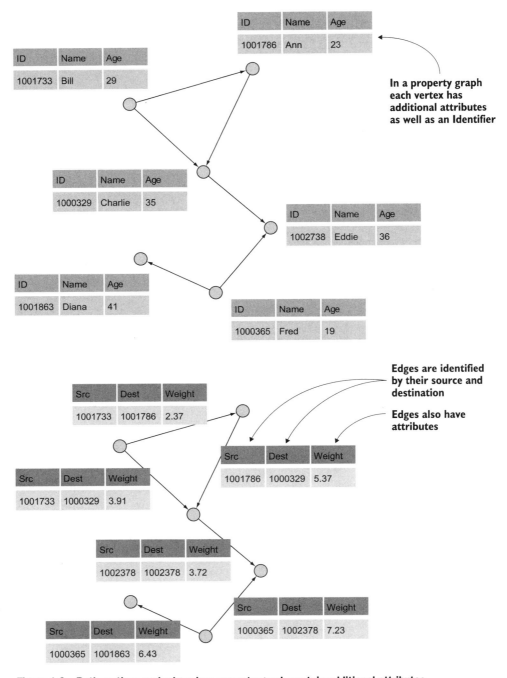

Figure 1.9   Both vertices and edges in a property graph contain additional attributes.

1.3.2　*Graph partitioning: graphs meet Big Data*

If we have a graph too large to fit in the memory of a single computer, Spark lets us divide it among multiple computers in a cluster of computers. But what's the best way to split up a graph?

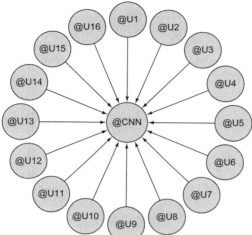

Figure 1.10　A graph with a high-degree vertex

The naïve way, and the way in which it was done for many years, was to assign different vertices to different computers in the cluster. But this led to computational bottlenecks because real-world graphs always seem to have some extremely high-degree vertices (see figure 1.10). The vertex degrees of real-world graphs tend to follow the *Power Law* (see the sidebar on the following page).

> **DEFINITION**　The word *degree* also has two meanings when it comes to graphs. Earlier we used it in the context of the Six Degrees of Kevin Bacon, meaning the number of hops, or edges, from one actor to another, where an edge means the two actors appeared in the same film. But the degree of a vertex is completely different: it's the combined number of edges going out of or coming into a particular vertex. We won't be referring to Kevin Bacon anymore, so we'll use the word *hop* for those types of uses going forward, and *degree* only in the context of a vertex and the number of edges incident to it.

Partitioning a graph by vertices is called *edge-cut* because it's the edges that are getting cut. But a graph processing system that instead employs *vertex-cut*, which evenly distributes the edges among the machines/nodes, more evenly balances the data across the cluster. This idea came from research in 2005, was popularized by a graph processing system called GraphLab (now called PowerGraph), and was adopted by GraphX as the default partitioning scheme.

GraphX supports four different partitioning schemes for edges, described in section 9.4. GraphX partitions vertices independently of edges. By avoiding piling all the edges from a high-degree vertex onto a single machine, GraphX avoids the load imbalance suffered by earlier graph processing systems and graph databases.

Power Law of Graphs

Graphs in the real world have been found to obey the Power Law, which in the context of ranking the vertices by degree (intuitively, by popularity) means that the most popular vertex will be, say, 40% more popular than the second most popular vertex, which in turn will be 40% more popular than the third most popular vertex to it, and so on.

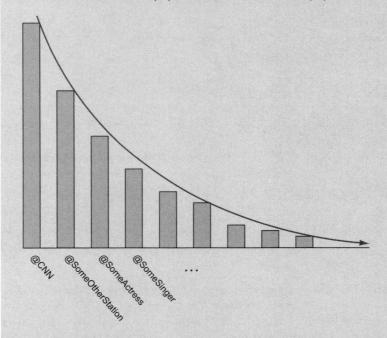

In this context of ranking, it is also known as Zipf's Law. These are the realities of graphs, and distributing graph data by the vertex-cut strategy balances graph data across a cluster. Spark GraphX employs the vertex-cut strategy by default.

1.3.3   GraphX lets you choose: graph parallel or data parallel

As we've seen, GraphX stores a graph's edges in one table and vertices in another. This allows graph algorithms implemented in GraphX to efficiently traverse graphs as graphs, along edges from one vertex to another, or as tables of edges or vertices (see figure 1.11). This latter mode of access permits efficient bulk transforms of edge or vertex data.

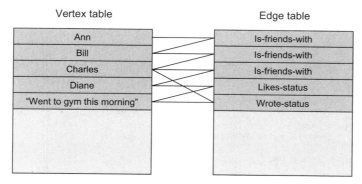

Figure 1.11   GraphX facilitates data access for either graph-parallel or data-parallel operations.

Although GraphX stores edges and vertices in separate tables as one might design an RDBMS schema to do, internally GraphX has special indexes to rapidly traverse the graph, and it exposes an API that makes graph querying and processing easier than trying to do the same in SQL.

1.3.4   Various ways GraphX fits into a processing flow

GraphX is inherently a batch-processing system. It doesn't integrate with Spark Streaming, for example (at least not in any straightforward way). There isn't one cookie-cutter way to use GraphX. There are many different batch processing data flows into which GraphX can fit, and the data flows in figures 1.12 and 1.13 cover some of these.

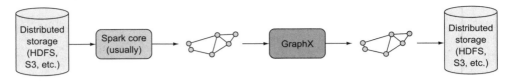

In this common workflow, a graph is transformed into a new graph (for example, vertices or edges may
have new property values). An example of this is PageRank covered in sections 2.3 and 5.1.

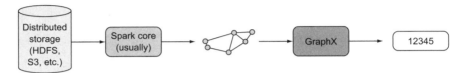

Some graph algorithms, like the Global Clustering Coefficient from section 8.4,
output only a global metric that describes the whole graph.

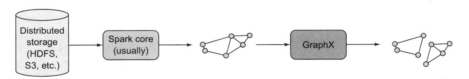

Other graph algorithms, like Connected Components from section 5.4, output subgraphs.

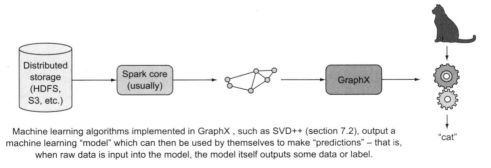

Machine learning algorithms implemented in GraphX , such as SVD++ (section 7.2), output a
machine learning "model" which can then be used by themselves to make "predictions" – that is,
when raw data is input into the model, the model itself outputs some data or label.

**Figure 1.12   Various possible GraphX data flows. Because GraphX's capabilities for reading graph data
files are so limited, data files usually have to be massaged and transformed using the Spark Core API
into the graph format that GraphX uses. The output of a GraphX algorithm can be another graph, a
number, some subgraphs, or a machine learning model.**

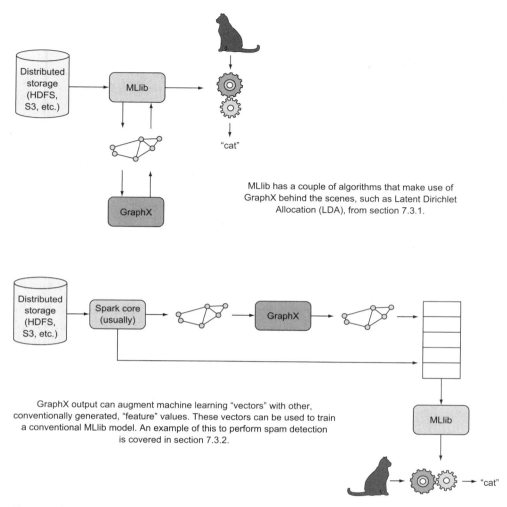

Figure 1.13   Data flows that involve using MLlib, the Spark machine learning component. A couple of algorithms use GraphX behind the scenes, but GraphX can also be used alongside any MLlib algorithm.

1.3.5   *GraphX vs. other systems*

Graph systems can be divided into two broad categories: graph processing systems and graph databases. Many are memory-based, and some even support cluster computing. Spark GraphX is a graph processing system rather than a graph database. A graph database has the great advantage of providing database transactions, a query language, and easy incremental updates and persistence, but if it's a disk-based graph database, it doesn't have the performance of a fully in-memory graph processing system like

GraphX. Graph processing systems are useful, for example, for fielding web service requests or performing one-off, long-running standalone computations.

Most graph analytics tasks require other types of processing as well. Graph analytics is usually one part of a larger processing pipeline. Often there's a need to generate a graph from raw data—say, from CSV or XML files. To generate the required property graph attributes, we may have to join data from another table. Once the graph processing task is completed, the resulting graph may need to be joined with other data. For example, we could use PageRank to find the most influential people in a social network. We could then use sales data from an RDBMS to find customers who are both influential and high-value to select the most promising recipients of a marketing promotion. Spark makes it easy to compose complex pipelines using both data-parallel and graph-parallel processing.

If you have a system that's already using Spark for other things and you also need to process graph data, Spark GraphX is a way to efficiently do that without having to learn and administer a completely different cluster technology, such as a separate distributed graph database. Because of GraphX's fast processing, you can even couple it to a graph database such as Neo4j and realize the best of both worlds: database transactions on the graph database and fast processing when you need it.

Apache Giraph is another example of a graph processing system, but again, Giraph is limited to slow Hadoop Map/Reduce. GraphX, Giraph, and GraphLab are all separate implementations of the ideas expressed in the Google Pregel paper. Neo4j, Titan, and Oracle Spatial and Graph are examples of graph databases. Graph databases have query languages that are convenient for finding information about a particular vertex or set of vertices. Pregel-based graph processing systems, in contrast, are bad at that and instead are good at executing massively parallel algorithms like PageRank. Now, GraphX does have the Spark REPL Shell, which provides an interactive command line interface into GraphX (as opposed to having to compile a program every time), and this speeds along development of GraphX applications and algorithms—but given the current syntax, it's still too cumbersome for querying, as shown in section 3.3.4.

GraphX is still young, and some of its limitations stem from the limitations of Spark. For example, GraphX datasets, like all Spark datasets, can't normally be shared by multiple Spark programs unless a REST server add-on like Spark JobServer is used. Until the IndexedRDD capability is added to Spark (Jira ticket SPARK-2365), which is effectively a mutable (that is, updatable) HashMap version of an RDD (Resilient Distributed Dataset, the foundation of Spark), GraphX is limited by the immutability of Spark RDDs, which is an issue for large graphs. Although faster for some uses, GraphX is often slower than systems written in C++, such as GraphLab/PowerGraph, due to GraphX's reliance on the JVM.

1.3.6 *Storing the graphs: distributed file storage vs. graph database*

Because GraphX is strictly an in-memory processing system, you need a place to store graph data. Spark expects distributed storage, such as HDFS, Cassandra, or S3, and storing graphs in distributed storage is the usual way to go.

But some use GraphX, a graph processing system, in conjunction with a graph database to get the best of both worlds (see figure 1.14). GraphX versus Neo4j is a frequent debate, but for some use cases, both are better than one or the other. The open source project Mazerunner is an extension to Neo4j that offloads graph analytics such as PageRank to GraphX.

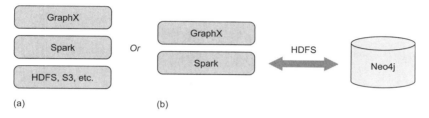

Figure 1.14 The conventional and by far most common way for GraphX to store its data is out to HDFS or to some other distributed storage system (a). Some, however, use the power of a full-fledged graph database, and realize the best of both worlds: transactions in a graph database and fast processing in GraphX (b).

1.4 Summary

- Graphs are a natural and powerful way to model connected data.
- Like Hadoop, Spark provides a Map/Reduce API (distributed computation) plus distributed storage. The main difference is that Spark stores data in RAM throughout the cluster, whereas Hadoop stores data on disk throughout the cluster.
- GraphX builds on the foundations of Spark to provide flexible and efficient graph-parallel processing.
- Spark also provides data-parallel processing that makes it ideal for real-world Big Data problems that often call for both graph-parallel and data-parallel processing.
- GraphX isn't a graph database and isn't suited to querying individual vertices or small groups of vertices. Rather, it's a graph processing system suited for massively parallel algorithms such as PageRank.
- Types of graph data include network, tree, relational, kitchen sink, and the graph equivalent to a sparse matrix.
- Graph algorithms include PageRank, recommender systems, shortest paths, community detection, and much more.

GraphX quick start

This chapter covers

- Finding graph data to play with
- First steps with GraphX using the Spark Shell
- Invoking the PageRank algorithm

The Spark Shell is the easiest way to quickly start using Spark and is a great way to explore graph datasets. No compilation is necessary, which means you can focus on running commands and seeing their output. Even though Spark Shell uses Scala as its programming language, there's no need to worry if you haven't used Scala before. This chapter will guide you every step of the way.

The chapter is intended to walk you through the steps of working with GraphX without delving into the details. You'll download some sample graph data consisting of bibliographic citations. Using the Spark Shell, you'll quickly determine which paper has been cited the most frequently. More interestingly, you'll invoke the PageRank algorithm built into GraphX to find the "most influential" paper in the graph network. In subsequent chapters, we'll see what's going on under the covers.

2.1   *Getting set up and getting data*

Although normally you would write a Spark program in Scala (or Java or Python), compile it, and submit it to a Spark cluster, Spark also offers the Spark Shell, which is an interactive shell where you can quickly test out ideas.

The first thing to do is to install Spark (this is covered in Appendix A if you haven't done this already).

Now, assuming you have Spark installed, type

```
spark-shell
```

That assumes the `spark/bin` directory is in your path (which it is if you're using the Cloudera QuickStart VM). Otherwise, you'll first need to `cd` to the `spark/bin` directory and then type `./spark-shell`. You should see something like this:

```
[mmalak@localhost bin]$ ./spark-shell
Welcome to                         <--- Many lines of log output not shown here

      ____              __
     / __/__  ___ _____/ /__
    _\ \/ _ \/ _ `/ __/  '_/
   /___/ .__/\_,_/_/ /_/\_\   version 1.6.0
      /_/

Using Scala version 2.10.5 (Java HotSpot(TM) 64-Bit Server VM, Java 1.8.0_60)
Type in expressions to have them evaluated.
Type :help for more information.
Spark context available as sc.    <--- More log lines not shown here

scala>
```

You'll notice toward the end that the Spark Shell helpfully alerts you that the variable `sc` is available. The Spark Shell instantiates an `org.apache.spark.SparkContext` for you with the variable name `sc`. `SparkContext` is our handle to the Spark world, providing the entry point to much of Spark's functionality (as you'll see later). In this chapter, you'll need `SparkContext` to load data into Spark.

The next step is getting some data to work with. Perhaps you have your own. But in this chapter you'll download some data from the Stanford Network Analysis Project (SNAP) at http://snap.stanford.edu/data.

You'll use the Arxiv-HEP-TH (high energy physics theory) citation network dataset (not to be confused with the collaboration network also available there), available for download from http://snap.stanford.edu/data/cit-HepTh.html. It's a little over 1 MB compressed as cit-HepTh.txt.gz; it decompresses to 6 MB. The start of this cit-HepTh .txt looks like this:

```
# Directed graph (each unordered pair of nodes is saved once):
# Paper citation network of Arxiv High Energy Physics Theory category
# Nodes: 27770 Edges: 352807
# FromNodeId   ToNodeId
1001          9304045
1001          9308122
1001          9309097
```

```
1001         9311042
1001         9401139
1001         9404151
1001         9407087
1001         9408099
```

Comment lines begin with #, and each data line represents one edge of the graph, with the vertex IDs of the source and destination vertices. In this case, each vertex ID refers to a particular physics paper listed in the companion file cit-HepTh-abstracts.tar.gz, which you can optionally download if you want to try to match up these bare numbers with something tangible. In the context of a paper citation, the source vertex is the newer paper, and the destination vertex is the older paper being cited by the newer paper.

This happens to be the file format recognized by GraphX.

NOTE The other major standard graph file format is called Resource Description Framework (RDF), along with derivatives such as N3 (Notation 3). As of Spark 1.6, GraphX doesn't have the built-in capability to read RDF. Chapter 8 shows you how to read RDF, but for now, we'll stick with the simpler format of edge lists of vertex IDs.

2.2   *Interactive GraphX querying using the Spark Shell*

Now we'll use the Spark Shell to load the HEP-TH dataset and query it. With a few lines of code you'll discover which paper in the dataset was the most frequently cited. Because the data remains loaded into memory, the next section shows how to perform further analytics on the dataset. This ability to undertake interactive querying is one of the key features of Spark.

DEFINITION The Spark Shell is an example of a REPL, which stands for Read-Eval Print Loop. A REPL is an interactive shell where each line of code you enter is executed (evaluated) immediately, and the result displayed in the console. Scala, Python, and other languages commonly have REPLs now, and the Spark REPL builds on the Scala REPL. Read, Eval, Print, and Loop are the names of the four LISP programming language primitives used to implement the first interactive LISP shell in the 1960s.

To avoid worrying about paths, copy cit-HepTh.txt into the same directory as spark-shell:

1 cp cit-HepTh.txt into the same directory as spark-shell.

2 ./spark-shell.

3 Now, with three lines entered into the Spark Shell, we can find the most-referenced paper:

```
import org.apache.spark.graphx._
val graph = GraphLoader.edgeListFile(sc, "cit-HepTh.txt")
graph.inDegrees.reduce((a,b) => if (a._2 > b._2) a else b)
```

We'll enter these lines one-by-one and explain each one as we go:

```
scala> import org.apache.spark.graphx._
import org.apache.spark.graphx._

scala>
```

> **SCALA TIP** Scala uses the underscore character in about a dozen different distinct ways. All the ways are some sort of wildcard or placeholder capacity, which makes it seem like the underscore has one solitary meaning. But it doesn't. Just because you've seen and understood how an underscore was used in one context, don't assume it means the same thing in a new context.

Scala's import is similar to a Java import. Here Scala uses an underscore as a wildcard, whereas Java uses an asterisk for the same purpose. After you enter each line, the REPL responds with some output on the next line. In the case of import statements, you get a confirmation of the input. If there's an error, you get some feedback on the source of that error:

```
scala> val graph = GraphLoader.edgeListFile(sc, "cit-HepTh.txt")
14/12/14 23:04:06 INFO MemoryStore: ensureFreeSpace...   ◁──┐ Many log lines
graph: org.apache.spark.graphx.Graph[Int,Int] =              │ not shown
 org.apache.spark.graphx.impl.GraphImpl@15721cbd

scala>
```

What happened? `GraphLoader` is the GraphX library object, imported in the previous step. `GraphLoader` contains a method `edgeListFile` that loads a graph from a text file in edge-list format—exactly what we need for our purposes. `edgeListFile` takes two parameters, where the first parameter is the SparkContext that was created for us earlier and the second parameter is the file path of the edge-list file. Because we copied cit-HepTh.txt into the current directory before starting Spark Shell, we can reference it by name.

The Spark Shell tells us it successfully created a variable called `graph` of type `org.apache.spark.graphx.Graph[Int,Int]`. Figure 2.1 looks at that line in more detail.

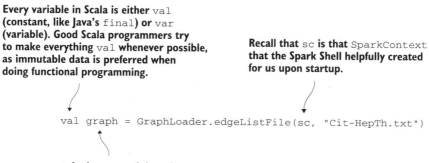

Every variable in Scala is either `val` **(constant, like Java's** `final`) **or** `var` **(variable). Good Scala programmers try to make everything** `val` **whenever possible, as immutable data is preferred when doing functional programming.**

Recall that `sc` **is that** `SparkContext` **that the Spark Shell helpfully created for us upon startup.**

```
val graph = GraphLoader.edgeListFile(sc, "Cit-HepTh.txt")
```

`graph` **is the name of the value (variable) and could contain an optional type definition.**

Figure 2.1   Creating a graph object from a file in edge-list format

NOTE graph is the name of the value (variable) being declared here, but where is the type? Scala is statically typed but uses inferred typing. The Scala compiler knows what type to make graph due to the return type of the edge-ListFile() method, and that return type is org.apache.spark.graphx .Graph. Once the compiler makes its decision, the type for graph can never change. Scala isn't an interpreted scripting language like Perl, though it might look like one due to its brevity. Perl's variables can change types while the program is running. Scala is a strictly and statically typed language, but it's not wordy.

Spark now has the HEP-TH graph loaded into memory, so let's look in more detail at that last line:

```
graph.inDegrees.reduce((a,b) => if (a._2 > b._2) a else b)
```

We call the inDegrees method on the graph object to obtain an RDD of VertexID/ in-degree pairs (note that in Scala we don't need to provide parentheses if a method has no arguments). For now think of an RDD as an array.

An RDD has a reduce method that takes a function as input. The function passed to reduce expects to receive as input two elements from the RDD and returns a single value. The reduce method then repeatedly calls the function on pairs of elements from the RDD until only a single value is left. This single value is returned from the reduce method.

Rather than separately define a function to give to reduce, we've taken advantage of Scala's anonymous functions (see figure 2.2). We'll look at anonymous functions in more detail in the next chapter, but for now, you only need to know that functions can be passed as parameters into other functions and that we can define functions inline without having to bother with a separate declaration. The output of reduce will end up being the (VertexID, in-degree) of the full RDD that has the maximum in-degree.

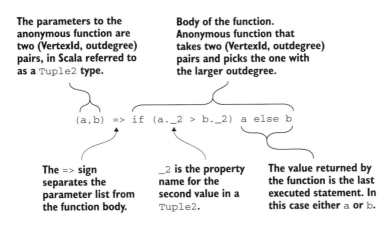

The parameters to the anonymous function are two (VertexId, outdegree) pairs, in Scala referred to as a Tuple2 **type.**

Body of the function. Anonymous function that takes two (VertexId, outdegree) pairs and picks the one with the larger outdegree.

```
(a,b) => if (a._2 > b._2) a else b
```

The => **sign separates the parameter list from the function body.**

_2 is the property name for the second value in a Tuple2.

The value returned by the function is the last executed statement. In this case either a **or** b.

Figure 2.2   Defining an anonymous function

When we enter that line into the Spark Shell, it gives us the ID of the theoretical physics paper that's most frequently cited:

```
scala> graph.inDegrees.reduce((a,b) => if (a._2 > b._2) a else b)
14/12/14 23:50:56 INFO SparkContext: Starting job: ...
14/12/14 23:50:59 INFO SparkContext: Job finished: reduce at          Many log lines
  <console>:18, took 3.16079562 s                                       not shown
res0: (org.apache.spark.graphx.VertexId, Int) = (9711200,2414)

scala>
```

As you can see, paper ID 9711200 (the 200th paper from November 1997) was cited the most—by 2,414 other papers, to be exact. But take a look at the breakdown of that line of code for everything that's going on there.

We were able to get the most cited paper with only three lines of code, one of which was an import, and the last two of which we could have combined into a single line if we really wanted to show off.

But this example hasn't taken advantage of the power of graphs. We could have done this in SQL on a relational database using a GROUP BY. In the next section, we'll use the power of GraphX by using its PageRank algorithm on this same data.

2.3   *PageRank example*

In this section you'll learn how easy it is to run PageRank, one of the best-known algorithms in graph processing. Although Larry Page of Google invented the PageRank algorithm (hence the name) to rank webpages on the World Wide Web, the algorithm can be used to measure the influence of vertices in any graph. Before applying Page-Rank to our theoretical physics citation network, though, note that one thing lurks behind the scenes. Let's take a look at the vertices of our graph:

```
scala> graph.vertices.take(10)
res2: Array[(org.apache.spark.graphx.VertexId, Int)] = Array((9405166,1),
  (108150,1), (110163,1), (204100,1), (9407099,1), (9703222,1),
  (9709148,1), (9905115,1), (103184,1), (211245,1))
```

> **NOTE**   For the rest of the book, we'lll omit all the log lines that Spark Shell spews out and won't mention that we're omitting them. Whenever you see a Spark Shell interaction, assume that a bunch of log output isn't shown.

You might have expected that the vertices in the graph would be the vertex IDs from the cit-HepTh.txt file. They're Scala pairs where the second number of the pair is always the number 1. As discussed in Chapter 3, GraphX is natively a property graph processor, which means it allows vertices and edges to have their own properties. Here, the 1 values are the properties of the vertices, and these 1 values are arbitrarily attached to the vertices by that GraphLoader.edgeListFile() function we used—so the vertices have some properties, even though they have no meaning. GraphX can handle vertices with properties, but edge-list files have no properties.

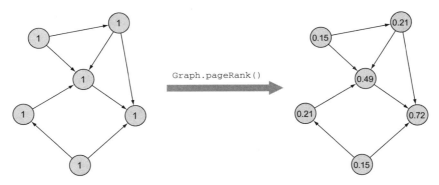

Figure 2.3   Running `pageRank()` creates a new graph where the vertex attributes are the PageRank values.

We bring this up now because the `pageRank()` method of `Graph` returns a new `Graph`, where each vertex has a property of type `Double` and is the PageRank for that vertex. This is a key idea in Spark: existing graph structures aren't updated. Instead, a transformation takes place on an existing graph to create a new graph, as shown in figure 2.3.

What does `pageRank()` do? It assigns to each vertex a number (a `Double`) that is a measure of how "influential" that vertex is in the overall network. Chapter 5 discusses exactly how PageRank works, but for now, let's see how easy it is to run PageRank on an existing graph using GraphX:

```
scala> val v = graph.pageRank(0.001).vertices
v: org.apache.spark.graphx.VertexRDD[Double] = VertexRDD[1264] at RDD at
 VertexRDD.scala:58
```

The value 0.001 passed to `pageRank()` is the tolerance, a parameter that sets the trade-off between speed and accuracy of the final result. If we set it too high, we'll stop the algorithm too early and our results won't be that accurate; too low, and the algorithm will continue on for too long without adding anything to the accuracy of the results.

Now look at the first 10 vertices of our PageRank graph:

```
scala> v.take(10)
res3: Array[(org.apache.spark.graphx.VertexId, Double)] =
 Array((9405166,1.336783076434938), (108150,0.5836164464324066),
 (110163,0.15), (204100,0.19080382117882116),
 (9407099,0.8271044254712047), (9703222,0.16521611205688394),
 (9709148,0.22176221523472583), (9905115,0.38267418598941183),
 (103184,0.20437621370972553), (211245,0.2298299371239072))
```

Those floating point numbers are the PageRanks; as you can see, for at least the first 10, they range from 0.15 up to 1.34.

Now let's run `reduce()` on v to find the vertex with the highest PageRank:

```scala
scala> v.reduce((a,b) => if (a._2 > b._2) a else b)
res4: (org.apache.spark.graphx.VertexId, Double) =
  (9207016,85.27317386053808)
```

The paper with ID 9207016 is the most influential, at least according to the PageRank algorithm. If you've downloaded the abstracts archive as well, you can locate the abstract for paper 9207016 using a search tool. The paper in question turns out to be from 1992, "Noncompact Symmetries in String Theory," by Jnan Maharana and John H. Schwarz.

Chapter 5 discusses the PageRank algorithm in much more detail.

2.4   Summary

- Spark Shell can be used for interactive querying and to quickly explore graph datasets.
- Many existing graph datasets are stored in edge-list format and can be loaded with `GraphLoader.edgeListFile`.
- PageRank can be run on a graph using the `graph.pageRank()` method. The graph returned by `pageRank` contains the PageRanks in the vertex data.
- Graphs in GraphX are immutable. Transformations of graphs return new graphs.

Some fundamentals

This chapter covers

- Scala philosophy, functional programming, and basics like class declarations
- Spark RDDs and common RDD operations, serialization, and Hello World with sbt
- Graph terminology

Using GraphX requires some basic knowledge of Spark, Scala, and graphs. This chapter covers the basics of all three—enough to get you through this book in case you're not up to speed on one or more of them.

Scala is a complex language, and this book ostensibly requires no Scala knowledge (though it would be helpful). The bare basics of Scala are covered in the first section of this chapter, and Scala tips are sprinkled throughout the remainder of the book to help beginning and intermediate Scala programmers.

The second section of this chapter is a tiny crash course on Spark—for a more thorough treatment, see *Spark In Action* (Manning, 2016). The functional programming philosophy of Scala is carried over into Spark, but beyond that, Spark is not nearly as tricky as Scala, and there are fewer Spark tips in the rest of the book than Scala tips.

Finally, regarding graphs, in this book we don't delve into pure "graph theory" involving mathematical proofs—for example, about vertices and edges. We do, however, frequently refer to structural properties of graphs, and for that reason some helpful terminology is defined in this chapter.

3.1 Scala, the native language of Spark

The vast majority of Spark, including GraphX, is written in Scala—pretty much everything inside Spark is implemented in Scala except for the APIs to support languages other than Scala. Because of this Scala flavor under the hood, everything in this book is in Scala, except for section 10.2 on non-Scala languages. This section is a crash course on Scala. It covers enough to get you started and, combined with the Scala tips sprinkled throughout the book, will be enough for you to use Spark. Scala is a rich, deep language that takes years to fully learn.

We also look at functional programming because some of its ideas have had a strong influence on the design of Spark and the way it works. Although much of the syntax of Scala will be intelligible to Java or C++ programmers, certain constructs, such as inferred typing and anonymous functions, are used frequently in Spark programming and need to be understood. We cover all the essential constructs and concepts necessary to work with GraphX.

Its complexity is not without controversy. Although Scala affords power, expressiveness, and conciseness, that same power can sometimes be abused to create obfuscated code. Some companies that have attempted to adopt Scala have tried to establish coding standards to limit such potential abuses and emphasize more explicit and verbose code and more conventional (purists would say less functional) programming styles, only to find that incorporating third-party Scala libraries forces them to use the full gamut of Scala syntax anyway, or that their own team of Java programmers weren't able to become fully productive in Scala. But for small high-performance teams or the solo programmer, Scala's conciseness can enable a high degree of productivity.

3.1.1 Scala's philosophy: conciseness and expressiveness

Scala is a philosophy unto itself. You may have heard that Scala is an *object-functional* programming language, meaning it blends the functional programming of languages like Lisp, Scheme, and Haskell with the object-oriented programming of languages like C++ and Java. And that's true. But the Scala philosophy embodies so much more. The two overriding maxims of the designers and users of Scala are as follows:

1 Conciseness. Some say that it takes five lines of Java code to accomplish the same thing as one line of Scala.

2 Expressiveness sufficient to allow things that look like language keywords and operators to be added via libraries rather than through modifying the Scala compiler itself. Going by the name Domain Specific Languages (DSL), examples include Akka and ScalaStorm. Even on a smaller scale, the Scala Standard

Library defines functions that look like part of the language, such as `&()` for `Set` intersection (which is usually combined with Scala's *infix notation* to look like A = B & C, hiding the fact that it's just a function call).

> **NOTE** The term *infix* commonly refers to the way operators are situated between the operands in a mathematical expression—for example, the plus sign goes between the values in the expression 2 + 2. Scala has the usual method-calling syntax familiar to Java, Python, and C++ programmers, where the method name comes first followed by a list of parameters surrounded by round brackets, as in `add(2,2)`. However Scala also has a special infix syntax for single argument methods that can be used as an alternative.

Many Scala language features (besides the fact the Scala is a functional programming language) enable conciseness: inferred typing, implicit parameters, implicit conversions, the dozen distinct uses of the wildcard-like underscore, case classes, default parameters, partial evaluation, and optional parentheses on function invocations. We don't cover all these concepts because this isn't a book on Scala (for recommended books on Scala, see appendix C). Later in this section we talk about one of these concepts: inferred typing. Some of the others, such as some of the uses of underscore, are covered in appendix D. Many of the advanced Scala language features aren't covered at all in this book. But first, let's review what is meant by *functional programming*.

3.1.2 *Functional programming*

Despite all the aforementioned language features, Scala is still first and foremost a functional language. Functional programming has its own set of philosophies:

- *Immutability* is the idea that functions shouldn't have side-effects (changing system state) because this makes it harder to reason at a higher level about the operation of the program.
- Functions are treated as first-class objects—anywhere you would use a standard type such as `Int` or `String`, you can also use a function. In particular, functions can be assigned to variables or passed as arguments to other functions.
- Declarative iteration techniques such as recursion are used in preference to explicit loops in code.

IMMUTABLE DATA: VAL

When data is immutable—akin to Java `final` or C++ `const`—and there's no state to keep track of, it makes it easier for both the compiler and the programmer to conceptualize. Nothing useful can happen without state; for example, any sort of input/output is by its nature stateful. But in the functional programming philosophy, the programmer out of habit cringes whenever a stateful variable or collection has to be declared because it makes it harder for the compiler and the programmer to understand and reason about. Or, to put it more accurately, the functional programmer understands where to employ state and where not to, whereas in contrast, the Java or

C++ programmer may not bother to declare final or const where it might make sense. Besides I/O, examples where state is handy include implementing classic algorithms from the literature or performance-optimizing the use of large collections.

Scala "variable" declarations all start off with var or val. They differ in just one character, and that may be one reason why programmers new to Scala and functional programming in general—or perhaps familiar with languages like JavaScript or C# that have var as a keyword—may declare everything as var. But val declares a fixed value that must be initialized on declaration and can never be reassigned thereafter. On the other hand, var is like a normal variable in Java. A programmer following the Scala philosophy will declare almost everything as val, even for intermediate calculations, only resorting to var under extraordinary situations. For example, using the Scala or Spark shell:

```
scala> val x = 10
x: Int = 10

scala> x = 20
<console>:12: error: reassignment to val
       x = 20
         ^
scala> var y = 10
y: Int = 10

scala> y = 20
y: Int = 20
```

IMMUTABLE DATA: COLLECTIONS

This idea of everything being constant is even applied to collections. Functional programmers prefer that collections—yes, entire collections—be immutable. Some of the reasons for this are practical—a lot of collections are small, and the penalty for not being able to update in-place is small—and some are idealistic. The idealism is that with immutable data, the compiler should be smart enough to optimize away the inefficiency and possibly insert mutability to accomplish the mathematically equivalent result.

Spark realizes this fantasy to a great extent, perhaps better than functional programming systems that preceded it. Spark's fundamental data collection, the Resilient Distributed Dataset (RDD), is immutable. As you'll see in the section on Spark later in this chapter, operations on RDDs are queued up in a lazy fashion and then executed all at once only when needed, such as for final output. This allows the Spark system to optimize away some intermediate operations, as well as to plan data shuffles which involve expensive communication, serialization, and disk I/O.

IMMUTABLE DATA: GOAL OF REDUCING SIDE EFFECTS

The last piece of the immutability puzzle discussed here is the goal of having functions with no side effects. In functional programming, the ideal function takes input and produces output—the same output consistently for any given input—without affecting any state, either globally or that referenced by the input parameters. Functional compilers and interpreters can reason about such stateless functions more effectively and optimize execution. It's idealistic for everything to be stateless, because truly stateless means no I/O, but it's a good goal to be stateless unless there's a good reason not to be.

FUNCTIONS AS FIRST-CLASS OBJECTS

Yes, other languages like C++ and Java have pointers to functions and callbacks, but Scala makes it easy to declare functions inline and to pass them around without having to declare separate "prototypes" or "interfaces" the way C++ and Java (pre-Java 8) do. These anonymous inline functions are sometimes called *lambda expressions.*

To see how to do this in Scala, let's first define a function the normal way by declaring a function prototype:

```
scala> def welcome(name: String) = "Hello " + name
welcome: (name: String)String
```

Function definitions start with the keyword def followed by the name of the function and a list of parameters in parentheses. Then the function body follows an equals sign. We would have to wrap the function body with curly braces if it contained several lines, but for one line this isn't necessary.

Now we can call the function like this:

```
scala> welcome("World")
res12: String = Hello World
```

The function returns the string Hello World as we would expect. But we can also write the function as an anonymous function and use it like other values. For example, we could have written the welcome function like this:

```
(name: String) => "Hello " + name
```

To the left of the => we define a list of parameters, and to the right we have the function body. We can assign this literal to a variable and then call the function using the variable:

```
scala> var f = (name: String) => "Hello " + name
scala> f("World")
res14: String = Hello World
```

Because we are treating functions like other values, they also have a type—in this case, the type is String => String. As with other values, we can also pass a function to another function that is expecting a function type—for example, calling map() on a List as shown at the top of the next page.

Scala intelligently handles what happens when a function references global or local variables declared outside the function. It wraps them up into a neat bundle with the function in an operation behind the scenes called *closure.* For example, in the following code, Scala wraps up the variable n with the function addn() and respects its

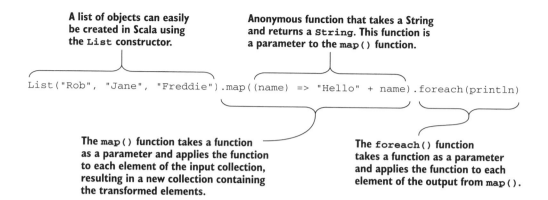

A list of objects can easily be created in Scala using the `List` constructor.

Anonymous function that takes a String and returns a `string`. This function is a parameter to the `map()` function.

```
List("Rob", "Jane", "Freddie").map((name) => "Hello" + name).foreach(println)
```

The `map()` function takes a function as a parameter and applies the function to each element of the input collection, resulting in a new collection containing the transformed elements.

The `foreach()` function takes a function as a parameter and applies the function to each element of the output from `map()`.

subsequent change in value, even though the variable n falls out of scope at the completion of doStuff():

```
scala> var f:Int => Int = null
f: Int => Int = null
scala> def doStuff() = {
     |    var n = 3;
     |    def addn(m:Int) = {
     |       m+n
     |    }
     |    f = addn
     |    n = n+1
     | }
doStuff: ()Unit
scala> doStuff()
scala> f(2)
res0: Int = 6
```

ITERATION DECLARATIVE RATHER THAN IMPERATIVE

If you see a for-loop in a functional programming language, it's because it was shoe-horned in, intended to be used only in exceptional circumstances. The two native ways to accomplish iteration in a functional programming language are map() and recursion. map() takes a function as a parameter and applies it to a collection. This idea goes all the way back to the 1950s in Lisp, where it was called mapcar (just five years after FORTRAN's DO loops).

Recursion, where a function calls itself, runs the risk of causing a stack overflow. For certain types of recursion, though, Scala is able to compile the function as a loop instead. Scala provides an annotation @tailrec to check whether this transformation is possible, raising a compile-time exception if not.

Like other functional programming languages, Scala does provide a for loop construct for when you need it. One example of where it is appropriate is coding a classic numerical algorithm such as the Fast Fourier Transform. Another example is a recursive function where @tailrec cannot be used. There are many more examples.

Scala also provides another type of iteration called the *for comprehension*, which is nearly equivalent to map(). This isn't imperative iteration like C++ and Java for loops, and choosing between for comprehension and map() is largely a stylistic choice.

3.1.3   Inferred typing

Inferred typing is one of the hallmarks of Scala, but not all functional programming languages have inferred typing. In the declaration

```
val n = 3
```

Scala infers that the type for n is Int based on the fact that the type of the number 3 is Int. Here's the equivalent declaration where the type is included:

```
val n:Int = 3
```

Inferred typing is still static typing. Once the Scala compiler determines the type of a variable, it stays with that type forever. Scala is not a dynamically-typed language like Perl, where variables can change their types at runtime. Inferred typing is a convenience for the coder. For example,

```
val myList = new ListBuffer[Int]();
```

In Java, you would have had to type out ArrayList<int> twice, once for the declaration and once for the new. Notice that type-parameterization in Scala uses square brackets—ListBuffer[Int]—rather than Java's angle brackets.

At other times, inferred typing can be confusing. That's why some teams have internal Scala coding standards that stipulate types always be explicitly stated. But in the real world, third-party Scala code is either linked in or read by the programmer to learn what it's doing, and the vast majority of that code relies exclusively on inferred typing. IDEs can help, providing hover text to display inferred types.

One particular time where inferred typing can be confusing is the return type of a function. In Scala, the return type of a function is determined by the value of the last statement of the function (there isn't even a return). For example:

```
def addOne(x:Int) = {
    val xPlusOne = x+1.0
    xPlusOne
}
```

The return type of addOne() is Double. In a long function, this can take a while for a human to figure out. The alternative to the above where the return type is explicitly declared is:

```
def addOne(x:Int):Double = {
    val xPlusOne = x+1.0
    xPlusOne
}
```

TUPLES

Scala doesn't support multiple return values like Python does, but it does support a syntax for tuples that provides a similar facility. A *tuple* is a sequence of values of miscellaneous types. In Scala there's a class for 2-item tuples, Tuple2; a class for 3-item tuples, Tuple3; and so on all the way up to Tuple22.

The individual elements of the tuple can be accessed using fields _1, _2, and so forth. Now we can declare and use a tuple like this:

```
scala> val t = Tuple2("Rod", 3)
scala> println(t._1 + " has " + t._2 + " coconuts")
Rod has 3 coconuts
```

Scala has one more trick up its sleeve: we can declare a tuple of the correct type by surrounding the elements of the tuple with parentheses. We could have written this:

```
scala> val t = ("Rod", 3)
scala> println(t._1 + " has " + t._2 + " coconuts")
Rod has 3 coconuts
```

3.1.4 Class declaration

There are three ways (at least) to declare a class in Scala.

JAVA-LIKE

```
class myClass(initName:String, initId:Integer) {
    val name:String = initName
    private var id:Integer = initId          Everything is public
    def makeMessage = {                      by default in Scala.
        "Hi, I'm a " + name + " with id " + id
    }
}
val x = new myClass("cat", 3)
```

Notice that although there's no explicit constructor as in Java, there are class parameters that can be supplied as part of the class declaration: in this case, initName and initId. The class parameters are assigned to the variables name and id respectively by statements within the class body.

In the last line, we create an instance of myClass called x. Because class variables are public by default in Scala, we can write x.name to access the name variable.

Calling the makeMessage function, x.makeMessage, returns the string:

```
Hi, I'm a cat with id 0
```

SHORTHAND

One of the design goals of Scala is to reduce boilerplate code with the intention of making the resulting code more concise and easier to read and understand, and class definitions are no exception. This class definition uses two features of Scala to reduce the boilerplate code:

```
class myClass(val name:String, id:Integer = 0) {
    def makeMessage = "Hi, I'm a " + name + " with id " + id
```

```
}
val y1 = new myClass("cat",3)          ⟵── Name is set to "cat" and id to 3.
val y2 = new myClass("dog")            ⟵── Name is set to "dog" and id to 0.
```

Note that we've added the val modifier to the name class parameter. The effect of this is to make the name field part of the class definition without having to explicitly assign it, as in the first example.

For the second class parameter, id, we've assigned a default value of 0. Now we can construct using the name and id or just the name.

CASE CLASS

```
case class myClass(name:String, id:Integer = 0) {
    def makeMessage = "Hi, I'm a " + name + " with id " + id
}
val z = myClass("cat",3)
```

> With case classes, there's no need for the new keyword.

Case classes were originally intended for a specific purpose: to serve as cases in a Scala match clause (called *pattern matching*). They've since been co-opted to serve more general uses and now have few differences from regular classes, except that all the variable members implicitly declared in the class declaration/constructor are public by default (val doesn't have to be specified as for a regular class), and equals() is automatically defined (which is called by ==).

3.1.5　Map and reduce

You probably recognize the term *map and reduce* from Hadoop (if not, section 3.2.3 discusses them). But the concepts originated in functional programming (again, all the way back to Lisp, but by different names).

Say we have a grocery bag full of fruits, each in a quantity, and we want to know the total number of pieces of fruit. In Scala it might look like this:

```
class fruitCount(val name:String, val num:Int)
val groceries = List(new fruitCount("banana",5), new fruitCount("apple",3))
groceries.map(f => f.num).reduce((a:Int, b:Int) => a+b)
```

map() converts a collection into another collection via some transforming function you pass as the parameter into map(). reduce() takes a collection and reduces it to a single value via some pairwise reducing function you pass into reduce(). That function—call it f—should be commutative and associative, meaning if reduce(f) is invoked on a collection of List(1,2,7,8), then reduce() can choose to do f(f(1,2),f(7,8)), or it can do f(f(7,1),f(8,2)), and so on, and it comes up with the same answer because you've ensured that f is commutative and associative. Addition is an example of a function that is commutative and associative, and subtraction is an example of a function that is not.

This general idea of mapping followed by reducing is pervasive throughout functional programming, Hadoop, and Spark.

UNDERSCORE TO AVOID NAMING ANONYMOUS FUNCTION PARAMETERS

Scala provides a shorthand where, for example, instead of having to come up with the variable name f in `groceries.map(f => f.num)`, you can instead write

```
groceries.map(_.num)
```

This only works, though, if you need to reference the variable only once and if that reference isn't deeply nested (for example, even an extra set of parenthesis can confuse the Scala compiler).

THE _ + _ IDIOM

`_ + _` is a Scala idiom that throws a lot of people new to Scala for a loop. It is frequently cited as a tangible reason to dislike Scala, even though it's not that hard to understand. Underscores, in general, are used throughout Scala as a kind of wildcard character. One of the hurdles is that there are a dozen distinct uses of underscores in Scala. This idiom represents two of them. The first underscore stands for the first parameter, and the second underscore stands for the second parameter. And, oh, by the way, neither parameter is given a name nor declared before being used. It is shorthand for `(a,b) => (a + b)`. (which itself is shorthand because it still omits the types, but we wanted to provide something completely equivalent to `_ + _`). It is a *Scala idiom for reducing/aggregating* by addition, two items at a time. Now, we have to admit, it would be our personal preference for the second underscore to refer again to the first parameter because we more frequently need to refer multiply to a single parameter in a single-parameter anonymous function than we do to refer once each to multiple parameters in a multiple-parameter anonymous function. In those cases, we have to trudge out an x and do something like `x => x.firstName + x.lastName`. But Scala's not going to change, so we've resigned ourselves to the second underscore referring to the second parameter, which seems to be useful only for the infamous `_ + _` idiom.

3.1.6 *Everything is a function*

As already shown, all functions in Scala return a value because it's the value of the last line of the function. There are no "procedures" in Scala, and there is no `void` type (though Scala functions returning `Unit` are similar to Java functions returning `void`). Everything in Scala is a function, and that even goes for its versions of what would otherwise seem to be classic imperative control structures.

IF/ELSE

In Scala, if/else returns a value. It's like the "ternary operator" `?:` from Java, except that `if` and `else` are spelled out:

```
val s = if (2.3 > 2.2) "Bigger" else "Smaller"
```

Now, we can format it so that it looks like Java, but it's still working functionally:

```
def doubleEvenSquare(x:Int) = {
    if (x % 2 == 0) {
        val square = x * x
```

```
        2 * square
    }
    else
        x
}
```

Here, a block surrounded by braces has replaced the "then" value. The `if` block gives the appearance of not participating in a functional statement, but recall that this is the last statement of the `doubleEvenSquare()` function, so the output of this `if/else` supplies the return value for the function.

MATCH/CASE

Scala's `match/case` is similar to Java's `switch/case`, except that it is, of course, functional. `match/case` returns a value. It also uses an infix notation, which throws off Java developers coming to Scala. The order is `myState match { case ... }` as opposed to `switch (myState) { case ... }`. The Scala match/case is also many times more powerful because it supports "pattern matching"—cases based on both data types and data values, not to be confused with Java regular expression pattern matching—but that's beyond the scope of this book.

Here's an example of using match/case to transition states in part of a string parser of floating point numbers:

```
class parserState
case class mantissaState() extends parserState
case class fractionalState() extends parserState
case class exponentState() extends parserState
def stateMantissaConsume(c:Char) = c match {
    case '.' => fractionalState
    case 'E' => exponentState
    case _ => mantissaState
}
```

Because case classes act like values, `stateMantissaConsume('.')`, for example, returns the case class `fractionalState`.

3.1.7   *Java interoperability*

Scala is a JVM language. Scala code can call Java code and Java code can call Scala code. Moreover, there are some standard Java libraries that Scala depends upon, such as Serializable, JDBC, and TCP/IP.

Scala being a JVM language also means that the usual caveats of working with a JVM also apply, namely dealing with garbage collection and type erasure.

> ## Type erasure in a nutshell
>
> Although most Java programmers will have had to deal with garbage collection, often on a daily basis, type erasure is little more esoteric.
>
> When Generics were introduced into Java 1.5, the language designers had to decide how the feature would be implemented. Generics are the feature that allows you to parameterize a class with a type. The typical example is the Java Collections where you can add a parameter to a collection like `List` by writing `List<String>`. Once parameterized, the compiler will only allow `String`s to be added to the list.
>
> The type information is not carried forward to the runtime execution, though—as far as the JVM is concerned, the list is still just a `List`. This loss of the runtime type parameterization is called *type erasure*. It can lead to some unexpected and hard-to-understand errors if you're writing code that uses or relies on runtime type identification. In this context of ranking, it is also known as Zipf's Law. These are the realities of graphs, and distributing graph data by the vertex-cut strategy balances graph data across a cluster. Spark GraphX employs the vertex-cut strategy by default.

3.2 Spark

Spark extends the Scala philosophy of functional programming into the realm of distributed computing. In this section you'll learn how that influences the design of the most important concept in Spark: the Resilient Distributed Dataset (RDD). This section also looks at a number of other features of Spark so that by the end of the section you can write your first full-fledged Spark program.

3.2.1 Distributed in-memory data: RDDs

As you saw in chapter 1, the foundation of Spark is RDD. An RDD is a collection that distributes data across nodes (computers) in a cluster of computers. An RDD is also immutable—existing RDDs cannot be changed or updated. Instead, new RDDs are created from transformation of existing RDDs. Generally, an RDDs is unordered unless it has had an ordering operation done to it such as `sortByKey()` or `zip()`.

Spark has a number of ways of creating RDDs from data sources. One of the most common is `SparkContext.textFile()`. The only required parameter is a path to a file:

```
val file = sc.textFile("path/to/file.txt")     ◁─┐  textFile() returns an RDD[String]
                                                  └ where each line is an entry in the RDD.
println(file.count)     ◁──── count returns the number of lines in the file.
```

The object returned from `textFile()` is a type-parameterized RDD: `RDD[String]`. Each line of the text file is treated as a `String` entry in the RDD.

By distributing data across a cluster, Spark can handle data larger than would fit on a single computer, and it can process said data in parallel with multiple computers in the cluster processing the data simultaneously.

Figure 3.1   Hadoop configured with replication factor 3 and Spark configured with replication factor 2.

By default, Spark stores RDDs in the memory (RAM) of nodes in the cluster with a replication factor of 1. This is in contrast to HDFS, which stores its data on the disks (hard drives or SSDs) of nodes in the cluster with typically a replication factor of 3 (figure 3.1). Spark can be configured to use different combinations of memory and disk, as well as different replication factors, and this can be set at runtime on a per-RDD basis.

RDDs are type-parametrized similar to Java collections and present a functional programming style API to the programmer, with `map()` and `reduce()` figuring prominently.

Figure 3.2 shows why Spark shines in comparison to Hadoop MapReduce. Iterative algorithms, such as those used in machine learning or graph processing, when implemented in terms of MapReduce are often implemented with a heavy Map and no Reduce (called *map-only jobs*). Each iteration in Hadoop ends up writing intermediate results to HDFS, requiring a number of additional steps, such as serialization or decompression, that can often be much more time-consuming than the calculation. On the other hand, Spark keeps its data in RDDs from one iteration to the next. This means it can skip the additional steps required in MapReduce, leading to processing that is many times faster.

3.2.2   *Laziness*

RDDs are *lazy*. The operations that can be done on an RDD—namely, the methods on the Scala API class RDD—can be divided into *transformations* and *actions*. Transformations are the lazy operations; they get queued up and do nothing immediately. When an action is invoked, that's when all the queued-up transformations finally get

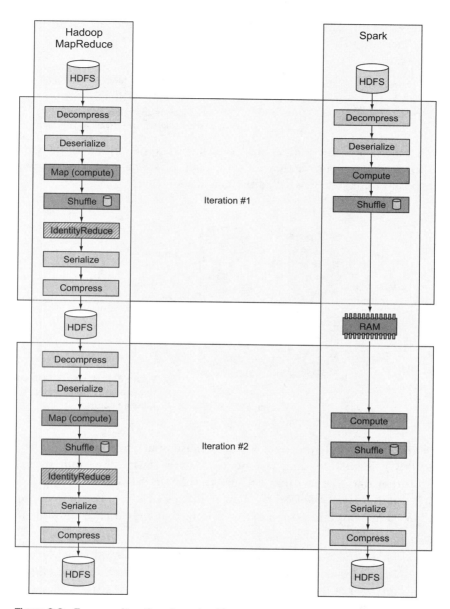

Figure 3.2 From one iteration of an algorithm to the next, Spark avoids the six steps of serialize, compress, write to disk, read from disk, decompress, and deserialize.

executed (along with the action). As an example, `map()` is a transformation, whereas `reduce()` is an action. These aren't mentioned in the main Scaladocs. The only documentation that lists transformations versus actions is the Programming Guide at http://spark.apache.org/docs/1.6.0/programming-guide.html#transformations. The key point is that functions that take RDDs as input and return new RDDs are transformations, whereas other functions are actions.

As an example:

```
val r = sc.makeRDD(Array(1,2,3))
val r2 = r.map(x => 2*x)
val result = r2.reduce(_ + _)
```

← **No computation takes place; map() transformation is queued up.**

← **reduce() is an action, so both map() and reduce() take place on this line.**

Figure 3.3 shows how the original array is transformed into a number of RDDs. At this point the transformations are queued up. Finally, a `reduce` method is called to return a value; it isn't until `reduce` is called that any work is done.

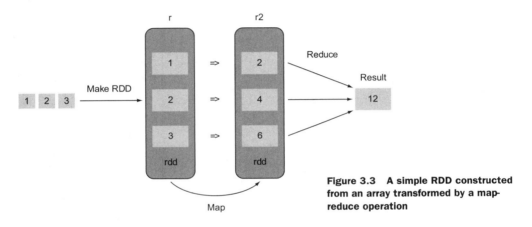

Figure 3.3   A simple RDD constructed from an array transformed by a map-reduce operation

Well, *queued* isn't exactly the right word, because Spark maintains a directed acyclic graph (DAG) of the pending operations. These DAGs have nothing to do with GraphX, other than the fact that because GraphX uses RDDs, Spark is doing its own DAG work underneath the covers when it processes RDDs. By maintaining a DAG, Spark can avoid computing common operations that appear early multiple times.

CACHING

What would happen if we took the RDD r2 and performed another action on it—say, a `count` to find out how many items are in the RDD? If we did nothing else, the entire history (or lineage) of the RDD would be recalculated starting from the `makeRDD` call.

In many Spark processing pipelines, there can be many RDDs in the lineage, and the initial RDD will usually start by reading in data from a data store. Clearly it doesn't make sense to keep rerunning the same processing over and over.

Spark has a solution in `cache()` or its more flexible cousin `persist()`. When you call `cache` (or `persist,`) this is an instruction to Spark to keep a copy of the RDD so that it doesn't have to be constantly recalculated. It's important to understand that the caching only happens on the next action, not at the time cache is called. We can extend our previous example like this:

```
val r = sc.makeRDD(Array(1,2,3))
val r2 = r.map(x => 2*x).cache
val result = r2.reduce(_ + _)
val count  = r2.count
```

No computation takes place even though cache() has been called.

The computation takes place due to the action reduce().

The elements of r2 are counted without having to re-execute the whole pipeline.

Chapter 9 looks in more detail at when and how to use cache/persist.

3.2.3 Cluster requirements and terminology

Spark doesn't live alone on an island. It needs some other pieces to go along with it (see figure 3.4).

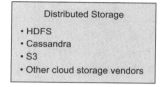

Distributed Storage

• HDFS
• Cassandra
• S3
• Other cloud storage vendors

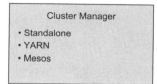

Cluster Manager

• Standalone
• YARN
• Mesos

Figure 3.4   Spark requires two major pieces to be present: a distributed file system and a cluster manager. There are options for each.

As mentioned in appendix A and elsewhere, having distributed storage or a cluster manager isn't strictly necessary for testing and development. Most of the examples in this book assume neither.

The pros and cons of each technology are beyond the scope of this book, but to define terms, *standalone* means the cluster manager native to Spark. Such a cluster can usually be effectively used only for Spark and can't be shared with other applications such as Hadoop/YARN. YARN and Mesos, in contrast, facilitate sharing an expensive cluster asset among multiple users and applications. YARN is more Hadoop-centric and has the potential to support HDFS data locality (see SPARK-4352), whereas Mesos is more general-purpose and can manage resources more finely.

Terminology for the parts of a standalone cluster is shown in figure 3.5. There are four levels:

- Driver
- Master
- Worker
- Task

The driver contains the code you write to create a SparkContext and submit jobs to the cluster, which is controlled by the Master. Spark calls the individual nodes (machines) in the cluster *workers*, but in these days of multiple CPU cores, each worker has one task per CPU core (for example, for an 8-core CPU, a worker would be able to handle 8 tasks). Tasks are each single-threaded by default.

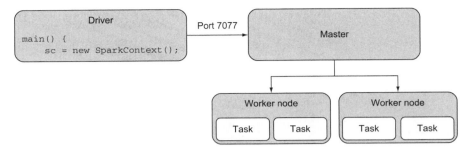

Figure 3.5   Terminology for a standalone cluster. Terminology for YARN and Mesos clusters varies slightly.

One final term you'll run into is *stage*. When Spark plans how to distribute execution across the cluster, it plans out a series of stages, each of which consists of multiple tasks. The Spark Scheduler then figures out how to map the tasks to worker nodes.

3.2.4   Serialization

When Spark ships your data between driver, master, worker, and tasks, it serializes your data. That means, for example, that if you use an RDD[MyClass], you need to make sure MyClass can be serialized. The simplest and easiest way to do this is to append extends Serializable to the class declaration (yes, the good old Serializable Java interface, except in Scala the keyword is extends instead of implements), but it's also the slowest.

There are two alternatives to Serializable that afford higher performance. One is Kryo, and the other is Externalizable. Kryo is much faster and compresses more efficiently than Serializable. Spark has first-class, built-in support for Kryo, but it's not without issues. In earlier versions of Spark 1.1, there were many major bugs in Spark's support for Kryo, and even as of Spark 1.6, there are still a dozen Jira tickets open for various edge cases.

Externalizable allows you to define your own serialization, such as forwarding the calls to a serialization/compression library like Avro. This is a reasonable approach to getting better performance and compression than Serializable, but it requires a ton of boilerplate code to pull it off.

This book uses Serializable for simplicity, and we recommend it through the prototype stage of any project, switching to an alternative only during performance-tuning.

3.2.5   Common RDD operations

MAP/REDUCE

You've already seen a couple examples of map/reduce in Spark, but here's where we burst the bubble about Spark being in-memory. Data is indeed held in memory (for the default storage level setting), but between map() and reduce(), and more generally between transformations and actions, a shuffle usually takes place.

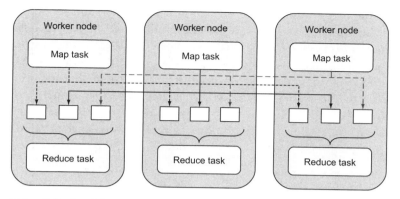

Figure 3.6 Spark has to do a shuffle between a map and a reduce, and as of Spark 1.6, this shuffle is always written to and read from disk.

A *shuffle* involves the map tasks writing a number of files to disk, one for each reduce task that's going to need data (see figure 3.6). The data is read by the reduce task, and if the map and reduce are on different machines, a network transfer takes place.

Ways to avoid and optimize the shuffle are covered in chapter 9.

KEY-VALUE PAIRS

Standard RDDs are collections, such as `RDD[String]` or `RDD[MyClass]`. Another major category of RDDs that Spark explicitly provides for is key-value pairs (PairRDD). When the RDD is constructed from a Scala `Tuple2`, a PairRDD is automatically created for you. For example, if you have tuples consisting of a `String` and an `Int`, the type of the RDD will be `RDD[(String, Int)]` (as mentioned earlier, in Scala the parenthesis notation with two values is shorthand for a `Tuple2`).

Here's a typical way that a PairRDD is constructed:

```
val r = sc.makeRDD(Array("Apples", "Bananas", "Oranges"))
val pairrdd = r.map(x => (x.substring(0,1), x)).cache
```

Anonymous function passed to map outputs a (String, String) tuple with type PairRDD[(String, String)].

The transformation is shown in Figure 3.7.

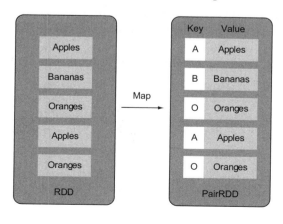

Figure 3.7 A simple `RDD[String]` converted to `PairRDD[(String, String)]`

In the `Tuple2`, the first of the two values is considered the key, and the second is considered the value, and that's why you see things like `RDD[(K,V)]` throughout the `PairRDDFunctions` Scaladocs.

Spark automatically makes available to you additional RDD operations that are specific to handling key-value pairs. The documentation for these additional operations can be found in the Scaladocs for the `PairRDDFunctions` class. Spark automatically converts from an RDD to a `PairRDDFunctions` whenever necessary, so you can treat the additional `PairRDDFunctions` operations as if they were part of your RDD. To enable these automatic conversions, you must include the following in your code:

```
import org.apache.spark.SparkContext
import org.apache.spark.SparkContext._
```

You can use either a Scala built-in type for the key or a custom class, but if you use a custom class, be sure to define both `equals()` and `hashCode()` for it.

A lot of the `PairRDDFunctions` operations are based on the general `combineByKey()` idea, where first items with the same key are grouped together and an operation is applied to each group. For example, `groupByKey()` is a concept that should resonate with developers familiar with SQL. But in the Spark world, `reduceByKey()` is often more efficient. Performance considerations are discussed in chapter 9.

Another `PairRDDFunctions` operation that will resonate with SQL developers is `join()`. Given two RDDs of key-value pairs, `join()` will return a single RDD of key-value pairs where the values contain the values from both of the two input RDDs.

Finally, `sortByKey()` is a way to apply ordering to your RDDs, for which ordering is otherwise not guaranteed to be consistent from one operation to the next. For primitive types such as `Int` and `String`, the resulting ordering is as expected, but if your key is a custom class, you will need to define a custom `compare()` function using a Scala `implicit`, and that is out of scope of this book.

OTHER USEFUL FUNCTIONS

`zip()` is an immensely useful function from functional programming. It's another way (besides `map()` and recursion) to avoid imperative iteration, and it's a way to iterate over two collections simultaneously. If in an imperative language you had a loop that accessed two arrays in each iteration, then in Spark these collections would presumably be stored in RDDs and would `zip()` them together (see figure 3.8) and then perform a `map()` (instead of a loop).

A common use of zip in functional programming is to zip with the sequential integers 1,2,3,.... For this, Spark offers `zipWithIndex()`.

There are two other useful functions to mention here. `union()` appends one RDD to another (though not necessarily to the "end" because RDDs don't generally preserve ordering). `distinct()` is yet another operation that has a direct SQL correspondence.

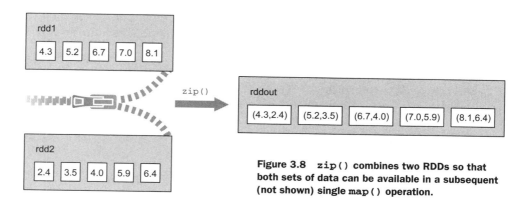

Figure 3.8 `zip()` **combines two RDDs so that both sets of data can be available in a subsequent (not shown) single** `map()` **operation.**

MLLIB

MLlib is the machine-learning library component that comes with Spark. But besides machine learning, it also contains some basic RDD operations that shouldn't be overlooked even if you're not doing machine learning:

- *Sliding window*—For when you need to operate on groups of sequential RDD elements at a time, such as calculating a moving average (if you're familiar with technical analysis in stock charting) or doing finite impulse response (FIR) filtering (if you're familiar with digital signal processing (DSP)). The `sliding()` function in `mllib.rdd.RDDFunctions` will do this grouping for you by creating an `RDD[Array[T]]` where each element of the `RDD` is an array of length of the specified window length. Yes, this duplicates the data in memory by a factor of the specified window length, but it's the easiest way to code sliding window formulas.
- *Statistics*—RDDs are generally one-dimensional, but if you have `RDD[Vector]`, then you effectively have a two-dimensional matrix. If you have `RDD[Vector]` and you need to compute statistics on each "column," then `colStats()` in `mllib.stat.Statistics` will do it.

3.2.6   *Hello World with Spark and sbt*

sbt, or *Simple Build Tool*, is the "make" or "Maven" native to Scala. If you don't already have it installed, download and install it from www.scala-sbt.org (if you're using the Cloudera QuickStart VM as suggested in appendix A, then it's already installed). Like most modern build systems, sbt expects a particular directory structure. As in listings 3.1 and 3.2, put helloworld.sbt into ~/helloworld and helloworld.scala into ~/helloworld /src/main/scala. Then, while in the helloworld directory, enter this command:

```
sbt run
```

You don't need to install the Scala compiler yourself; sbt will automatically download and install it for you. sbt has Apache Ivy built in, which does package management similar to what Maven has built-in. Ivy was originally from the Ant project. In helloworld

.sbt in the following listing, the `libraryDependencies` line instructs sbt to ask Ivy to download and cache the Spark 1.6 Jar files (and dependencies) into ~/.ivy2/cache.

Listing 3.1   helloworld.sbt

```
scalaVersion := "2.10.5"
libraryDependencies += "org.apache.spark" %% "spark-core" % "1.6.0"
```

Listing 3.2   hellworld.scala

```
import org.apache.spark.SparkContext
import org.apache.spark.SparkConf

object helloworld {
  def main(args: Array[String]) {
    val sc = new SparkContext(new SparkConf().setMaster("local")
                                        .setAppName("helloworld"))
    val r = sc.makeRDD(Array("Hello", "World"))
    r.foreach(println(_))
    sc.stop
  }
}
```

When creating applications that use GraphX, you will also need to add the following line to your sbt file to bring in the GraphX jar and dependencies:

```
libraryDependencies += "org.apache.spark" %% "spark-graphx" % "1.6.0"
```

3.3   *Graph terminology*

This book avoids graph "theory." There are no proofs involving numbers of edges and vertices. But to understand the practical applications that this book focuses on, some terminology and definitions are helpful.

3.3.1   *Basics*

In this book we use graphs to model real-world problems, which begs the question: what options are available for modeling problems with graphs?

DIRECTED VS. UNDIRECTED GRAPHS

As discussed in chapter 1, a graph models "things" and relationships between "things." The first distinction we should make is between directed and undirected graphs, shown in figure 3.9. In a directed graph, the relationship is from a source vertex to a destination vertex. Typical examples are the links from one web page to another in the World Wide Web or references in academic papers. Note that in a directed graph, the two ends of the edge play different roles, such as parent-child or page A links to page B.

In an undirected graph, our edge has no arrow; the relationship is symmetrical. This is a typical type of relationship in a social network, as generally if A is a friend of B, then we are likely to consider B to be friend of A. Or to put it another way, if we are six degrees of separation from Kevin Bacon, then Kevin Bacon is six degrees of separation from us.

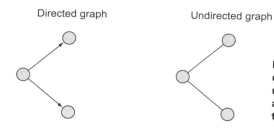

Figure 3.9 **All graphs in GraphX are inherently directed graphs, but GraphX also supports undirected graphs in some of its built-in algorithms that ignore the direction. You can do the same if you need undirected graphs.**

One important point to understand is that in GraphX, all edges have a direction, so the graphs are inherently directed. But it's possible to treat them as undirected graphs by ignoring the direction of the edge.

CYCLIC VS. ACYCLIC GRAPHS

A *cyclic graph* is one that contains cycles, a series of vertices that are connected in a loop (see figure 3.10). An *acyclic graph* has no cycles. One of the reasons to be aware of the distinction is that if you have an algorithm that traverses connected vertices by following the connecting edges, then cyclic graphs pose the risk that naive implementations can get stuck going round forever.

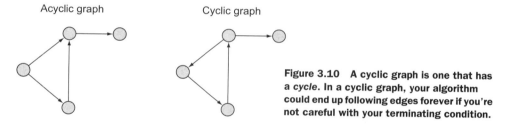

Figure 3.10 **A cyclic graph is one that has a *cycle*. In a cyclic graph, your algorithm could end up following edges forever if you're not careful with your terminating condition.**

One feature of interest in cyclic graphs is a triangle—three vertices that each have an edge with the other two vertices. One of the many uses of triangles is as a predictive feature in models to differentiate spam and non-spam mail hosts.

UNLABELED VS. LABELED GRAPHS

A *labeled graph* is one where the vertices and/or edges have data (labels) associated with them other than their unique identifier (see figure 3.11). Unsurprisingly, graphs with labeled vertices are called *vertex-labeled graphs*; those with labeled edges, *edge-labeled graphs*.

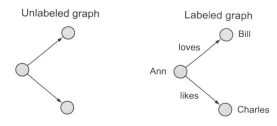

Figure 3.11 **A completely unlabeled graph is usually not useful. Normally at least the vertices are labeled. GraphX's basic `GraphLoader.edgeListFile()` supports labeled vertices but only unlabeled edges.**

We saw in chapter 2 that when GraphX creates an `Edge` with `GraphLoader.edge-ListFile()`, it will always create an attribute in addition to the source and destination vertex IDs, though the attribute is always 1.

One specific type of edge-labeled graph to be aware of is a weighted graph. A weighted graph can be used, for example, to mode the distance between towns in a route-planning application. The weights in this case are edge labels that represent the distance between two vertices (towns).

PARALLEL EDGES AND LOOPS

Another distinction is whether the graph allows multiple edges between the same pair of vertices, or indeed an edge that starts and ends with the same vertex. The possibilities are shown in figure 3.12. GraphX graphs are pseudographs, so extra steps must be taken if parallel edges and loops are to be eliminated, such as calling `groupEdges()` or `subgraph()`.

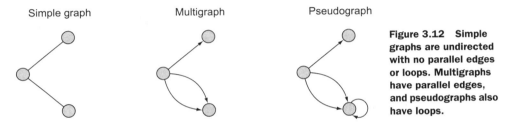

Figure 3.12   Simple graphs are undirected with no parallel edges or loops. Multigraphs have parallel edges, and pseudographs also have loops.

BIPARTITE GRAPHS

Bipartite graphs have a specific structure, as shown in figure 3.13. The vertices are split into two different sets, and edges can only be between a vertex in one set and a vertex in another—no edge can be between vertices in the same set.

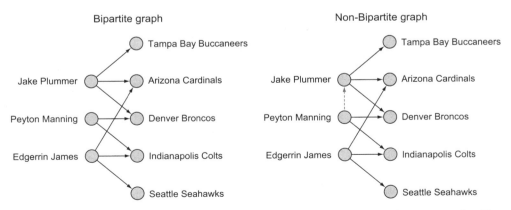

Figure 3.13   Bipartite graphs frequently arise in social network analysis, either in group membership as shown here, or for separating groups of individuals, such as males and females on a heterosexual dating website. In a bipartite graph, all edges go from one set to another. Non-bipartite graphs cannot be so divided, and any attempt to divide them into two sets will end up with at least one edge fully contained in one of the two sets.

Bipartite graphs can be used to model relationships between two different types of entities. For example, for students applying to college, each student would be modeled by vertices in one set and the colleges they apply to by the other set. Another example is a recommendation system where users are in one set and the products they buy are in another.

3.3.2 RDF graphs vs. property graphs

Resource Description Framework (RDF) is a graph standard first proposed in 1997 by the World Wide Web Consortium (W3C) for the *semantic web*. It realized a mini-resurgence starting in 2004 with its updated standard called RDFa. Older graph database/processing systems support only RDF *triples* (subject, predicate, object), whereas newer graph database/processing systems (including GraphX) support property graphs (see figure 3.14).

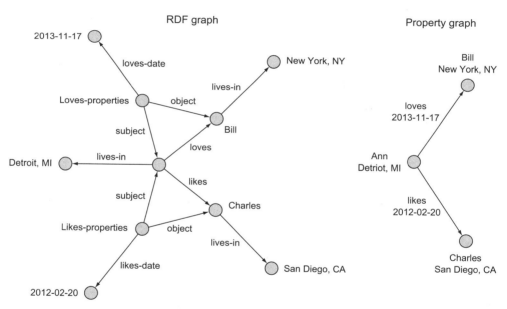

Figure 3.14 Without properties, RDF graphs get unwieldy, in particular when it comes to edge properties. GraphX supports property graphs, which can contain vertex properties and edge properties without adding a bunch of extra vertices to the base graph.

Due to its limitations, RDF triples have had to be extended to quads (which include some kind of ID) and even quints (which include some kind of so-called *context*). These are ways of dancing around the fact that RDF graphs don't have properties. But despite their limitations, RDF graphs remain important due to available graph data, such as the YAGO2 database derived from Wikipedia, WordNet, and GeoNames.

For new graph data, property graphs are easier to work with.

3.3.3   *Adjacency matrix*

Another way graph theorists represent graphs is by an *adjacency matrix* (see figure 3.15). It's not the way GraphX represents graphs, but, separate from GraphX, Spark's MLlib machine learning library has support for adjacency matrices and, more generally, sparse matrices. If you don't need edge properties, you can sometimes find faster-performing algorithms in MLlib than in GraphX. For example, for a recommender system, strictly from a performance standpoint, `mllib.recommendation.ALS` can be a better choice than `graphx.lib.SVDPlusPlus`, although they are different algorithms with different behavior. SVDPlusPlus is covered in section 7.1.

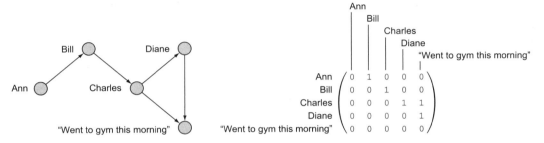

Figure 3.15   A graph and its equivalent adjacency matrix. Notice that an adjacency matrix doesn't have a place to put edge properties.

3.3.4   *Graph querying systems*

There are dozens of graph querying languages, but this section discusses three of the most popular ones and compares them to stock GraphX 1.6. Throughout, we use the example of "Tell me the friends of friends of Ann."

SPARQL

SPARQL is a SQL-like language promoted by W3C for querying RDF graphs:

```
SELECT ?p

{
    "Ann" foaf:knows{2} ?p
}
```

CYPHER

Cypher is the query language used in Neo4j, which is a property graph database.

```
MATCH (ann { name: 'Ann' })-[:knows*2..2]-(p)
RETURN p
```

TINKERPOP GREMLIN

Tinkerpop is an attempt to create a standard interface to graph databases and processing systems—like the JDBC of graphs, but much more. There are several components to Tinkerpop, and Gremlin is the querying system. There is an effort, separate from the main Apache Spark project, to adapt Gremlin to GraphX. It's called the Spark-Gremlin project, available on GitHub at https://github.com/kellrott/spark-gremlin. As of January 2015, the project status was "Nothing works yet."

```
g.V("name", "ann").out('knows').aggregate(x).out('knows').except(x)
```

GRAPHX

GraphX has no query language out of the box as of Spark GraphX 1.6. The GraphX API is better suited to running algorithms over a large graph than to finding some specific information about a specific vertex and its immediate edges and vertices. Nevertheless, it is possible, though clunky:

```
val g2 = g.outerJoinVertices(g.aggregateMessages[Int](
  ctx => if (ctx.srcAttr == "Ann" && ctx.attr == "knows") ctx.sendToDst(1),
  math.max(_,_)))((vid, vname, d) => (vname, d.getOrElse(0)))
g2.outerJoinVertices(g2.aggregateMessages[Int](
  ctx => if (ctx.srcAttr._2 == 1 && ctx.attr == "knows") ctx.sendToDst(2),
  math.max(_,_)))((vid, vname, d) => (vname, d.getOrElse(0))).
  vertices.map(_._2).filter(_._2 == 2).map(_._1._1).collect
```

This is far too complex to dissect in this chapter, but by the end of part 2 of this book, this miniature program will make sense. The point is to illustrate that GraphX, as of version 1.6.0, does not have a quick and easy query language. Two things make the preceding code cumbersome: looking for a specific node in the graph and traversing the graph exactly two steps (as opposed to one step or, alternatively, an unlimited number of steps bound by some other condition).

There is some relief, though. In chapter 10 you'll see GraphFrames, which is a library on GitHub that does provide a subset of Neo4j's Cypher language, together with SQL from Spark SQL, to allow for fast and convenient querying of graphs.

3.4 Summary

- Doing GraphX has a lot of prerequisites: Scala, Spark, and graphs.
- Scala is an object-functional programming language that carries not only the functional philosophy, but also its own philosophy that includes conciseness and implementing features in its library rather than the language itself.
- Spark is effectively a distributed version of Scala, introducing the Resilient Distributed Dataset (RDD).
- GraphX is a layer on top of Spark for processing graphs.
- Graphs have their own vocabulary.
- GraphX supports property graphs.
- GraphX has no query language in the way that graph databases do.

Part 2

Connecting vertices

Graphx has a large API with a number of built-in algorithms. But not all of the API is well-documented. Chapter 4 walks you through how to do basic operations in GraphX, including the cornerstone operations like `pregel()`, which is modeled after Google's Pregel graph system.

Chapter 5 covers the core algorithms that GraphX provides, such as Page-Rank, and discusses how each can be used to solve a real-world problem.

After all that groundwork covered in the first five chapters, chapters 6 and 7 are where we finally really start putting GraphX into action. Chapter 6 shows how to implement some of the classical graph algorithms, such as Minimum Spanning Tree, in GraphX. You'll also see an example of what Minimum Spanning Trees can be used for.

Machine learning has become pervasive. Although Spark's MLlib is the primary way to do machine learning on Spark, graph-oriented machine learning can be done with GraphX. In the extensive chapter 7 you'll learn the basics of machine learning on up through recommender systems (like those used by Netflix or Amazon) and document classification. Then you'll see how to combine MLlib together with GraphX in a spam-detection example.

GraphX Basics

This chapter covers

- The basic GraphX classes
- The basic GraphX operations, based on Map/Reduce and Pregel
- Serialization to disk
- Stock graph generation

Now that we have covered the fundamentals of Spark and of graphs in general, we can put them together with GraphX. In this chapter you'll use both the basic GraphX API and the alternative, and often better-performing, Pregel API. You'll also read and write graphs, and for those times when you don't have graph data handy, generate random graphs.

4.1   Vertex and edge classes

As discussed in chapter 3, Resilient Distributed Datasets (RDDs) are the fundamental building blocks of Spark programs, providing for both flexible, high-performance, data-parallel processing and fault-tolerance. The basic graph class in GraphX is called `Graph`, which contains two RDDs: one for edges and one for vertices (see figure 4.1).

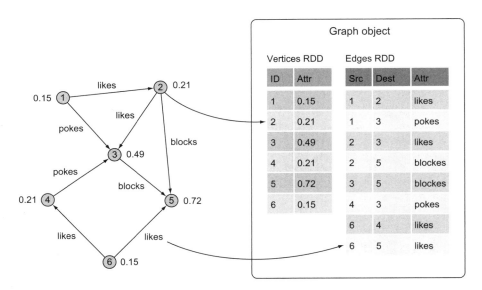

Figure 4.1   A GraphX Graph object is composed of two RDDs: one for the vertices and one for the edges.

One of the big advantages of GraphX over other graph processing systems and graph databases is its ability to treat the underlying data structures as both a graph, using graph concepts and processing primitives, and also as separate collections of edges and vertices that can be mapped, joined, and transformed using data-parallel processing primitives.

In GraphX, it's not necessary to "walk" a graph (starting from some vertex) to get to the edges and vertices you're interested in. For example, transforming vertex property data can be done in one fell swoop in GraphX, whereas in other graph-processing systems and graph databases, such an operation can be contrived in terms of both the necessary query and how such a system goes about performing the operation.

You can construct a graph given two RDD collections: one for edges and one for vertices. Once the graph has been constructed, you can access these collections via the edges() and vertices() accessors of Graph.

Because Graph defines a property graph (as described in chapter 3), each edge and each vertex carries its own custom properties, described by user-defined classes.

In the UML diagram in figure 4.2, VD and ED serve as placeholders for these user-defined classes. Graph is a type-parameterized generic class Graph[VD, ED]. For example, if you had a graph showing cities and their population size as vertices connected by roads, one representation would be Graph[Long, Double], where the vertex data attribute is a Long type for the population size and the edge type a Double for the distance between cities.

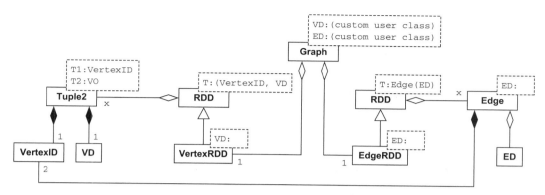

Figure 4.2   UML diagram of GraphX's `Graph` and its dependencies. Note that GraphX defines `VertexId` to be a type synonym of a 64-bit Long.

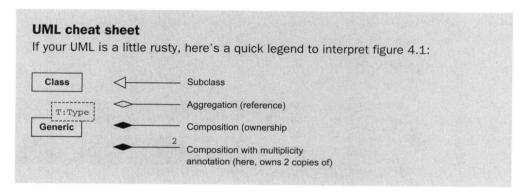

You always have to supply some type of class for VD or ED, even if it's `Int` or `String`. It could be considered a slight limitation in GraphX that there is no inherent support for a "property-less" graph, because the closest you can come is to, for example, make `Int` the type parameter and set every edge and vertex to the same dummy value.

GraphX defines `VertexId` to be of type 64-bit `Long`. You have no choice in the matter. Notice that `Edge` contain `VertexIds` rather than references to the vertices (which are the `(VertexId,VD)` Scala `Tuple2` pairs). That's because graphs are distributed across the cluster and don't reside within a single JVM, and an edge's vertices may be physically residing on a different node in the cluster!

To construct a graph, we can call `Graph()` as if it were a constructor. The example in listing 4.1 (see page 65) constructs the same graph we saw in chapter 1. We'll use this same graph (see figure 4.3) throughout this chapter in other examples.

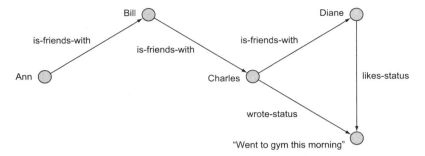

Figure 4.3   Example graph to be constructed and used throughout this chapter

The other (object) half of the Scaladocs

Don't miss out on the "other half" of the Scaladocs. For example, the Graph class and the Graph object each have their own APIs.

Here, the API for the Graph object (as opposed to the Graph class) is being shown

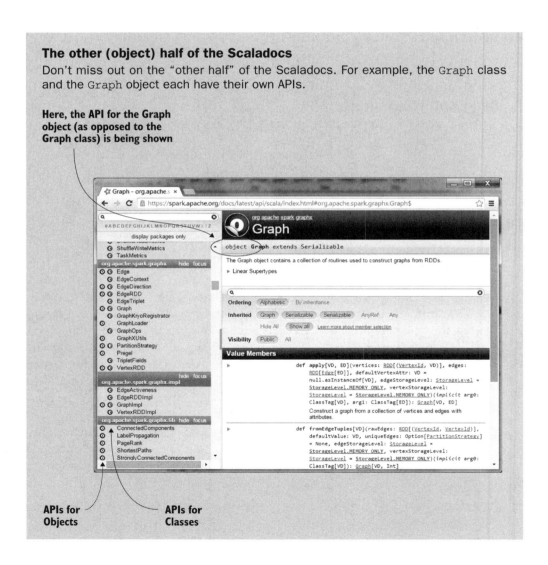

APIs for Objects

APIs for Classes

Listing 4.1 Construct a graph as shown in figure 4.3

```
import org.apache.spark.graphx._

val myVertices = sc.makeRDD(Array((1L, "Ann"), (2L, "Bill"),
 (3L, "Charles"), (4L, "Diane"), (5L, "Went to gym this morning")))

val myEdges = sc.makeRDD(Array(Edge(1L, 2L, "is-friends-with"),
 Edge(2L, 3L, "is-friends-with"), Edge(3L, 4L, "is-friends-with"),
 Edge(4L, 5L, "Likes-status"), Edge(3L, 5L, "Wrote-status")))

val myGraph = Graph(myVertices, myEdges)

myGraph.vertices.collect

res1: Array[(org.apache.spark.graphx.VertexId, String)] = Array((4,Diane),
(1,Ann), (3,Charles), (5,Went to gym this morning), (2,Bill))
```

SCALA TIP Using the Scala keyword `object` (as opposed to `class`) defines a singleton object. When such a singleton object has the same name as a class, it's called a *companion object*. `Graph` from the GraphX API is an example of a class that has a companion object, and as shown in the sidebar, each has its own API. A companion object, besides being a place where `apply()` can be defined (for example, to implement the Factory pattern), is also a place where functions akin to Java `static` functions can be defined.

SCALA TIP When a Scala class or object has a method called `apply()`, the `apply` can be omitted. Thus, although `Graph()` looks like a constructor, it's an invocation of the `apply()` method. This is an example of using Scala's `apply()` to implement the Factory pattern described in the book *Design Patterns* by Gamma et al (Addison-Wesley Professional, 1994).

SPARK TIP In GraphX tutorials you'll often see `parallelize()` instead of `makeRDD()`. They are synonyms. `makeRDD()` is your author Michael Malak's personal preference because he feels it is more descriptive and specific.

Listing 4.1 constructed the graph that was shown in figure 4.3. You can also get the edges, as shown in the following listing.

Listing 4.2 Retrieve the edges from the just-constructed graph

```
myGraph.edges.collect

res2: Array[org.apache.spark.graphx.Edge[String]] = Array(Edge(1,2,
is-friends-with), Edge(2,3,is-friends-with), Edge(3,4,is-friends-with),
    Edge(3,5,Wrote-status), Edge(4,5,Likes-status))
```

Being regular (unordered) RDDs, the vertex and edge RDDs aren't guaranteed any particular order.

You can also use the `triplets()` method to join together the vertices and edges based on `VertexId`. Although `Graph` natively stores its data as separate edge and vertex

RDDs, `triplets()` is a convenience function that joins them together for you, as shown in the following listing.

Listing 4.3   Get a `triplet(s)` version of the graph data

```
myGraph.triplets.collect

res3: Array[org.apache.spark.graphx.EdgeTriplet[String,String]] =
Array(((1,Ann),(2,Bill),is-friends-with),
((2,Bill),(3,Charles),is-friends-with),
((3,Charles),(4,Diane),is-friends-with),
((3,Charles),(5,Went to gym this morning),Wrote-status),
((4,Diane),(5,Went to gym this morning),Likes-status))
```

The return type of `triplets()` is an RDD of `EdgeTriplet[VD,ED]`, which is a subclass of `Edge[ED]` that also contains references to the source and destination vertices associated with the edge. As shown in figure 4.4, the `EdgeTriplet` gives access to the `Edge` (and the edge attribute data) as well as the vertex attribute data for the source and destination vertices. As you will see, having easy access to both the edge and vertex data makes many graph-processing tasks easier.

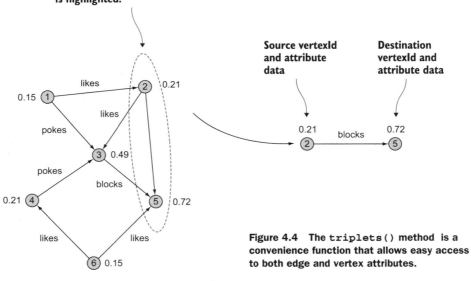

The **`triplets()` function transforms all edges into `EdgeTriplets` that each contain references to the edge and to the source and destination vertices for that edge. The processing done by `Triplets()` for one of the edges is highlighted.**

Source vertexId and attribute data

Destination vertexId and attribute data

Figure 4.4   The `triplets()` method is a convenience function that allows easy access to both edge and vertex attributes.

Table 4.1 shows some of the useful fields available on EdgeTriplet.

Table 4.1 Key fields provided by `EdgeTriplet`

Field	Description
Attr	Attribute data for the edge
srcId	Vertex id of the edge's source vertex
srcAttr	Attribute data for the edge's source vertex
dstId	Vertex id of the edge's destination vertex
dstAttr	Attribute data for the edge's destination vertex

4.2   *Mapping operations*

The real meat of GraphX Map/Reduce operations is called aggregateMessages() (which supplants the deprecated mapReduceTriplets()), but to get our feet wet, let's first look at the much simpler mapTriplets(). Doing so will also serve to introduce another important idea in GraphX. Many of the operations we'll look at in this book return a new Graph that's a transformation of the original Graph object. Though the end result might be the same as if we had transformed edges and vertices ourselves and created a new Graph, we won't benefit from optimizations that GraphX provides under the covers.

4.2.1   *Simple graph transformation*

To the graph constructed in the previous section, let's add an annotation to each "is-friends-with" edge whenever the person on the initiating side of the friendship has a name that contains the letter *a*. How will we add this annotation? By transforming the Edge type from String to a tuple (String, Boolean) as shown in the next listing. The EdgeTriplet class comes in handy here as we need access to both the edge attribute and the attribute for the source vertex.

Listing 4.4   Add Boolean annotation to edges indicating a condition

```
myGraph.mapTriplets(t => (t.attr, t.attr=="is-friends-with" &&
  t.srcAttr.toLowerCase.contains("a"))).triplets.collect

res4: Array[org.apache.spark.graphx.EdgeTriplet[String,(String, Boolean)]]
  = Array(((1,Ann),(2,Bill),(is-friends-with,true)),
((2,Bill),(3,Charles),(is-friends-with,false)),
((3,Charles),(4,Diane),(is-friends-with,true)),
((3,Charles),(5,Went to gym this morning),(Wrote-status,false)),
((4,Diane),(5,Went to gym this morning),(Likes-status,false)))
```

The resulting graph is shown in figure 4.5. Note that our original graph, myGraph (without the extra Boolean annotation on each edge), is still around. And, actually, the

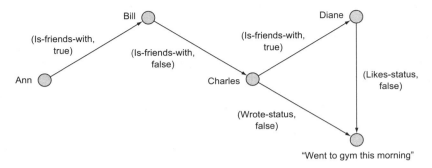

Figure 4.5   We opted to change the Edge type, compared to figure 4.3, as part of the way we invoked `mapTriplets()`. Whereas the Edge type was `String` in figure 4.3, this resulting graph's Edge type is the `Tuple2` of type `(String,Boolean)`.

graph in the figure isn't permanent in any sense of the word because we didn't bother to capture it into a Scala `val` or `var` before handing it off immediately to `triplets()`.

Although `mapTriplets()` can optionally take two parameters, here we used the first parameter, an anonymous function that takes as input an `EdgeTriplet` and returns as output our new Edge type of the `Tuple2` of `(String,Boolean)`.

> **SCALA TIP**   If you don't declare the return type of an anonymous function, Scala will infer the type by the type of what you are returning. In the preceding example, if we wanted to ask the Scala compiler to double-check our intentions (as well as document the types to the human reader of our code), we could have instead written this:

```
myGraph.mapTriplets((t => (t.attr, t.attr=="is-friends-with" &&
                      t.srcAttr.toLowerCase.contains("a"))) :
                 (EdgeTriplet[String,String] =>
                     Tuple2[String,Boolean]) )
          .triplets.collect
```

There's a similar `mapVertices()` API call that allows you to transform the `Vertex` class on the fly, similar to how `mapTriplets()` allows you to change the `Edge` class. You can explore `mapVertices()` on your own.

4.2.2   *Map/Reduce*

Many graph processing tasks involve aggregating information from around the local neighborhood of a vertex. By *neighborhood* we mean the associated edges and vertices around a vertex. You'll see examples of aggregating information from the local neighborhood in the next chapter when we look at some of the classic graph algorithms, such as triangle counting.

> **DEFINITION**   A *triangle* occurs when one vertex is connected to two other vertices and those two vertices are also connected. In a social media graph showing

which people are friends, a triangle occurs when people who are my friends are also friends with each other. We could say that how many triangles a person is involved with gives a sense of how connected the community is around that person.

To identify whether a vertex is part of a triangle, you need to consider the set of edges that connect to that vertex, the set of vertices at the other end of those edges, and whether any of the associated vertices also have an edge between them. For each vertex this involves considering information in its neighborhood.

We'll leave triangle counting to the next chapter and look at a simpler example that will allow us to concentrate on some of the key concepts underlying processing and aggregating information from the neighborhood of a vertex. This idea has strong parallels with the classic Map/Reduce paradigm (see chapter 1). Much like in Map/Reduce, we'll define transformations (map) that are applied to individual structures in the neighborhood of the vertex. Then the output from those transformations will be merged to update the vertex information (reduce).

Our example will count the out-degree of each vertex—for each vertex, the count of edges leaving the vertex. To do this we'll process each vertex indirectly by acting on the edges and their associated source and destination vertices. Rather than explicitly counting edges coming out of each vertex we'll get the edges to "emit" a message to the relevant source vertex, which amounts to the same thing. Aggregating these messages gives us the answer we want.

The following listing uses the `aggregateMessages()` method and is all we need to carry out this task in GraphX.

> **Listing 4.5   Using `aggregateMessages[]()` to compute the out-degree of each vertex**

```
myGraph.aggregateMessages[Int](_.sendToSrc(1), _ + _).collect

res5: Array[(org.apache.spark.graphx.VertexId, Int)] = Array((4,1), (1,1),
(3,2), (2,1))
```

The array returned contains pairs (`Tuple2s`) that show us the ID of the vertex and the vertex's out-degree. Vertex #4 has only one outgoing edge, but vertex #3 has two.

How did it do that? To understand what this code is doing, we'll break it down into its constituent parts. First here's the method signature for `aggregateMessages`:

```
def aggregateMessages[Msg](
    sendMsg: EdgeContext[VD, ED, Msg] => Unit,
    mergeMsg: (Msg, Msg) => Msg)
  : VertexRDD[Msg]
```

The first thing to note is the type parameterization of the method: `Msg` (short for *message*, and you'll see why in a moment). The `Msg` type represents the answer we want to generate; in this case, we want a count of edges emanating from a vertex, so `Int` is the appropriate type to parameterize `aggregateMessages`.

SCALA TIP   With all the type inference the Scala compiler does for you, you might expect it to be able to infer the type parameter for `aggregate-Messages[]()` based on the return type of the anonymous function it takes as its first parameter. After all, they're both declared as type `Msg` in the function declaration for `aggregateMessages[]()`. The reason the Scala compiler can't infer the type in this case is because Scala is a *left-to-right compiler*, and the anonymous function appears (slightly) later in the source code than the name of the function you're invoking.

The two parameters to `aggregateMessages`, `sendMsg` and `mergeMsg`, provide the transformation and reduce logic.

SENDMSG

`sendMsg` is a method that takes an `EdgeContext` as parameter and returns nothing (recall from earlier chapters that `Unit` is the Scala equivalent of Java's `void`). `Edge-Context` is a type-parameterized class similar to `EdgeTriplet`. `EdgeContext` contains the same fields as `EdgeTriplet` but also provides two additional methods for message sending:

- `sendToSrc`—Sends a message of type `Msg` to the source vertex.
- `sendToDst`—Sends a message of type `Msg` to the destination vertex.

These two methods are the key to how `aggregateMessages` works. A message is nothing more than a piece of data sent to a vertex. For each edge in the graph, we can choose to send a message to either the source or the destination vertex (or both). Inside the `sendMsg` method the `EdgeContext` parameter can be used to inspect the values of the edge attributes and the source and destination vertices as part of the logic. For our example, we're counting how many edges exit from a vertex, so we'll send a message containing the integer 1 to the source vertex.

MERGEMSG

All the messages for each vertex are collected together and delivered to the `mergeMsg` method. This method defines how all the messages for the vertex are reduced down to the answer we're looking for. In the example code, we want to sum each 1 that's sent to the source vertex to find the total number of outgoing edges. That is what the `_` anonymous function using + does.

The result of applying `mergeMsg` for each of the vertices is returned as a `Vertex-RDD[Int]`. `VertexRDD` is an RDD containing `Tuple2`s consisting of the `VertexId` and the `mergeMsg` result for that vertex. One thing to notice is that since vertex #5 didn't have any outgoing edges, it won't receive any messages and therefore doesn't appear in the resulting `VertexRDD`.

CLEANING UP THE RESULTS

Interpreting these raw `VertexId`s is inconvenient, so let's join with the original vertices to get the human-readable names. In the following listing we use Spark RDD `join()`, which is a method from `PairRDDFunctions`.

Listing 4.6 RDD `join()` to match up `VertexId`s with vertex data

```
myGraph.aggregateMessages[Int](_.sendToSrc(1),
 _ + _).join(myGraph.vertices).collect

res6: Array[(org.apache.spark.graphx.VertexId, (Int, String))] =
Array((4,(1,Diane)), (1,(1,Ann)), (3,(2,Charles)), (2,(1,Bill)))
```

SPARK TIP Whenever you have an RDD of `Tuple2`, Spark provides an automatic conversion when needed from `RDD[]` to `PairRDDFunctions[]` under the assumption that the `Tuple2` is a key/value pair (K,V). `join()` is one of many functions that become available for `RDD[Tuple2]`s. The conversion is automatically available in the REPL, but in a compiled Scala program you need to `import org.apache.spark.SparkContext._` (in addition to the regular `import org.apache.spark.SparkContext`).

Well, that's a little verbose. We don't need those `VertexId`s anymore, so we can get rid of them by using the `map()` method of RDD. Then we can use the `swap()` method of `Tuple2` to swap the order within each pair so that the human-readable vertex name appears before its out-degree numerical value, for the purposes of providing pretty output, as shown in the following listing.

Listing 4.7 `map()` and `swap()` to clean up output

```
myGraph.aggregateMessages[Int](_.sendToSrc(1),
 _ + _).join(myGraph.vertices).map(_._2.swap).collect

res7: Array[(String, Int)] = Array((Diane,1), (Ann,1), (Charles,2),
(Bill,1))
```

Now for some final mopping up. How can we get back that missing vertex #5? By using `rightOuterJoin()` instead of `join()`, as shown in the following listing.

Listing 4.8 `rightOuterJoin()` instead of `join()` to pull in "forgotten" vertices

```
myGraph.aggregateMessages[Int](_.sendToSrc(1),
 _ + _).rightOuterJoin(myGraph.vertices).map(_._2.swap).collect

res8: Array[(String, Option[Int])] = Array((Diane,Some(1)), (Ann,Some(1)),
 (Charles,Some(2)), (Went to gym this morning,None), (Bill,Some(1)))
```

Ugh! What is all that `Some` and `None` stuff? Well, outer joins can give `null` or empty fields when there's no corresponding record in the joining table. It's Scala's way of avoiding problems with `null` (though it still does have `null` for when you need it, and often there's no way around it when you need to interface with Java code). `Some` and `None` are values from Scala's `Option[]`, and to get rid of them we can use the `getOrElse()` method from `Option[]`. In the process, we have to dig inside our `Tuple2`, so we won't be able to use the convenience of `swap()` anymore, as shown in the following listing.

Listing 4.9   `Option[]`'s `getOrElse()` to clean up `rightOuterJoin()` output

```
myGraph.aggregateMessages[Int](_.sendToSrc(1),
  _ + _).rightOuterJoin(myGraph.vertices).map(
  x => (x._2._2, x._2._1.getOrElse(0))).collect
```

```
res9: Array[(String, Int)] = Array((Diane,1), (Ann,1), (Charles,2), (Went to
  gym this morning,0), (Bill,1))
```

SCALA TIP   Using `Option[]` instead of `null` in Scala opens up a world of possibilities for more functional programming because `Option[]` can be considered a mini-collection (containing either zero or one element). Functional programming constructs such as `flatmap()`, for comprehensions and partial functions, can be used on `Option[]`s, whereas they can't be used on `null`s.

4.2.3   ITERATED MAP/REDUCE

Most algorithms involve more than a single step or iteration. `aggregateMessages` can be used to implement algorithms where we continuously update each vertex based only on information obtained from neighboring edges and vertices.

To see this idea in action, we'll implement an algorithm that finds the vertex with the greatest distance from its ancestor in the graph. At the end of the algorithm we hope to have each vertex labeled with the farthest distance from an ancestor.

We'll assume our graphs don't have cycles (cycles occur when we have edges that go around from one vertex and eventually loop back to the same vertex). Dealing with cyclic graphs usually makes for added complexity in our algorithms, and we'll show you some strategies for dealing with those later on.

First we define the `sendMsg` and `mergeMsg` functions that will be called by `aggregate-Messages`. We define them up front rather than as anonymous functions in the body of the aggregate messages function, as sometimes the code can become a little cluttered.

The common way to express iteration in functional programming is through recursion, so next we'll define a helper recursive function, `propagateEdgeCount`, which will continuously call `aggregateMessages` (see the following listing).

Listing 4.10   Iterated (via recursion) Map/Reduce to find distance of furthest vertex

```
// sendMsg  function that will be given to aggregateMessages.
// Remember this function will be called for each edge in the
// graph.  Here it simply passes on an incremented counter.
def sendMsg(ec: EdgeContext[Int,String,Int]): Unit = {
  ec.sendToDst(ec.srcAttr+1)
}

// Here we define a mergeMsg function that will be called
// repeatedl for all messages delivered to a vertex. The end
// result is the vertex will contain the highest value, or
// distance, over all the messages
def mergeMsg(a: Int, b: Int): Int = {
  math.max(a,b)
}
```

Generate new set of vertices ...

... and generate updated version of graph containing the new info.

```
def propagateEdgeCount(g:Graph[Int,String]):Graph[Int,String] = {
  val verts = g.aggregateMessages[Int](sendMsg, mergeMsg)
  val g2 = Graph(verts, g.edges)
  // Let's see whether the updated graph has any new information
  // by joining the two sets of vertices together – this results
  // in Tuple2[vertexId, Tuple2[old vertex data, new vertex data]]
  val check = g2.vertices.join(g.vertices).
      map(x => x._2._1 - x._2._2).
      reduce(_ + _)
  if (check > 0)
    propagateEdgeCount(g2)
  else
    g
}
```

Look at each element of the joined sets of vertices and calculate the difference between them. If there is no difference we get zero.

Add up all the differences—if all the vertices are the same, the total is zero.

Continue recursion if graph has changed.

No change so return the graph originally passed into our function.

In this listing, propagateEdgeCount() adds 1 to the distance traveled so far and sends that to the destination vertex of each edge. The destination vertex then does a max() across all the distance messages it receives and makes that the new distance for itself.

An important point to note is that we define when to stop the recursion by comparing the original graph and the updated graph after each iteration. When there's no difference between the graphs, we stop. Note that the reduce(_ + _) check works because we know that the new distance between vertices must be at least as big as the old distance and therefore the difference must be non-negative; we can't have a situation where we add a negative to a positive and get a zero that way.

> **TIP** Alternatively, for better performance, we could avoid doing the join() completely by adding another vertex property—a Boolean that indicates whether the value has been updated. Then we can reduce() on that Boolean and not involve the VertexRDD from the previous iteration in our recursion exit condition.

Now we have the recursive pump primed, we need to invoke it. We'll feed in our myGraph graph, but first we need to initialize it. This is a key question for any iterative algorithm: how do we start? We need to think of the task in terms of what information we know for each vertex at the start and what answer we'll want at the end. We're looking for an integer value that tells us the farthest distance we would have to travel. At the start we have no idea about the distance, so we'll set each vertex to zero and have the algorithm gradually diffuse new information across the graph:

```
val initialGraph = myGraph.mapVertices((_,_) => 0)
propagateEdgeCount(initialGraph).vertices.collect

res10: Array[(org.apache.spark.graphx.VertexId, Int)] = Array( (1,0), (2,1)),
    (3,2), (4,3), (5,4) )
```

Vertex #5 has the longest distance to an ancestor vertex, which is a distance of 4.

You've seen how quick it is to implement an iterative algorithm. The key point is to think how information ("messages") can be delivered across edges and accumulated to reach the answer you're looking for.

4.3   *Serialization/deserialization*

You saw how to read in edge pairs in chapter 2 using GraphX's `GraphLoader` API. But that data had neither vertex properties nor edge properties, and one of the main advantages of GraphX is that it handles property graphs. Here we provide some custom code to read and write property graphs in binary and JSON formats. The RDF format, a standard format for graphs of "triples" (not property graphs), is shown in chapter 8.

4.3.1   *Reading/writing binary format*

In this section, we read and write a standard Hadoop sequence file, which is a binary file containing a sequence of serialized objects. The Spark RDD API function `saveAsObjectFile()` saves to a Hadoop sequence file, relying upon standard Java serialization to serialize the vertex and edge objects, as shown in the following listing.

Listing 4.11   Round-trip persisting to and reading from file

```
myGraph.vertices.saveAsObjectFile("myGraphVertices")
myGraph.edges.saveAsObjectFile("myGraphEdges")
val myGraph2 = Graph(
    sc.objectFile[Tuple2[VertexId,String]]("myGraphVertices"),
    sc.objectFile[Edge[String]]("myGraphEdges"))
```

> To save to HDFS instead, use
> **"hdfs://localhost:8020/myGraphVertices"**.

> **SPARK TIP**   Despite its name, `saveAsObjectFile()` saves to multiple files in a directory, with one file per Spark partition inside that directory. The parameter you pass in is the name of that directory.

Although our simple graph uses `String` as the vertex and edge property classes, because the preceding technique uses Java `Serializable`, it generalizes to handle any complex class you might want to attach to vertices or edges. Substitute the class name for `String` in the type parameter for `objectFile[]()`.

The preceding code doesn't specify a file system, so it saves to the local file system. In a real Spark cluster, prepend the destination directory name with the appropriate URI prefix; for example, `hdfs://localhost:8020/myGraphVertices`.

Serialization of GraphX objects

In the Spark core, everything has to be serializable so that objects can be serialized and transmitted to worker nodes. Java `Serializable` is the default, but Spark has first-class integration with Kryo, a more efficient serialization alternative. Prior to Spark 1.0, Kryo had lots of problems with Spark, and as of Spark 1.6, there are still several dozen Kryo-related Jira tickets open. A third serialization option is to use Java `Externalizable` and implement your own serialization scheme—or, more likely, delegate to a third-party library such as Avro or Pickling—but this route is far from transparent and clean. Thankfully, Spark's `saveAsObjectFile()` provides another last-ditch opportunity for tuning via compression. After the objects are serialized, they can optionally be run through a codec. Even though `Serializable` doesn't compress, `saveAsObjectFile()` can still perform compression post-serialization.

SAVING TO A SINGLE FILE: THE CHEATER WAY

To avoid the multiple part files when saving to HDFS or S3 using `saveAsObjectFile()`, you can cheat by adding a `coalesce(1,true)`, such as the following:

```
myGraph.vertices.coalesce(1,true).saveAsObjectFile("myGraphVertices")
```

The downside of this trick is that the entire RDD has to fit inside a single partition, meaning it has to fit inside a single executor. That's fine for experimenting with small graphs, but not in production with big graphs.

SAVING TO A SINGLE FILE: THE RIGHT WAY

Assuming you're working in HDFS, the right way to produce a single file is to first allow Spark to create the part files (which it does in parallel) and then, as a second step, merge them into a single file. There are two ways to do this: at the command line or through the Hadoop Java API.

For the following example, first make sure you're saving to HDFS rather than the local file system. The following URL assumes use of the Cloudera Quickstart VM; it will be different for other environments:

```
myGraph.vertices.saveAsObjectFile(
    "hdfs://localhost:8020/user/cloudera/myGraphVertices")
```

To merge the part files contained in the myGraphVertices directory, one option is to use the command line, which reads the HDFS part files and creates a single file on the local file system:

```
hadoop fs -getmerge /user/cloudera/myGraphVertices myGraphVerticesFile
```

The API equivalent to `getmerge` is called `copyMerge()`, which has the option for the destination to be HDFS, as shown in the following listing.

Listing 4.12   Saving to a single file in HDFS using the Hadoop Java API

```
import org.apache.hadoop.fs.{FileSystem, FileUtil, Path}
val conf = new org.apache.hadoop.conf.Configuration
conf.set("fs.defaultFS", "hdfs://localhost")
val fs = FileSystem.get(conf)
FileUtil.copyMerge(fs, new Path("/user/cloudera/myGraphVertices/"),
  fs, new Path("/user/cloudera/myGraphVerticesFile"), false, conf, null)
```

> **SCALA TIP**   You can combine multiple imports from the same package on the same line by enclosing the multiple class names in curly braces.

You're still stuck with two files: one for vertices produced by the preceding code, and one for edges (created similarly). To truly create a single file, you can choose to persist the triplets instead with `graph.triplets.saveAsObjectFile()`, but note that this would be a wastel of disk space because full vertex data would be repeated for every edge that uses that vertex. In this example, saving triplets to a single file would take about 20 times as much disk space as saving the edges and vertices separately in two files.

If you're using S3 instead of HDFS, the `hadoop fs -getMerge` command line and the Hadoop API `copyMerge()` won't work. There are various shell scripts and GUI-based tools found on the Web that accomplish the same thing for S3.

4.3.2   *JSON format*

If you prefer to serialize to a human-readable format, you can use a JSON library. In the realm of Scala for JSON, wrappers around the venerable Jackson library for Java are popular. The wrapper Jerkson was popular until it was abandoned in 2012. In its place, Jackson has since released jackson-module-scala. Its syntax is not as concise as most Scala libraries, but it works. Although Jackson is already available in the Spark REPL, we need to do the following in listing 4.13 at the OS command line to make jackson-module-scala also available there.

Listing 4.13   Command line commands to use jackson-module-scala in the REPL

```
wget http://repo1.maven.org/maven2/com/fasterxml/jackson/module/
➥ jackson-module-scala_2.10/2.4.4/jackson-module-scala_2.10-2.4.4.jar
wget http://repo1.maven.org/maven2/com/google/guava/guava/14.0.1/
➥ guava-14.0.1.jar
./spark-shell --jars jackson-module-scala_2.10-2.4.4.jar,guava-14.0.1.jar
```

Note that the version numbers given (Scala 2.10 and Jackson 2.4.4, and its dependency Guava 14.0.1) are specific to Spark 1.6. If you're using a different version of Spark, find out which version of Scala it's using from the banner when you start up the REPL and which version of Jackson and Guava it's using from the Maven pom.xml. In Spark 1.6, the version numbers of all the dependent jars are centralized into the root pom.xml in the Spark source tree. The version of jackson-module-scala has to match the version of Jackson that Spark is built with.

First we look at how to use Jackson to serialize the graph to JSON using the features of Spark we've looked at so far. Then we introduce a new feature, `mapPartitions`, which can give significant performance improvement in some situations.

Once you have the REPL set up, go ahead and once again create `myGraph` as in listing 4.1. Then you might naively serialize to JSON, as shown in the following listing.

Listing 4.14   Naïve approach to serialize to JSON

```
myGraph.vertices.map(x => {
    val mapper = new com.fasterxml.jackson.databind.ObjectMapper()
    mapper.registerModule(
        com.fasterxml.jackson.module.scala.DefaultScalaModule)
    val writer = new java.io.StringWriter()
    mapper.writeValue(writer, x)
    writer.toString
}).coalesce(1,true).saveAsTextFile("myGraphVertices")
```

> **NOTE** The output file is itself not JSON-compliant; rather, each line within the file is valid JSON. This is more conducive to distributed storage and distributed processing than trying to put commas at the end of every line except for the last line and putting open and close brackets at the beginning and end of the file.

Notice that for every vertex, we're constructing an entirely new JSON parser! For such purposes, the Spark API provides an alternative to `map()` called `mapPartitions()`. This is what we do in the better performing version in listing 4.15.

> **SPARK TIP** Whenever you have heavyweight initialization that should be done once for many RDD elements rather than once per RDD element, and if this initialization, such as creation of objects from a third-party library, cannot be serialized (so that Spark can transmit it across the cluster to the worker nodes), use `mapPartitions()` instead of `map()`. `mapPartitions()` provides for the initialization to be done once per worker task/thread/partition instead of once per RDD data element.

Listing 4.15   Better performing way to serialize/deserialize to/from JSON

```
import com.fasterxml.jackson.core.`type`.TypeReference
import com.fasterxml.jackson.module.scala.DefaultScalaModule

myGraph.vertices.map(x => {
    val mapper = new com.fasterxml.jackson.databind.ObjectMapper()
    mapper.registerModule(
        com.fasterxml.jackson.module.scala.DefaultScalaModule)
    val writer = new java.io.StringWriter()
    mapper.writeValue(writer, x)
    writer.toString
}).coalesce(1,true).saveAsTextFile("myGraphVertices")

myGraph.vertices.mapPartitions(vertices => {
    val mapper = new com.fasterxml.jackson.databind.ObjectMapper()
```

```
    mapper.registerModule(DefaultScalaModule)
    val writer = new java.io.StringWriter()
    vertices.map(v => {writer.getBuffer.setLength(0)
                       mapper.writeValue(writer, v)
                       writer.toString})
}).coalesce(1,true).saveAsTextFile("myGraphVertices")

myGraph.edges.mapPartitions(edges => {
    val mapper = new com.fasterxml.jackson.databind.ObjectMapper();
    mapper.registerModule(DefaultScalaModule)
    val writer = new java.io.StringWriter()
    edges.map(e => {writer.getBuffer.setLength(0)
                    mapper.writeValue(writer, e)
                    writer.toString})
}).coalesce(1,true).saveAsTextFile("myGraphEdges")

val myGraph2 = Graph(
    sc.textFile("myGraphVertices").mapPartitions(vertices => {
        val mapper = new com.fasterxml.jackson.databind.ObjectMapper()
        mapper.registerModule(DefaultScalaModule)
        vertices.map(v => {
            val r = mapper.readValue[Tuple2[Integer,String]](v,
                new TypeReference[Tuple2[Integer,String]]{})
            (r._1.toLong, r._2)
        })
    }),
    sc.textFile("myGraphEdges").mapPartitions(edges => {
        val mapper = new com.fasterxml.jackson.databind.ObjectMapper()
        mapper.registerModule(DefaultScalaModule)
        edges.map(e => mapper.readValue[Edge[String]](e,
            new TypeReference[Edge[String]]{}))
    })
)
```

SCALA TIP   If you need to use a reserved Scala keyword, surround it with a backtick on either side (`—also known as the *grave accent* character). This comes up often when using Java libraries in Scala.

Notice that due to a weakness in Jackson, we had to read in the vertex IDs as Integers and then convert them to Longs. This limits vertex IDs to the 2 billion range. Also notice that Jackson made us repeat the vertex and edge property class type parameters (String, in this case) twice each for readValue[](), so if you use a custom class, replace it in both places. Finally, as with the binary example, when using a distributed file system, remember to eliminate the coalesce(1,true).

4.3.3   *GEXF format for Gephi visualization software*

Gephi is a powerful open source graph visualization tool, and GEXF is its native XML format. In this section, we serialize to .gexf, as shown in the following listing and in figure 4.6. Gephi is open source and free to download from gephi.github.io. Its use is described in appendix B.

Listing 4.16 Export to GEXF for Gephi visualization software

```scala
def toGexf[VD,ED](g:Graph[VD,ED]) =
    "<?xml version=\"1.0\" encoding=\"UTF-8\"?>\n" +
    "<gexf xmlns=\"http://www.gexf.net/1.2draft\" version=\"1.2\">\n" +
    " <graph mode=\"static\" defaultedgetype=\"directed\">\n" +
    "  <nodes>\n" +
    g.vertices.map(v => "      <node id=\"" + v._1 + "\" label=\"" +
                    v._2 + "\" />\n").collect.mkString +
    "  </nodes>\n" +
    "  <edges>\n" +
    g.edges.map(e => "      <edge source=\"" + e.srcId +
                "\" target=\"" + e.dstId + "\" label=\"" + e.attr +
                "\" />\n").collect.mkString +
    "  </edges>\n" +
    " </graph>\n" +
    "</gexf>"

val pw = new java.io.PrintWriter("myGraph.gexf")
pw.write(toGexf(myGraph))
pw.close
```

SCALA TIP Sometimes the REPL gets confused about when you want to continue a line of code to the next line, such as when you end a line on a plus sign for string concatenation. In those cases, enter paste mode by entering the command `:paste`. Exit paste mode by pressing Ctrl-D.

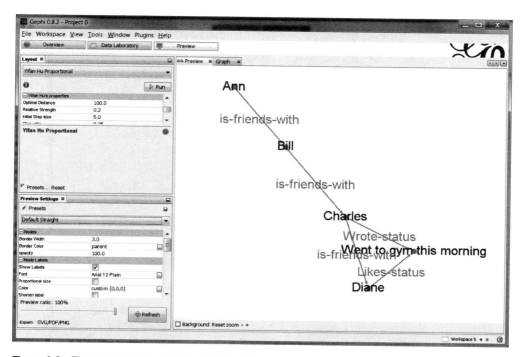

Figure 4.6 The generated .gexf file loaded into Gephi

4.4   Graph generation

If you don't have graph data available, the GraphGenerators object can generate some random graphs for you. This approach can be useful when you need to test out some ideas about a graph function or an algorithm and you need to get something working quickly. One of them, generateRandomEdges(), is a helper function for the main graph-generating functions; it's not that useful on its own because it takes as a parameter a single vertex ID from which all the generated edges will emanate. But let's take a look at the four full graph generators that are available in Spark 1.6.

4.4.1   Deterministic graphs

The first two graph structures we cover are non-random: the grid and the star. The following listings assume you've already done import org.apache.spark.graphx._. For example, util.GraphGenerators refers to org.apache.spark.graphx.util.Graph-Generators.

GRID GRAPH

A grid graph has a specific configuration of vertices and edges that are laid out as if in a 2-D grid or matrix. Each vertex is labeled with the row and column of its position in the grid (for example, the top left vertex is labeled (0,0)). Then each vertex is connected to its neighbor immediately above, below, left, and right. The following listing demonstrates how to create a 4x4 grid graph. The layout of the graph is show in figure 4.7.

> **Listing 4.17   Generate a grid graph**

```
val pw = new java.io.PrintWriter("gridGraph.gexf")
pw.write(toGexf(util.GraphGenerators.gridGraph(sc, 4, 4)))
pw.close
```

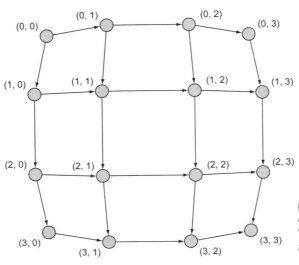

Figure 4.7   A generated gridGraph() visualized in Gephi. There is no randomness to a grid graph; the grid is always complete.

STAR GRAPH

A star graph has one vertex connected by edges to all other vertices—there are no other edges in the graph. As figure 4.8 shows, the name comes from its star-like layout.

The graph is generated by calling `GraphGenerators.starGraph` with the number of vertices as the second parameter to the method. Vertex 0 is always the center of the star, so the call `GraphGenerators.starGraph(sc, 8)` in the following listing results in a graph with Vertex 0 connected to 7 other vertices.

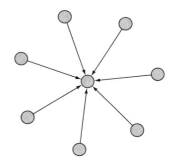

Figure 4.8   A generated `starGraph()` visualized in Gephi. Like `gridGraph()`, it is not random.

Listing 4.18   Generate a star graph

```
val pw = new java.io.PrintWriter("starGraph.gexf")
pw.write(toGexf(util.GraphGenerators.starGraph(sc, 8)))
pw.close
```

4.4.2   Random graphs

GraphX provides two ways to generate graphs randomly: a single-step algorithm (called log normal) that attaches a particular number of edges to each vertex, and a multistep procedural algorithm (called R-MAT) that generates graphs that are closer to what is found in the real world.

DEGREE-BASED: LOG NORMAL GRAPH

The log normal graph focuses on the out-degrees of the vertices in the graphs it generates. It ensures that if you take a histogram of all the out-degrees, they form a log normal graph, which means that log(d) forms a normal distribution (Gaussian bell shape), where the ds are the vertex degrees. The following listing incorporates the code from listing 4.5 that counted the out-degrees, and as you can see, there are a lot of vertices of degree 6, with it tailing off to the left (lower-degree vertices) and a longer tail to the right (higher-degree vertices). Figure 4.9 shows a possible output graph.

Listing 4.19   Generate a log normal graph

```
val logNormalGraph = util.GraphGenerators.logNormalGraph(sc, 15)
val pw = new java.io.PrintWriter("logNormalGraph.gexf")
pw.write(toGexf(logNormalGraph))
pw.close
logNormalGraph.aggregateMessages[Int](
    _.sendToSrc(1), _ + _).map(_._2).collect.sorted

Res11: Array[Int] = Array(2, 3, 4, 6, 6, 6, 6, 8, 9, 9, 9, 10, 10, 13, 14)
```

2nd parameter to logNormalGraph specifies the number of vertices in the resulting graph.

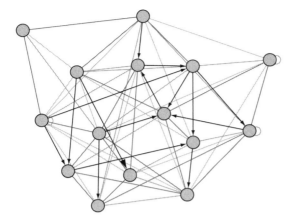

Figure 4.9 A generated `logNormalGraph()` visualized in Gephi. The only constraint in `logNormalGraph()` is the out-degree of each vertex, and otherwise there are no restrictions on where edges are placed. Some edges have the same source and destination vertices. And some pairs of vertices have multiple parallel edges, represented in the Gephi visualization (which does not render parallel edges directly) by darker edges and larger arrowheads.

PROCEDURAL-BASED: R-MAT GRAPH

R-MAT, which stands for *recursive matrix,* is intended to simulate the structure of typical social networks. As opposed to the "degree-based" approach of the earlier `logNormal-Graph()`, `rmatGraph()` takes a "procedural" approach. It adds edges one at a time into quadrants of the graph (and quadrants within quadrants, and so on), based on predetermined probabilities for each quadrant, as shown in the following listing. A possible output graph is shown in figure 4.10.

Listing 4.20   Generate an R-MAT graph

```
val pw = new java.io.PrintWriter("rmatGraph.gexf")
pw.write(toGexf(util.GraphGenerators.rmatGraph(sc, 32, 60)))
pw.close
```

2nd and 3rd parameters to rmatGraph are the requested number of vertices and edges respectively—number of vertices is rounded up to the next power of 2.

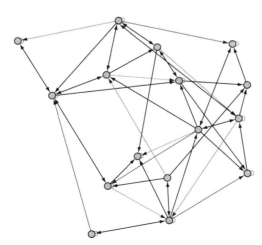

Figure 4.10 `rmatGraph`'s recursive quadrant subdivision leaves some relative loner vertices and also makes for some groups of vertices having a high number of interconnections.

rmatGraph assumes the number of vertices passed in as a parameter is a power of 2. If it's not, rmatGraph rounds it up to the next power of 2 for you. It needs the number of vertices to be a power of 2 for the recursive quadrant subdivision, as shown in figure 4.11. rmatGraph starts out by laying the vertices out in a grid (the non-grid layout in figure 4.10 is caused by Gephi trying to make the resultant graph look nice) and then randomly places edges one by one, choosing vertices based on probabilities arising from the recursive quadrants. Some vertices may by chance end up with zero edges, which is why the Gephi rendering in figure 4.10 shows only 16 vertices, even though listing 4.20 specifies 32 vertices.

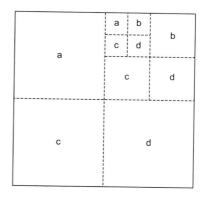

Figure 4.11   Recursive quadrants from the 2004 paper "R-MAT: A Recursive Model for Graph Mining" by Chakrabarti et al. GraphX uses the hard-coded probabilities a=0.45, b=0.15, c=0.15, d=0.25.

4.5   *Pregel API*

Section 2.3 states that complete algorithms can be built by repeated application of aggregateMessages. This is such a common requirement that GraphX provides an API based on Google's Pregel to accomplish such iterative algorithms in a concise manner. It is so concise that an entire algorithm can be expressed with a single Pregel call. In fact, many of GraphX's pre-canned algorithms are implemented in terms of a single Pregel call.

GraphX's Pregel API provides a concise functional approach to algorithm design. It also provides some performance benefits through caching and uncaching intermediate data sets; getting this right is generally tricky for programmers and relieves them of the burden of having to deal with low-level performance tuning.

In GraphX the implementation of Pregel is a form of Bulk Synchronous Parallel (BSP) processing. As its name suggests, BSP is a parallel processing model developed in the 1980s. BSP is not specifically designed for graph processing, but when Google implemented its graph processing framework, Pregel, it used the principles behind BSP. Google's Pregel is the inspiration for Spark's own Pregel API.

As shown in figure 4.12, the algorithm is decomposed into a series of *supersteps*, with each superstep being a single iteration. Within each superstep, per-vertex calculations can be performed in parallel. At the end of the superstep, each vertex generates messages for other vertices that are delivered in the next superstep. Due to the *synchronization barrier*, nothing from a subsequent superstep gets executed until the current superstep is fully completed. Unlike some general purpose, low-level libraries for distributed high-performance computing, the synchronization in the Pregel API is handled automatically for you by GraphX.

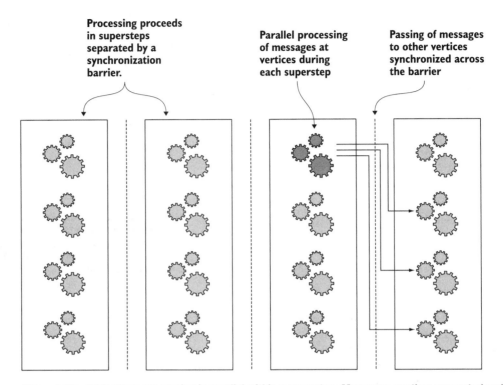

Processing proceeds in supersteps separated by a synchronization barrier.

Parallel processing of messages at vertices during each superstep

Passing of messages to other vertices synchronized across the barrier

Figure 4.12   BSP allows processing in parallel within a superstep. Messages are then generated and delivered for the next superstep. The next superstep does not begin until the current superstep is completed and all messages are delivered to the next superstep. This is illustrated by the synchronization barriers.

One of the benefits of having a framework like this is that it's useful to have a high-level abstraction that lets you specify program behavior that can then be efficiently parallelized by the framework.

Figure 4.13 shows how the Pregel API processes a single superstep in more detail. The messages sent in the previous superstep are grouped together by vertex and processed by a "merge message" (mergeMsg) function so that each vertex is associated with a single merged message (unless the vertex wasn't sent any messages). The mergeMsg function works in exactly the same way as the mergeMsg function used by aggregateMessages: it must be commutative and associative so that it can repeatedly process pairs of messages to arrive at a single result for each vertex.

Unlike aggregateMessages, though, the result of mergeMsg doesn't update the vertex directly but is passed to a vertex program that takes a vertex (both the VertexID and the data) and the message as input and returns new vertex data that's applied by the framework to the vertex.

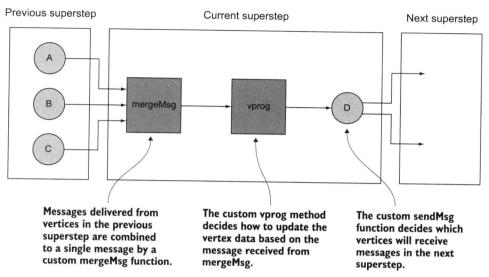

Previous superstep   Current superstep   Next superstep

Messages delivered from vertices in the previous superstep are combined to a single message by a custom mergeMsg function.

The custom vprog method decides how to update the vertex data based on the message received from mergeMsg.

The custom sendMsg function decides which vertices will receive messages in the next superstep.

Figure 4.13 Messages for a vertex from the previous superstep are processed by the `mergeMsg` and `vprog` functions to update the vertex data. The vertex then sends messages to be delivered in the next superstep.

In the last step of the superstep iteration, each vertex gets to send a message along each of its out-edges. The vertex can also choose not to send a message; if the destination vertex doesn't receive any messages from its source vertices, it will no longer be considered for processing in the next superstep. The logic for this decision is encapsulated in a sendMsg function. Figure 4.14 shows the complete flow of the Pregel method call.

Now that you have an idea of how this works, let's see what the Pregel method signature looks like:

```
def pregel[A]
    (initialMsg: A,
     maxIter: Int = Int.MaxValue,
     activeDir: EdgeDirection = EdgeDirection.Out)
    (vprog: (VertexId, VD, A) => VD,
     sendMsg: EdgeTriplet[VD, ED] => Iterator[(VertexId, A)],
     mergeMsg: (A, A) => A)
  : Graph[VD, ED]
```

As with aggregateMessages, the method is type-parameterized by the message (A) that will be received and delivered by each vertex. Unlike aggregateMessages, though, pregel does some extra work for you by returning a new Graph object rather than a VertexRDD.

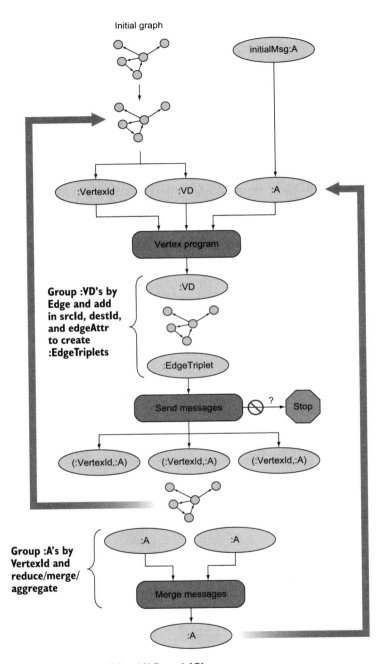

Figure 4.14   Flow of GraphX Pregel API

SCALA TIP Notice that the function has two sets of parameters. In Scala you can split parameters up into *multiple parameter lists.* You can invoke the function by providing all the parameters, although you have to use the syntax of surrounding each list of parameters in its own set of parentheses. This is how we call `pregel` in the upcoming example. Alternatively, you can use *partial function application.* For example, you could do `val p = Pregel(g,0)_` (note the underscore is required when using partial application). Then at some later point, you could do `p(myVprog, mySendMsg, myMergeMsg)`. Later still, you could reuse `p` again for some other similar `Pregel` invocation.

The first set of parameters defines some settings or algorithm parameters. `initialMsg` is a value that will be delivered to the vertex to kick-start the processing. Often this is some sort of zero value that represents our lack of knowledge at the beginning of the algorithm.

`maxIter` defines how many iterations or supersteps will be carried out. Some algorithms have convergence guarantees that ensure an accurate answer will be reached within a reasonable number of iterations. But many algorithms don't give this guarantee, giving rise to the possibility that the algorithm will continue forever. In this latter case, it's definitely a good idea to specify a number smaller than the default `Int.Max-Value`!

The second set of parameters defines the three functions already outlined: `vprog`, `sendMsg`, and `mergeMsg`. These define the behavior we want to encode into the algorithm. The introduction to this section mentioned that Pregel provides similar functionality to the iterated MapReduce using `aggregateMessages`. There are some subtle differences between the two that we will call out here.

First, `aggregateMessages` only requires two functions to define its behavior: `send-Msg` and `mergeMsg`. What's the purpose of this vertex program, `vprog`? It provides greater flexibility in defining the logic. In some cases, the message and the vertex data type are the same, and only some simple logic is required to update the graph with a new value.

In other cases, the message and the vertex data will be different types. An example is the implementation of `LabelPropagation`, discussed in detail in the next chapter. `LabelPropagation` returns a `Graph` whose vertex data is a `VertexId`, but the message type is a Map relating `VertexIDs` to Long – `Map[VertexId, Long]`. The Map message passed to the vertex program is interrogated to find the `VertexId` with the highest `Long` value, and this is the ID that is used to update the vertex data.

The other key difference is the form of the `sendMsg` function signature, compared in table 4.2. Recall that `EdgeTriplet` contains information on an edge and its two vertex endpoints. `EdgeContext` adds two additional methods, `sendToSrc` and `sendToDst`.

Table 4.2 `sendMsg` function signature in `aggregateMessages` and Pregel

aggregateMessages	Pregel
`EdgeContext[VD, ED, Msg] => Unit`	`EdgeTriplet[VD, ED] => Iterator[(VertexId, A)]`

You may ask why there is this difference. The answer is that Pregel still relies on the deprecated `mapReduceTriplets` method to do its work and hasn't been updated to use `aggregateMessages`. The work to implement Pregel using `aggregateMessages` is being tracked in SPARK-5062.

The following listing shows the iterated MapReduce example of listing 4.10, converted to Pregel.

Listing 4.21   `Pregel` to find distance of furthest vertex

```
val g = Pregel(myGraph.mapVertices((vid,vd) => 0), 0,
               activeDirection = EdgeDirection.Out)(
               (id:VertexId,vd:Int,a:Int) => math.max(vd,a),
               (et:EdgeTriplet[Int,String]) =>
                   Iterator((et.dstId, et.srcAttr+1)),
               (a:Int,b:Int) => math.max(a,b))
g.vertices.collect
res12: Array[(org.apache.spark.graphx.VertexId, Int)] = Array((4,3), (1,0),
(3,2), (5,4), (2,1))
```

> **SCALA TIP**   You always have the option of using *named parameters*. Sometimes this can make the code easier to read. Other times, if there are several parameters with default values, some such parameters can be skipped if in your function invocation you use named parameters for the later parameters.

The terminating condition for Pregel is that there are no more messages to be sent. In each iteration, if an edge's vertices did not receive messages from the previous iteration, `sendMsg` will not be called for that edge. The `activeDirection` parameter to Pregel specifies this filter. For an edge with vertices `srcId` and `destId`,

- *EdgeDirection.Out*—`sendMsg` gets called if `srcId` received a message during the previous iteration, meaning this edge is considered an "out-edge" of `srcId`.
- *EdgeDirection.In*—`sendMsg` gets called if `dstId` received a message during the previous iteration, meaning this edge is considered an "in-edge" of `dstId`.
- *EdgeDirection.Either*—`sendMsg` gets called if either `srcId` or `dstId` received a message during the previous iteration.
- *EdgeDirection.Both*—`sendMsg` gets called if both `srcId` and `dstId` received messages during the previous iteration.

In the vertex distance example, we used `EdgeDirection.Out` because the vertex distance algorithm follows the edge directions of the graph. Once it reaches the "end" of the directed graph, it terminates.

If the graph has cycles, we have to be more careful because we're likely to run into situations where a group of vertices continuously sends and receives messages without termination. One thing we can do to deal with this situation is use the `maxIterations` parameter to ensure that our algorithm terminates in a reasonable amount of time.

Another approach is to try and detect situations where the algorithm is looping around and not doing any useful new work. For example, the ShortestPaths algorithm discussed in the next chapter progressively updates a map with vertices reachable from the current vertex. The `sendMsg` function only issues messages if there's new information to be added to the map that wouldn't have already been seen by the message target.

4.6 Summary

- `Pregel` and its little sibling `aggregateMessages()` are the cornerstones of graph processing in GraphX.
- Most of the canned algorithms that come with GraphX are implemented in terms of `Pregel`.
- Because the terminating condition for `Pregel` is that no messages happen to be sent, algorithms that require more flexibility for the terminating condition have to be implemented using `aggregateMessages()` instead.
- Because GraphX doesn't have built-in API functions to read and write property graphs (only to read in an edge list), we showed code to do that.
- If you don't have data to work with, the GraphX API provides ways to generate both random and deterministic graphs.

Built-in algorithms

In chapter 4 you learned about the foundational GraphX APIs that enable you to write your own custom algorithms. But there's no need for you to reinvent the wheel in cases where the GraphX API already provides an implemented standard algorithm. In this chapter, we describe some of those basic algorithms and discuss which situations they can be used in:

- PageRank
- Personalized PageRank
- Triangle Count
- Shortest Paths
- Connected Components
- Strongly Connected Components
- Label Propagation

We wait until chapter 7 to cover SVDPlusPlus, one of the more useful and advanced built-in algorithms.

5.1 *Seek out authoritative nodes: PageRank*

Chapter 2 covered an example invoking the PageRank algorithm, which was originally invented to rank web pages for a search engine, but there we used it to find influential papers in a citation network. Generally speaking, PageRank can be used to find the "important" nodes in almost any graph. Here we go more in depth into PageRank: what it does under the covers and parameters and different ways of invoking it. Note that PageRank is patented by Stanford University and trademarked by Google.

5.1.1 *PageRank algorithm explained*

PageRank is a way to measure the "authority" of vertices in a graph. We saw an example of this in chapter 2 where we measured the influence of scientific papers from within a collection of bibliographic citations. Although the original application of PageRank was to assign an authority number to each web page a search engine crawler encounters, PageRank can be used on any directed graph to establish the authority of every node in the graph. Other applications include ranking key people in a social network graph based on people-to-people connections, ranking influencers in a social network based on a graph of "shares," and employing several advanced machine-learning techniques, such as collaborative filtering and semantic relevance.

A simplistic alternative to PageRank is to measure the in-degrees at each vertex, similar to the way we calculated the out-degrees in section 4.2.2. The GraphX API even provides an `outDegrees()` function to compute the out-degrees without any additional code. Many people mistakenly believe that such a number of "inbound links" is all PageRank is. PageRank is much more.

PageRank seeks to optimize a recursive formula and is based not on the number of vertices that have edges which point to the vertex in question, but on the PageRanks of those vertices.

Although the definition of PageRank is recursive, its implementation is a straightforward iterative computation. Figure 5.1, adapted from the 1999 PageRank paper by Page and Brin, "The PageRank citation ranking: Bringing order to the web," illustrates the algorithm.

The algorithm can be described as follows:

1 Initialize vertices with a starting PageRank of 1/N, where N is the number of vertices in the graph.

2 Loop:

  a For each vertex, transmit a PageRank of 1/M along each outbound edge, where M is the out-degree of the vertex.

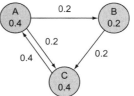

Figure 5.1   PageRank iteration. This particular iteration is also a steady and final state of the algorithm because after the redistribution of PageRank among the vertices, the resulting vertex PageRanks end up with the same values.

b   At each vertex receiving incoming PageRanks from adjacent vertices, sum these up and make that the new PageRank for the vertex.

c   If PageRanks haven't significantly changed across the graph since the previous iteration, then exit.

5.1.2   *Invoking PageRank in GraphX*

As we saw in chapter 2, GraphX has already implemented PageRank; we didn't need to code up the algorithm described in the previous subsection. In this section, you'll see two different ways to invoke PageRank and some of the parameters.

OBJECT-ORIENTED VS. OBJECT-BASED WAYS TO INVOKE PAGERANK

GraphX provides two ways to invoke PageRank: object-oriented and object-based. In chapter 2, we invoked the pageRank() function from our Graph object, which is the object-oriented way. The pageRank() function is a function of GraphOps, and Graph automatically creates a GraphOps and provides a conversion of itself to GraphOps whenever needed, much in the same way that an RDD will convert itself to a PairRDD as needed, as we saw in section 4.2.2. The relationships between the various classes are shown in figure 5.2.

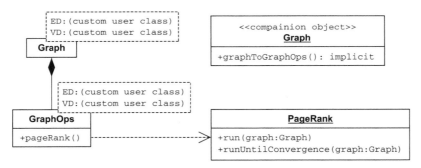

Figure 5.2   **The companion object `Graph` contains an `implicit` (automatic) conversion from `Graph` to its corresponding `GraphOps`, so all of the operations available in `GraphOps` can be invoked as if those operations were declared in the `Graph` class. `GraphOps` contains a `pageRank()` method, but it calls `run()` from the `PageRank` singleton object, passing in the graph as the first parameter.**

TIP   To find out all the methods you can invoke on an instance of Graph, be sure to look at the GraphOps API documentation in addition to the docs for Graph.

The other way of invoking PageRank—the object-based way—is to call the run() method of the singleton object org.apache.spark.graphx.lib.PageRank, passing in the graph as the first parameter. This is what the pageRank() method of GraphOps does. Which way to invoke PageRank is a matter of style; for example, if you're already performing a number of operations on your graph, the object-oriented style allows you to chain it as an additional operation.

FIXED NUMBER OF ITERATIONS ("STATIC") VS. TOLERANCE EXIT CONDITION ("DYNAMIC")

For each of the two invocation means (object-oriented and object-based), there's another choice to be made: whether to exit after a specified number of iterations or to continue iterating (potentially forever) and exit only after a tolerance condition has been met. The GraphX API documentation calls the former *static* and the latter *dynamic*.

Whereas the static versions take a parameter `numIter` (number of iterations), the dynamic versions take a parameter `tol` (tolerance). If a vertex's PageRank didn't change by more than `tol` between the previous iteration and the current iteration, it will pull itself out of the algorithm, neither distributing its PageRank to its neighbors nor paying attention to PageRank being sent to it by its neighbors. `tol` is also used to determine when the overall algorithm stops: if no vertex in the entire graph changes by more than `tol`, the algorithm terminates.

When we used `tol` in chapter 2, we picked a value of `0.001`, which is on the high side for quick algorithm termination. For more precise results, pick a smaller value, such as `0.0001`.

THE RANDOM RESET PROBABILITY

All four variations (object-oriented versus object-based and static versus dynamic) take an additional parameter, `resetProb`, which the API documentation also refers to as *alpha*. This `resetProb` parameter corresponds to what the 1998 Brin and Page paper, "The Anatomy of a Large-Scale Hypertextual Web Search Engine," refers to as a *damping factor*. You specify `resetProb` in the range [0,1], and it represents a sort of minimum PageRank value.

Conceptually, `resetProb` corresponds to the probability that an imaginary web surfer will suddenly visit a random page on the web instead of following one of the outbound links prescribed by the web page that the surfer is currently visiting. This is useful for accounting for *sinks*—web pages that have inbound links but no outbound links. `resetProb` ensures that all pages always have some minimum PageRank, and also the (1-resetProb) in the preceding formula *dampens* the contribution of the incoming PageRanks from the adjacent vertices. It is as if imaginary outbound edges are added from all sink vertices to every other vertex in the graph, and to keep things fair, this same thing is done to the non-sink vertices as well.

> **NOTE** The `resetProb` used in GraphX is the same as 1-*d* described in the PageRank literature, where *d* is the damping factor. The PageRank literature recommends a value of 0.85 for the damping factor, and the GraphX documentation recommends a value of 0.15 for `resetProb`.

The following formula incorporates `resetProb` to compute the new PageRank for a vertex v:

$$v'_{PageRank} = resetProb + (1 - resetProb) \sum_{u\ having\ outbound\ edge\ into\ v} \frac{u_{PageRank}}{u_{Outdegree}}$$

resetProb is in some sense a hack. For a true, ideal PageRank, resetProb should be set to zero; however, doing so leads to longer convergence times and can also lead to degenerate results: clusters of self-interconnected components getting all the Page-Rank, and the mainstream highly connected vertices getting zero as their PageRank. An example of what can happen is shown in figure 5.3.

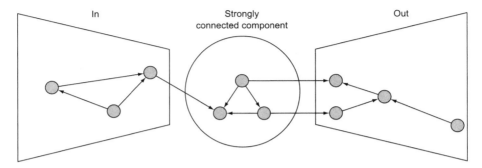

Figure 5.3   The real-world graph of web pages is said to resemble a bow-tie. With a damping factor of 1.0 (resetProb of .0.0), all the PageRanks would get trapped in the "OUT" vertices, and all the "IN" vertices would be left with a PageRank of 0.

Based on the name resetProb, you might think a random number generator is involved. Although in some implementations of PageRank a random number generator is employed, in the GraphX implementation it's strictly deterministic, and reset-Prob is treated as a constant. An example of an implementation that uses a random number generator is one that uses the Monte Carlo technique to estimate PageRank in a shorter amount of computation time.

5.1.3   *Personalized PageRank*

Suppose that instead of ranking web pages you want to recommend people on a social network. Such recommendations should be tailored to the user looking for other people; the user is more likely to be interested in other people who aren't too far away on the graph.

   Personalized PageRank is a variation on PageRank that gives a rank relative to a specified "source" vertex in the graph. Conceptually, the imaginary web surfer (or social network graph wanderer) described in the previous section, when suddenly deciding to visit another vertex, will always land on the specified source vertex. Within GraphX, this concept of an imaginary web surfer is implemented by enforcing a minimum PageRank only on the specified source vertex; the PageRanks of all the other vertices are allowed to fall to zero (for example, if they have no inbound links).

   In chapter 2 you saw PageRank run on a network of paper citations. In that example, the paper "Noncompact Symmetries in String Theory" had the highest Page-Rank. In the following listing, we specify the source vertex to be 9207016, the ID of that paper.

Listing 5.1   Personalized PageRank to find the most important related paper

```
import org.apache.spark.graphx._
val g = GraphLoader.edgeListFile(sc, "cit-HepTh.txt")
g.personalizedPageRank(9207016, 0.001)
 .vertices
 .filter(_._1 != 9207016)
 .reduce((a,b) => if (a._2 > b._2) a else b)
res1: (org.apache.spark.graphx.VertexId, Double) =
      (9201015,0.09211875000000003)
```

When we look up ID 9201015 in the abstracts from the SNAP site, we see it's "An Algorithm to Generate Classical Solutions for String Effective Action." According to the Personalized PageRank algorithm, this is the most important paper from the perspective of the paper "Noncompact Symmetries in String Theory."

The GraphX implementation of Personalized PageRank is limited in a couple of ways compared to implementations on other systems. First, only one source vertex can be specified. If specifying a group of vertices was allowed, this would permit, for example, finding the most important person to a group of people, such as 1992 Harvard alumni. Second, the weight for each source vertex cannot be specified; in the GraphX implementation it's hard-coded to 1.0, meaning the minimum PageRank for a vertex is either one of two extremes: 0 for vertices other than the source vertex, or 1.0 * resetProb for the source vertex. This isn't a big limitation right now, when GraphX only allows specifying a single source vertex, but when GraphX gains the capability in the future to specify multiple source vertices, being able to specify weights independently for each source vertex will allow one to conceptually specify some kind of affinity or importance to the rest of the vertices in the set of source vertices.

5.2   *Measuring connectedness: Triangle Count*

Where PageRank measured the influence of individual vertices, counting triangles can measure the connectedness of a graph or subgraph—how, collectively, the vertices together influence each other. For example, in a social network, if everyone influences everyone else—if everyone is connected to everyone else—there will be a lot of triangles.

A triangle is what it sounds like: three vertices that are all connected with edges. But there can be some subtleties when dealing with directed graphs, as GraphX does. When counting triangles, GraphX treats the graph as if it were undirected, ignoring the edge directions (see figure 5.4), collapsing duplicate edges into one, ignoring direction, and eliminating loop edges from a vertex back to itself.

Figure 5.4   When counting triangles, GraphX doesn't care about edge direction. These are both triangles, even though the triangle on the left forms a cycle and the triangle on the right has a dead end.

5.2.1 *Uses of Triangle Count*

The more triangles a graph or subgraph has, the more connected it is. This property can be used to identify cliques (parts of the graph that have a lot of interconnections), provide recommendations, and identify spammers. It's not always the case that more connectedness is always better. A fully connected graph, where every vertex connects to every other vertex, conveys no information about connectedness (though edge and vertex properties could still carry information). Sometimes a lack of connectedness identifies valuable vertices within the graph; for example, a research paper ("Visualizing the Signatures of Social Roles in Online Discussion Groups" by Welser et al) shows that those who answer questions on online forums are often loners with weak connections to a large number of other forum participants, leading to few triangles. Those helpful loner question-answerers may have edges to a bunch of unrelated question-askers, but those loners aren't part of any dense networks of people, so few triangles are formed (and only when question-askers happen to also be connected to each other). When trying to identify valuable question-answerers, a tell-tale sign might be a low Triangle Count.

Triangle Count serves as one factor in two other metrics known as the *clustering coefficient* and the *transitivity ratios*. These are more complicated to compute because they involve more than counting triangles. But being ratios, they're scaled/normalized with a denominator, making it easy to compare connectedness of graphs of different sizes. As of version 1.6, GraphX doesn't have algorithms built in to compute the clustering coefficient or transitivity ratio. Chapter 8 shows how to compute the global clustering coefficient.

5.2.2 *Slashdot friends and foes example*

Here we'll show an example of using Triangle Count to measure connectedness among various arbitrary subsets of users of Slashdot.org, the popular technology news and discussion site started in 1997. SNAP, the same Stanford repository of graph data we used in chapter 2, has an anonymized edge list of Slashdot "friends" and "foes." On Slashdot, a user reading comments can tag authors of forum comments as friends or foes to be reminded of that opinion the next time the user encounters a comment written by the same author. Even though the SNAP Slashdot data is anonymized—the vertex IDs don't match real-life Slashdot user IDs—the vertex IDs still appear to be in increasing order; longer-term users have lower vertex IDs.

In this data, the vertex IDs start at 0 and go up to over 70,000. We'll break this up into seven sets of 10,000 vertices each. That means we'll lose a lot of edges, namely the ones from one subgraph to another. We'll count the number of triangles within each of the seven subgraphs and see if there is a trend over time. Because long-term users tend to have interacted with each other often, there should be a high degree of interconnectedness. We would expect to see the first subgraph of 10,000 to be a tight-knit, highly connected group, and the second subgraph of 10,000 to have connections divided between themselves within this second subgraph and with the well-respected users in the first subgraph. But remember, we're discarding those edges from the second subgraph to the first subgraph when we cut out each subgraph. Continuing on, we would expect the third subgraph to have even fewer triangles.

Subgraphs in GraphX

Taking a subgraph in GraphX is straightforward. The `subgraph()` method of `Graph` takes two parameters: an edge predicate function and a vertex predicate function. Both are not required; you can specify one. The edge predicate function is presented with every edge in the graph and must return `true` or `false`—`true` if the edge is to be a part of the subgraph. It's similar with the vertex predicate function. If the edge predicate function filters out all edges to and from a vertex, that vertex remains in the subgraph as a naked vertex with no edges. If the vertex predicate function filters out one or both of the vertices from an edge, that edge doesn't make it into the subgraph.

NOTE In Spark 1.6 and earlier, `triangleCount()` imposed a couple of severe prerequisites on the graph: first, the graph has to be partitioned by one of the `PartitionStrategy` options described in section 9.4. Second, if there are any duplicate edges (two or more edges between the same two particular vertices), those duplicate edges have to point in the same direction. The GraphX documentation overstates this latter requirement; it says that all edges must be in canonical order, pointing from the lower-numbered vertex ID to the higher-numbered vertex ID. This is usually the easiest way to transform a graph to meet the second requirement, but if, for example, your graph has no duplicate edges, there's nothing to worry about (except for the partitioning from the first requirement). Jira ticket SPARK-3650, not targeted to any specific Spark release (as of Spark 1.6), would lift these requirements.

To get started, download the Slashdot friend and foe edge data from http://snap .stanford.edu/data/soc-Slashdot0811.html and uncompress it. Then from the Spark Shell, do what's shown in the following listing.

Listing 5.2 Triangle Counts on Slashdot friend and foe data

```
val g = GraphLoader.edgeListFile(sc, "soc-Slashdot0811.txt").cache
val g2 = Graph(g.vertices, g.edges.map(e =>
        if (e.srcId < e.dstId) e else new Edge(e.dstId, e.srcId, e.attr))).
    partitionBy(PartitionStrategy.RandomVertexCut)
(0 to 6).map(i => g2.subgraph(vpred =
        (vid,_) => vid >= i*10000 && vid < (i+1)*10000).
    triangleCount.vertices.map(_._2).reduce(_ + _))
res1: scala.collection.immutable.IndexedSeq[Int] = Vector(1352001, 61376,
10865, 3935, 1384, 786, 658)
```

Shorthand way to construct a
`scala.collection.immutable.Range.`
Pumping a `Range` **into a** `map()` **is a functional alternative to an imperative for loop.**

`vpred` **is the second parameter to**
`subgraph()` **and we omitted the first parameter (accepting its default value of a function that always returns** `true`**) so we have to specify the second parameter by name.**

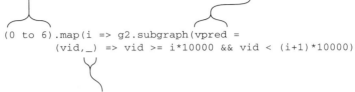

```
(0 to 6).map(i => g2.subgraph(vpred =
      (vid,_) => vid >= i*10000 && vid < (i+1)*10000)
```

Yet another distinct use of underscore in Scala. Here it stands for a parameter we don't care about.

This anonymous function takes two parameters. It looks like a `Tuple2`**, but it's really the Scala syntax for an anonymous function taking two distinct parameters.**

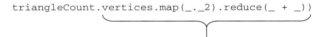

```
triangleCount.vertices.map(_._2).reduce(_ + _))
```

`triangleCount()` **actually calculates a Triangle Count on a per-vertex basis, returning a** `Graph[Int,ED]`**. Here we sum up all the Triangle Counts (stored in the vertex attribute, which we retrieve via** `_._2`**) over all the vertices.**

SCALA TIP   Scala allows two different syntaxes for invoking functions. One is the familiar Java-style, with the preceding period and parameters inside the parentheses. In the other, the period and the parentheses are omitted. Scala allows this if the function has zero parameters (where it's called *suffix notation*) or one parameter (where it is called *infix notation*). Stylistically, Scala programmers typically leave off parentheses whenever possible, especially when a function has no side effects (leaves the underlying object unchanged). In the preceding diagrammed line of code, `to` is a function of `scala.Int` (of which the zero (0) preceding it is an instance) and the subsequent 6 is its parameter. `to` is not a Scala keyword but merely part of the Scala standard library, and documentation on `to` can be found in the API documentation page on `scala.Int`.

The portion of the computation of g2 that ensures edge vertex IDs are in ascending order will be unnecessary once SPARK-3650 is fixed.

Our hypothesis was confirmed: each succeeding subgraph of 10,000 vertices had a lower triangle count.

In this simple example, we didn't care about Triangle Counts on a per-vertex basis, but such information is useful when considering local connectedness as opposed to global graph connectedness.

As with PageRank, there's an object-based `TriangleCount` version as well in the `graphx.lib` package.

5.3 Find the fewest hops: ShortestPaths

The `ShortestPaths` algorithm built into GraphX counts the number of hops (not using any distance values that may be attached to the edges) and returns the distance in terms of number of hops (not a full path of how to get from one vertex to another).

You might be tempted, based on the name, to use this to plot driving routes on a map, but an algorithm that uses distance values on edges will be covered in section 6.2.

An example where you would want to count hops is counting the shortest number of "friends" edges from each vertex in a social network graph to get to "Fred Marple." Or, because the GraphX API supports passing in a list of vertices known as `landmarks`, the shortest distance from each vertex in the graph to any of those could be computed—for example, anyone in the class of '79. An example from another domain is counting network hops in a computer network to the nearest tier-one node.

For a simple example, using the example graph from figure 1.5 and constructed in the Spark Shell in listing 4.1, the code in listing 5.3 computes the shortest number of hops from each vertex in the graph to Charles. Note that even though the algorithm is formally named "shortest paths," from an API perspective, the GraphX implementation only returns the shortest distances. The result is shown in figure 5.5.

> **Listing 5.3   Invoking `ShortestPaths`**

```
lib.ShortestPaths.run(myGraph,Array(3)).vertices.collect
res2: Array[(org.apache.spark.graphx.VertexId,
    org.apache.spark.graphx.lib.ShortestPaths.SPMap)] = Array((4,Map()),
    (1,Map(3 -> 2)), (3,Map(3 -> 0)), (5,Map()), (2,Map(3 -> 1)))
```

Note that `ShortestPaths` can be invoked only in the object-based style, as there is no corresponding method in `Graph` or `GraphOps`.

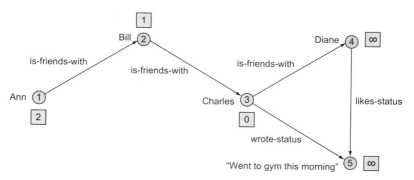

Figure 5.5   `ShortestPaths` finds the number of hops (shown in the squares) from every vertex to a particular specified vertex (in this case, vertex #3). It does not take into account any edge weights (which might, for example, represent distances on a map), and it only returns the number of hops, not any routes on how to achieve that shortest distance.

5.4   *Finding isolated populations: Connected Components*

Connected Components can find cliques in social network graphs and "partitioning" in a data center network. The Connected Components algorithm is relevant for both directed and undirected graphs. The code to construct the graph in figure 5.6 and find its Connected Components is shown in the following listing.

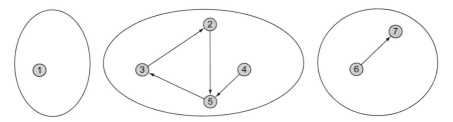

Figure 5.6   **This one graph of 7 vertices and 5 edges has three Connected Components. If this graph data were from a social network, each Connected Component would be considered a clique.**

Listing 5.4   Invoking connectedComponents()

```
val g = Graph(sc.makeRDD((1L to 7L).map((_,""))),
    sc.makeRDD(Array(Edge(2L,5L,""), Edge(5L,3L,""), Edge(3L,2L,""),
                Edge(4L,5L,""), Edge(6L,7L,"")))).cache
g.connectedComponents.vertices.map(_.swap).groupByKey.map(_._2).collect
res3: Array[Iterable[org.apache.spark.graphx.VertexId]] = Array(
CompactBuffer(1), CompactBuffer(6, 7), CompactBuffer(4, 3, 5, 2))
```

connectedComponents returns a new Graph object with the same structure as the input graph. Connected Components are identified by the lowest vertex ID in the component, and this value is assigned as an attribute to each vertex. We have the result shown in table 5.1.

Table 5.1   **Connected Components are identified by the lowest vertex ID.**

Component ID	Component members
1	1
2	2, 3, 4, 5
6	6, 7

As with PageRank and some of the other built-in algorithms, there are both object-oriented and object-based ways to invoke GraphX's Connected Components implementation.

5.4.1 Predicting social circles

Now that you've seen how easy it is to generate Connected Components in GraphX, let's put the algorithm to work on a real-world dataset. Not only will we get to run the Connected Components algorithm we've looked at, we'll also see how to import data, manipulate it into the structure that we need, and output the results in a particular format. We'll use a dataset derived from Facebook that was used in a 2014 Kaggle data science competition.

Kaggle (www.kaggle.com) hosts competitions in which a dataset is provided for download and the participants are set a task to predict a certain outcome for each record in the dataset. Over the course of the competition, competitors get to submit their predictions, which are scored for their accuracy compared to some ground truth known only to the competition organizers. At the end of the competition, the competitor with the best score wins, with prizes ranging from cash to job offers.

We're going to use data from the Learning Social Circles from Networks competition. The data was collected from a small number of Facebook users who had supplied information on friends in their network. In addition to the graph of their network, each contributing user was asked to allocate their friends to one or more *social circles*. A social circle is some grouping of the user's friends that made sense to that user. For example, it could be colleagues at work, people from the same school, or a group of friends they socialize with. What constitutes a social circle was left up to the user. Circles could overlap, be completely contained by one or more other circles, and could even be empty.

The aim of the competition was to use the network information to get the best prediction of how users would be grouped into circles. Clearly there are numerous ways that we could tackle the problem, but we'll use a simple approach of finding connected components within the graph of each user's connections. Our prediction of what circles each user has and how friends are allocated to those circles are then the Connected Components.

GETTING THE KAGGLE DATA ON SOCIAL NETWORKS

To download the data from Kaggle, you'll need to set up an account with Kaggle. Once you've done that, navigate to www.kaggle.com/c/learning-social-circles/data. This page lists a number of files, but you want the one called egonets.zip. You'll be asked to accept the competition rules even though the competition has ended, so go ahead and accept. Unzip the file and have a look at the directory—we saved the egonets folder underneath a folder structure called socialcircles/data, as shown in figure 5.7.

> **NOTE** The term *egonet* comes from a paper by Julian McAuley and Jure Leskovec from Stanford in which they describe individual users as *egos* and users' connections as *alters*. All very Freudian!

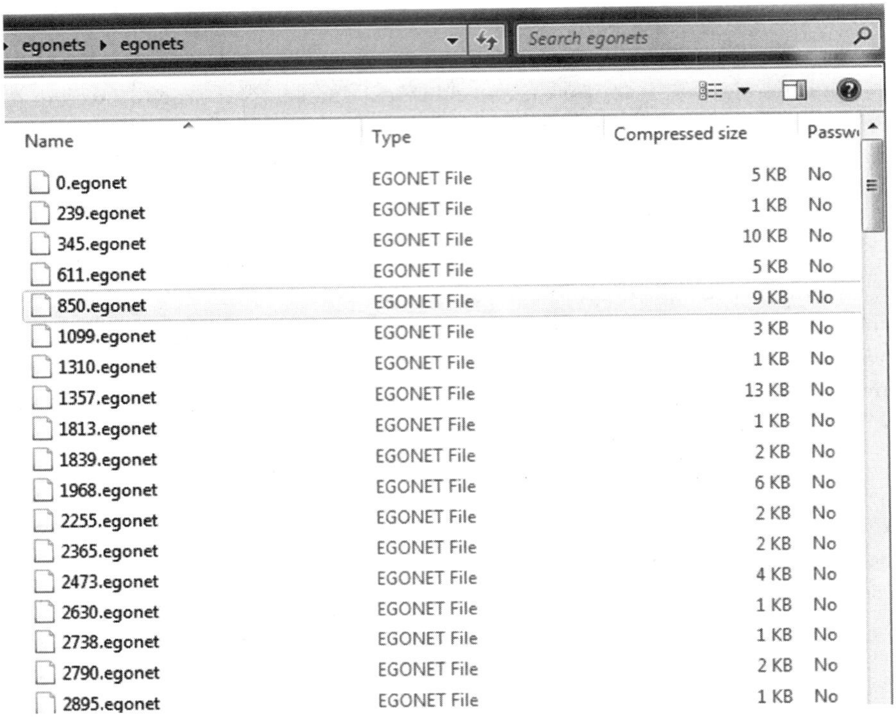

Figure 5.7   The egonets folder contains 111 egonet files, one for each user.

The dataset is anonymized so that each contributing user is given an ID, and you'll find an egonet file for each user. Open one up and look at its contents. We've chosen 3077.egonet because it is small enough to display on the page; here are its contents:

```
3078: 3085 3089
3079: 3082
3080: 3089
3081: 3085 3083 3089
3082: 3079 3086 3089
3083: 3085 3081 3089
3084:
3085: 3083 3078 3081 3088 3089
3086: 3082
3087:
3088: 3085 3089
3089: 3085 3080 3083 3078 3082 3081 3088
```

The egonet file lists each of the user's friends and, for each of those friends, who their connections are. There is one row for each of the user's friends (again anonymized and given numeric IDs). The format is

```
Friend-id: Space-seperated list of connection-ids
```

User 3077 has 12 friends (IDs 3078 to 3089). Friend 3078 is connected to two of 3077's other friends, 3085 and 3089. Friends 3084 and 3087 seem to be loners in the group who aren't connected to any of 3077's friends. Figure 5.8 shows a graph of these connections. In this instance we have one big graph for everyone but 3084 and 3087 and singleton vertices for the two loners. We should find three connected components which will form the basis for three social circles. Other egonets have a more complicated structure.

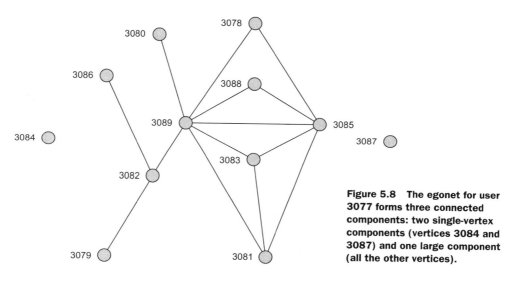

Figure 5.8 The egonet for user 3077 forms three connected components: two single-vertex components (vertices 3084 and 3087) and one large component (all the other vertices).

Reading folder contents with wholeTextFiles

Our task is to read in each of the egonet files, create a graph from the friends and their connections, find the connected components, and output the resulting social circles.

As with many real-world problems, we have to accept the input in the format it is given to us and convert that input into the structures we need to create graphs. In this case, the input data is not in a single convenient file but rather is scattered across the files of a directory. Luckily we can use a method on SparkContext called wholeText-Files to read the contents of a folder into an RDD:

```
val egonets = sc.wholeTextFiles("socialcircles/data/egonets")
```

wholeTextFiles returns a PairRDD with one element for each file; the key is the folder path to the file, and the value is the contents of the file (see figure 5.9).

Finding social circles

Listing 5.5 shows the full code to read in the input, generate the social circles, and output the predictions to the console. Once wholeTextFiles has loaded the egonets directory into an RDD called egonets, we generate two arrays, egonets_numbers and egonets_edges, using a map operation on each element of egonets.

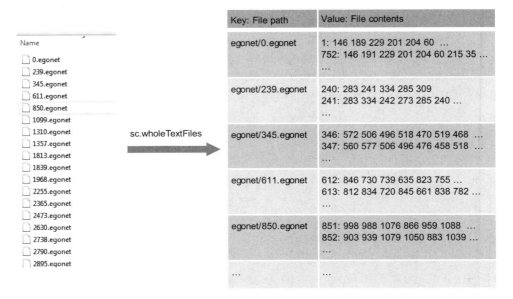

Figure 5.9   A folder path is passed to `wholeTextFiles` to generate a `PairRDD` with the file path as the key for each element and the file contents for the value. This is both good performing and a convenient way to read a directory of text files, resulting in all the data being in a single RDD.

The first map operation uses a method we define called `extract`. This uses a regular expression to extract the user ID from the filename.

> **SCALA TIP**   Regular expressions (or regexes) can be created by appending `r` to the end of a string. Regexes are usually a pain to write in Java because every backslash has to be delimited by another backslash. For this reason, Scala provides "raw" strings using a triple-quoting syntax as used in the example. Finally Scala regexes provide "extractor" methods that allow you to designate variables that a matching regex will populate. The code `val Pattern(num) = s` populates the `num` variable with the group matching the string `s`.

The second map expression calls a helper method, `make_edges`, which parses each egonet file's contents to create edges between each friend connection. Another helper method, `get_circles`, creates a graph of the egonet using `Graph.fromEdge-Tuples`. Once we have the graph, we call `connectedComponents` to derive the social circles (see the following listing).

Listing 5.5   Find and list social circles

```
// returns the userId from a file path with the format
//     <path>/<userId>.egonet
def extract(s: String) = {
    val Pattern = """^.*?(\d+).egonet""".r
    val Pattern(num) = s
    num
}
```

```
// Processes a line from an egonet file to return a
// Array of edges in a tuple
def get_edges_from_line(line: String): Array[(Long, Long)] = {
    val ary = line.split(":")
    val srcId = ary(0).toInt
    val dstIds = ary(1).split(" ")
    val edges = for {
        dstId <- dstIds
        if (dstId != "")
    } yield {
        (srcId.toLong, dstId.toLong)
    }

    // A subtle point: if the user is not connected to
    // anyone else then we generate a "self-connection"
    // so that the vertex will be included in the graph
    // created by Graph.fromEdgeTuples.
    if (edges.size > 0) edges else Array((srcId, srcId))
}

// Constructs Edges tuples from an egonet file
// contents
def make_edges(contents: String) = {
    val lines = contents.split("\n")
    val unflat = for {
      line <- lines
    } yield {
      get_edges_from_line(line)
    }
    // We want an Array of tuples to pass to Graph.fromEdgeTuples
    // but we have an Array of Arrays of tuples. Luckily we can
    // call flatten() to sort this out.
    val flat = unflat.flatten
    flat
}

// Constructs a graph from Edge tuples
// and runs connectedComponents returning
// the results as a string
def get_circles(flat: Array[(Long, Long)]) = {
    val edges = sc.makeRDD(flat)
    val g = Graph.fromEdgeTuples(edges,1)
    val cc = g.connectedComponents()
    cc.vertices.map(x => (x._2, Array(x._1))).
        reduceByKey( (a,b) => a ++ b).
        values.map(_.mkString(" ")).collect.mkString(";")
}

val egonets = sc.wholeTextFiles("socialcircles/data/egonets")
val egonet_numbers = egonets.map(x => extract(x._1)).collect
val egonet_edges   = egonets.map(x => make_edges(x._2)).collect
val egonet_circles = egonet_edges.toList.map(x => get_circles(x))
println("UserId,Prediction")
val result = egonet_numbers.zip(egonet_circles).map(x => x._1 + "," + x._2)
println(result.mkString("\n"))
```

Splits string into array of its parts based on a delimiter, like String.split() in Java

Scala for comprehension

SCALA TIP   A *for comprehension* is like a `map()` combined with a `filter()`. The syntax starts off with something like `x <- myCollection`, which is similar to enhanced for-loops introduced in Java 5. Immediately following is an optional *guard* which acts like the `filter()`. Finally comes the `yield {}` which acts like the function passed into a `map()`; the difference is that what would be the function parameter of the function passed into `map()` is declared at the beginning of the for comprehension.

The competition requires a particular format for predictions. Each social circle is represented as a space-separated list of user IDs, and each social circle is separated by a semicolon (;). The code we use to do this is as follows:

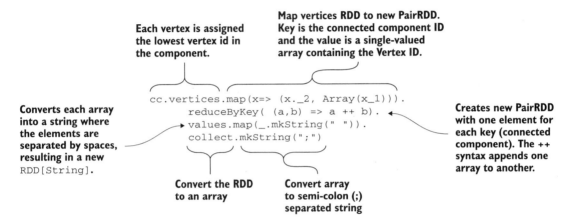

In this example, we have output the user ID and the social circles in the format required for the competition; but the choice of output depends on what subsequent use we want to make of the information. Spark allows you to easily push the data to an external database, output to a real-time system, or even integrate into a more extensive machine-learning pipeline.

5.5   *Reciprocated love only, please: Strongly Connected Components*

For directed graphs, sometimes we might want to eliminate dead ends from our components. In social networks, Strongly Connected Components can form a basis for a recommendation engine if other aspects are added to the engine. Another application is ensuring that in a state machine there are no dead ends where the state machine could get stuck. They are also useful in building optimizing compilers for when they do data flow analysis to identify expressions that never get used and would otherwise be wastefully computed.

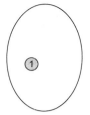 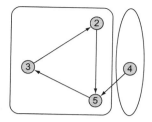 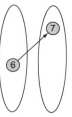

Figure 5.10 **In Strongly Connected Components, every vertex is reachable from every other vertex in the component. Within a Strongly Connected Component, no vertex can act as a dead end.**

Invoking `stronglyConnectedComponents()` is similar to invoking `connected-Components()` except that a parameter `numIter` is required. Assuming `g` is defined as in the previous section, the following listing finds its Strongly Connected Components.

Listing 5.6 Invoking `stronglyConnectedComponents()`

```
g.stronglyConnectedComponents(10).vertices.map(_.swap).groupByKey.
    map(_._2).collect
res4: Array[Iterable[org.apache.spark.graphx.VertexId]] = Array(
CompactBuffer(4), CompactBuffer(1), CompactBuffer(6), CompactBuffer(7),
CompactBuffer(3, 5, 2))
```

5.6 *Community detection: LabelPropagation*

To identify close-knit communities within a graph, GraphX provides the label propagation algorithm (LPA) as described by Raghavan et al in their 2007 paper "Near linear time algorithm to detect community structures in large-scale networks." The idea is to have densely connected groups of vertices form a consensus on a unique label and so define communities.

> **DEFINITION** Many iterative algorithms are guaranteed to get closer to a particular result on each iteration of the algorithm; they *converge*. With algorithms that have this property, it's reasonable to run the algorithm for as many iterations as required and use a tolerance test to exit the algorithm when they're "close enough." Algorithms that don't converge could continue forever without converging, so we need to specify an upper limit on the number of iterations that will be run. Inevitably in this situation there is a trade-off between the accuracy of the end result and the time the algorithm takes to run.

Unfortunately, LPA often doesn't converge. Figure 5.11 shows an example of non-convergence—the graph in step 5 is the same as in step 3, and the algorithm continues forever ping-ponging between the two graphs that look like steps 4 and 5. For that reason, GraphX only provides a static version that runs for a number of iterations you specify and doesn't provide a dynamic version with a tolerance-terminating condition.

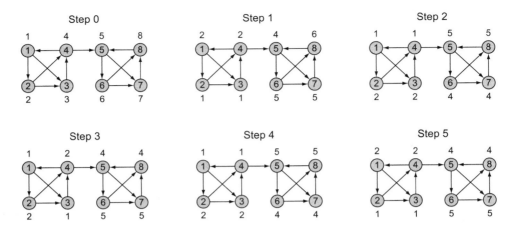

Figure 5.11   The LPA algorithm often doesn't converge. Step 5 is the same as step 3, meaning that steps 3 and 4 keep repeating forever.

Despite its name, LPA is also not applicable to the use case of propagating classifications of vertices—propagating labels from vertices of known classification to vertices of unknown classification. Section 7.3 explores this use case, called *semi-supervised learning*.

LPA, in contrast, uses as its initial labels the vertex ID, as shown in step 0 of figure 5.11 (see the following listing). LPA doesn't care about edge direction, effectively treating the graph as an undirected graph. The flip-flopping of two sets of labels that is shown in steps 3 through 5 in figure 5.11 is illustrated in a similar example in the original Raghavan paper.

Listing 5.7   Invoking `LabelPropagation`

```
val v = sc.makeRDD(Array((1L,""), (2L,""), (3L,""), (4L,""), (5L,""),
  (6L,""), (7L,""), (8L,""))))
val e = sc.makeRDD(Array(Edge(1L,2L,""), Edge(2L,3L,""), Edge(3L,4L,""),
  Edge(4L,1L,""), Edge(1L,3L,""), Edge(2L,4L,""), Edge(4L,5L,""),
  Edge(5L,6L,""), Edge(6L,7L,""), Edge(7L,8L,""), Edge(8L,5L,""),
  Edge(5L,7L,""), Edge(6L,8L,""))))
lib.LabelPropagation.run(Graph(v,e),5).vertices.collect.
  sortWith(_._1<_._1)
res5: Array[(org.apache.spark.graphx.VertexId,
    org.apache.spark.graphx.VertexId)] = Array((1,2), (2,1), (3,1), (4,2),
    (5,4), (6,5), (7,5), (8,4))
```

5.7   Summary

- GraphX's built-in algorithms range widely in their usefulness, power, and applicability.
- PageRank is useful for a number of different applications beyond ranking web pages for a search engine.

- Personalized PageRank is useful for ranking "people you may know" in a social network.
- Triangle Count can serve as a gross measure for connectedness, but another measure to be introduced in chapter 8, the Global Clustering Coefficient, has the advantage of always being within the range of 0 to 1, facilitating comparisons between graphs of different sizes.
- Connected Components and Strongly Connected Components can find social circles in social networks.
- GraphX's Label Propagation is less useful because it rarely converges.

Other useful
graph algorithms

This chapter covers

- Standard graph algorithms that GraphX doesn't provide out of the box
- Shortest Paths on graphs with weighted edges
- The Traveling Salesman problem
- Minimum Spanning Trees

In chapter 5 you learned the foundational GraphX APIs that will enable you to write your own custom algorithms. But there's no need for you to reinvent the wheel in those cases where the GraphX API already provides an implemented standard algorithm. There are some algorithms that have been historically associated with graphs for decades but are not in the GraphX API. This chapter describes some of those classic graph algorithms and discusses which situations they can be used in.

These classic graph algorithms were invented in the 1950s, long before Spark or any other sort of parallel computing. They are iterative in nature—for example, they add one edge at a time to the solution. GraphX's Pregel API isn't a good match because it operates on all the vertices simultaneously. The power of GraphX's parallel processing is still being used, though, because each step in these algorithms involves some kind of graph-wide search. You'll see how to use GraphX's iterative Map/Reduce facilities (`aggregateMessages()` together with `outerJoinVertices()`) to implement and parallelize these algorithms that were originally designed for serial computation.

The first of the three algorithms described in this chapter, Shortest Paths with Weights, fills a glaring hole in the GraphX API, which only provides a shortest-paths algorithm that assumes each edge has a weight of 1. Shortest Paths with Weights allows route planning on a map where each edge weight represents the distance between its two vertices (representing cities).

The second algorithm, called the Travelling Salesman, finds a path through a graph that hits every vertex. This algorithm is useful for package/mail delivery and other logistics applications.

The third and final algorithm, Minimum Spanning Tree, overlays a *tree* (a graph with no cycles) over the top of the graph where the sum of its edge weights is less than any other possible spanning tree. Although this sounds abstract (and is, in fact, one of the first algorithms presented in a graph theory course), it's useful for routing utilities and has other non-intuitive uses, such as creating hierarchical scientific or bibliographic taxonomies.

6.1 *Your own GPS: Shortest Paths with Weights*

Today, we take for granted the GPS capability in our smartphones and map apps. But how do they do it? Edsger Dijkstra figured it out in 1956, and this section implements a Spark version of that algorithm.

Section 5.3 showed GraphX's implementation of finding shortest-path lengths for graphs with unweighted edges, but Dijkstra's algorithm finds the shortest-path lengths for graphs with weighted edges (see figure 6.1). When way-finding on a geographical map, the vertices represent cities or road intersections, and the edge weights represent road distances.

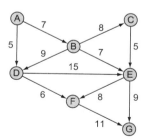 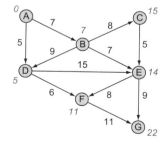

Figure 6.1 Example graph data and distances from vertex A after having been run through Dijkstra's algorithm. Given a graph with edge weights on the left, Dijkstra's algorithm annotates each vertex with a "shortest distance from vertex A." Graph data credit: the graph data comes from the Wikipedia article on Kruskal's algorithm (which, incidentally, is implemented in the last section of this chapter), which the contributor contributed to the public domain.

The Dijkstra algorithm calculates path distance from one particular vertex to every other vertex in the graph. It can be described like this:

1 Initialize the starting vertex to distance zero and all other vertices to distance infinity.

2 Set the current vertex to be the starting vertex.

3 For all the vertices adjacent to the current vertex, set the distance to be the lesser of either its current value or the sum of the current vertex's distance plus the length of the edge that connects the current vertex to that other vertex. For example, in figure 6.1, after the first iteration, vertex D has a value of 5, and vertex B has a value of 7. In the second iteration, there is a candidate alternative to get from A to D, which is through B, but that has a total path length of 16, so D keeps its old value of 5.

4 Mark the current vertex as having been visited.

5 Set the current vertex to be the unvisited vertex of the smallest distance value. If there are no more unvisited vertices, stop.

6 Go to step 3.

There are many variations of Dijkstra's algorithm, including versions for directed versus undirected graphs. The implementation in the following listing is geared toward directed graphs.

Listing 6.1 Dijkstra Shortest Paths distance algorithm

```
import org.apache.spark.graphx._
def dijkstra[VD](g:Graph[VD,Double], origin:VertexId) = {
  var g2 = g.mapVertices(
    (vid,vd) => (false, if (vid == origin) 0 else Double.MaxValue))

  for (i <- 1L to g.vertices.count-1) {
    val currentVertexId =
      g2.vertices.filter(!_._2._1)
        .fold((0L,(false,Double.MaxValue)))((a,b) =>
          if (a._2._2 < b._2._2) a else b)
        ._1

    val newDistances = g2.aggregateMessages[Double](
        ctx => if (ctx.srcId == currentVertexId)
                ctx.sendToDst(ctx.srcAttr._2 + ctx.attr),
        (a,b) => math.min(a,b))

    g2 = g2.outerJoinVertices(newDistances)((vid, vd, newSum) =>
      (vd._1 || vid == currentVertexId,
       math.min(vd._2, newSum.getOrElse(Double.MaxValue))))
  }

  g.outerJoinVertices(g2.vertices)((vid, vd, dist) =>
    (vd, dist.getOrElse((false,Double.MaxValue))._2))
}
```

SPARK TIP   The RDD API unfortunately doesn't include a `minBy()` function like regular Scala collections do, so a cumbersome and verbose `fold()` had to be used in the preceding code to accomplish the same thing.

In this implementation, we stoop to using a `var` (for g2) instead of a `val` because this is an iterative algorithm. When we initialize g2, we throw away any vertex data in the original g and attach our own: a pair of a Boolean and a Double. The Boolean indicates whether the vertex has been visited yet. The Double is the distance from the origin to that vertex.

As of GraphX 1.6 all graphs are immutable, so the only way to "update" these vertex values in our algorithm is to create a new graph. When we compute `newDistances`, we have to add that onto our graph g2 with `outerJoinVertices()`, which creates a new graph. We assign that new graph back to g2, relying on JVM garbage collection to get rid of the old graph that was in g2.

As the last line of the function, which is the return value, we restore the original vertex properties by adding the final results from g2 onto the original g with `outerJoinVertices`. In the process we make the type of the vertex properties for the return graph have an extra level of information; instead of `VD`, the vertex property type is a `Tuple2[VD,Double]`, where the Double contains the distance output from Dijkstra's algorithm.

The Pregel API would not have been easy to use due to the concept of the "current vertex," which for each iteration is the global overall minimum. The Pregel API is more suited for algorithms that treat all vertices as equals. The next listing shows how to execute our new `dijkstra()` function with the graph from figure 6.1.

Listing 6.2   Executing the Shortest Path distance algorithm

```
val myVertices = sc.makeRDD(Array((1L, "A"), (2L, "B"), (3L, "C"),
  (4L, "D"), (5L, "E"), (6L, "F"), (7L, "G")))
val myEdges = sc.makeRDD(Array(Edge(1L, 2L, 7.0), Edge(1L, 4L, 5.0),
  Edge(2L, 3L, 8.0), Edge(2L, 4L, 9.0), Edge(2L, 5L, 7.0),
  Edge(3L, 5L, 5.0), Edge(4L, 5L, 15.0), Edge(4L, 6L, 6.0),
  Edge(5L, 6L, 8.0), Edge(5L, 7L, 9.0), Edge(6L, 7L, 11.0)))
val myGraph = Graph(myVertices, myEdges)

dijkstra(myGraph, 1L).vertices.map(_._2).collect

res0: Array[(String, Double)] = Array((D,5.0), (A,0.0), (F,11.0), (C,15.0),
  (G,22.0), (E,14.0), (B,7.0))
```

These are the values shown in figure 6.1. But wait a minute—how would you know the path sequence to get to any of these destination vertices? The algorithm computes the distances, but not the paths.

The following listing adds the common embellishment of keeping track of the paths every step of the way by adding a third component to the vertex tuple, a Scala List that accumulates breadcrumbs.

Listing 6.3   Dijkstra's Shortest Path algorithm with breadcrumbs

```
import org.apache.spark.graphx._
def dijkstra[VD](g:Graph[VD,Double], origin:VertexId) = {
  var g2 = g.mapVertices(
    (vid,vd) => (false, if (vid == origin) 0 else Double.MaxValue,
                 List[VertexId]()))

  for (i <- 1L to g.vertices.count-1) {
    val currentVertexId =
      g2.vertices.filter(!_._2._1)
        .fold((0L,(false,Double.MaxValue,List[VertexId]())))((a,b) =>
          if (a._2._2 < b._2._2) a else b)
        ._1

    val newDistances = g2.aggregateMessages[(Double,List[VertexId])](
      ctx => if (ctx.srcId == currentVertexId)
               ctx.sendToDst((ctx.srcAttr._2 + ctx.attr,
                              ctx.srcAttr._3 :+ ctx.srcId)),
        (a,b) => if (a._1 < b._1) a else b)

    g2 = g2.outerJoinVertices(newDistances)((vid, vd, newSum) => {
      val newSumVal =
        newSum.getOrElse((Double.MaxValue,List[VertexId]()))
      (vd._1 || vid == currentVertexId,
       math.min(vd._2, newSumVal._1),
       if (vd._2 < newSumVal._1) vd._3 else newSumVal._2)})
  }

  g.outerJoinVertices(g2.vertices)((vid, vd, dist) =>
    (vd, dist.getOrElse((false,Double.MaxValue,List[VertexId]()))
           .productIterator.toList.tail))
}
```

SCALA TIP   The "operator" (Scala purists call them *functions*, even though they look like operators) :+ is a Scala List function that returns a new list with an element appended. Scala List has a large number of similar operators for prepending or appending lists or elements, and these are listed along with the other Scala List functions in the Scaladocs for List.

Listing 6.4   Executing the Shortest Path algorithm that uses breadcrumbs

```
dijkstra(myGraph, 1L).vertices.map(_._2).collect

res1: Array[(String, List[Any])] = Array((D,List(5.0, List(1))),
  (A,List(0.0, List())), (F,List(11.0, List(1, 4))),
  (C,List(15.0, List(1, 2))), (G,List(22.0, List(1, 4, 6))),
  (E,List(14.0, List(1, 2))), (B,List(7.0, List(1))))
```

That's much better. Now you can know the shortest path to take to get to any of the other vertices.

6.2   *Travelling Salesman: greedy algorithm*

The travelling salesman problem tries to find the shortest path through an undirected graph that hits every vertex. For example, if a salesperson needs to visit every city in a region, they would like to minimize the total distance traveled.

Unlike the shortest path problem in the previous section, there is no easy, straightforward, deterministic algorithm to solve the travelling salesman problem. Note that *travelling salesman* is a well-known math problem; the term was coined in the 1930s, so that term is used here rather than inclusive language.

The problem is of a class of problems known as *NP-hard*, which means it can't be solved in an amount of time that is a polynomial with respect to the number of vertices or edges. It is, rather, a combinatorial optimization problem that would require an exponential amount of time to solve optimally. Instead of trying to find the optimum, various approaches use heuristics to come close to the optimum. The implementation shown in figure 6.2 uses the greedy algorithm, which is the simplest algorithm but it also gives answers that can be far from optimal and don't necessarily hit all the vertices. (If hitting every vertex is a requirement, the algorithm might produce no acceptable answer at all.) This algorithm is called *greedy* because at every iteration it grabs the immediate shortest edge without doing any kind of deeper search.

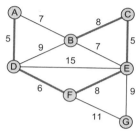

Figure 6.2   The greedy approach to the Travelling Salesman problem is the simplest, but it doesn't always hit all the vertices. In this example, it neglected to hit vertex G.

The greedy algorithm can be improved without much additional coding by iterating and rerunning the whole algorithm with different starting vertices, picking from the resulting solutions the one that goes to all the vertices and is the shortest. But the implementation shown in listing 6.5 only does one execution of the greedy algorithm for a given starting vertex passed in as a parameter.

The approach of the greedy algorithm is simple:

1 Start from some vertex.
2 Add the adjacent edge of lowest weight to the spanning tree.
3 Go to step 2.

Listing 6.5   Travelling Salesman greedy algorithm

```
def greedy[VD](g:Graph[VD,Double], origin:VertexId) = {
  var g2 = g.mapVertices((vid,vd) => vid == origin)
         .mapTriplets(et => (et.attr,false))
  var nextVertexId = origin
  var edgesAreAvailable = true

  do {
    type tripletType = EdgeTriplet[Boolean,Tuple2[Double,Boolean]]

    val availableEdges =
```

```
        g2.triplets
          .filter(et => !et.attr._2
                      && (et.srcId == nextVertexId && !et.dstAttr
                         || et.dstId == nextVertexId && !et.srcAttr))

      edgesAreAvailable = availableEdges.count > 0

      if (edgesAreAvailable) {
        val smallestEdge = availableEdges
            .min()(new Ordering[tripletType]() {
              override def compare(a:tripletType, b:tripletType) = {
                Ordering[Double].compare(a.attr._1,b.attr._1)
              }
            })

        nextVertexId = Seq(smallestEdge.srcId, smallestEdge.dstId)
                      .filter(_ != nextVertexId)(0)

        g2 = g2.mapVertices((vid,vd) => vd || vid == nextVertexId)
              .mapTriplets(et => (et.attr._1,
                                  et.attr._2 ||
                                   (et.srcId == smallestEdge.srcId
                                    && et.dstId == smallestEdge.dstId)))

      }
    } while(edgesAreAvailable)

    g2
}
greedy(myGraph,1L).triplets.filter(_.attr._2).map(et=>(et.srcId, et.dstId))
                  .collect

res1: Array[(org.apache.spark.graphx.VertexId,
 org.apache.spark.graphx.VertexId)] = Array((1,4), (2,3), (3,5), (4,6),
 (5,6))
```

> **SCALA TIP**   type is a convenient way to alias types at compile time to prevent having to type out long types over and over again. It's similar to typedef in C/C++, but there's no equivalent in Java. type in Scala also has another use— to introduce abstract type members in traits—but that's beyond the scope of this book.

Here we stoop to using three vars. The third one is for loop control because Scala has no break keyword (although there is a simulation of break in the standard library). In this implementation, during the looping the graph g2 has different vertex property types and a different edge property type than for g that was passed in. The vertex property type is Boolean, indicating whether the vertex has been incorporated into the solution yet. The edge property type is similar, except the edge weight is carried along as well because it's used by the algorithm; specifically, the Edge attribute type is Tuple2[Double,Boolean] where the Double is the edge weight and the Boolean indicates whether the edge has been incorporated as part of the solution.

The computation of availableEdges checks edges in both directions. This is what makes the algorithm treat graphs as if they were undirected. All GraphX graphs are directed in reality, with a source and a destination. Any implementation in GraphX of other algorithms meant for undirected graphs would have to take similar precautions of checking both directions.

Similar to the Shortest Paths algorithm in the previous section, we had to create a new graph at the end of the iteration due to the immutability of graphs in GraphX. For each iteration, the algorithm needs to set the Boolean on one vertex and the Boolean on one edge, but nevertheless, a new graph has to be created. Also similar to the Shortest Paths algorithm, the Pregel API would not be a good choice here because the greedy Travelling Salesman algorithm adds one edge at a time (to one vertex); it isn't treating all vertices equally.

The resulting graph finally returned by greedy is in perhaps not the most convenient form for the caller. We didn't bother to glom back on the original vertex properties from g. The reason we didn't is that we would have had to join the edge properties from g and g2 together, and GraphX provides no automatic way to do that. We do it in the next section, but it requires more than a line of code, which is a lot for Scala.

6.3   *Route utilities: Minimum Spanning Trees*

Minimum Spanning Trees sound abstract and not useful, but they can be considered to be like the Travelling Salesman problem where you don't care if you have to backtrack (and where backtracking is free of cost). One of the most immediate applications is routing utilities (roads, electricity, water, and so on) to ensure that all cities receive the utility, at minimum cost (for example, minimum distance, if the edge weights represent distance between cities). There are some non-obvious applications of Minimum Spanning Trees as well, including the creation of taxonomies among a collection of similar items, such as animals (for scientific classification) or newspaper headlines. See figure 6.3.

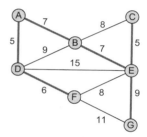

Figure 6.3   A Minimum Spanning Tree is a tree (a graph with no cycles) that covers every vertex of an undirected graph, of minimum total weight (sum of the edge weights).

Listing 6.6 is an implementation of Kruskal's algorithm. Again, the example graph used throughout this chapter is the same as the example graph on the Wikipedia page of Kruskal's algorithm, and because that Wikipedia page illustrates the execution of the algorithm through a sequence of graph illustrations, you can see exactly how the following implementation works.

Even though Kruskal's algorithm is greedy, it does find one of the Minimum Spanning Trees (there may be more than one Spanning Tree that has the same total weight). Finding a Minimum Spanning Tree isn't a combinatorial problem. Kruskal's algorithm is called greedy because at every iteration it grabs the edge of lowest weight. Unlike the Travelling Salesman greedy algorithm, the result is mathematically provably a Minimum Spanning Tree. See figure 6.4.

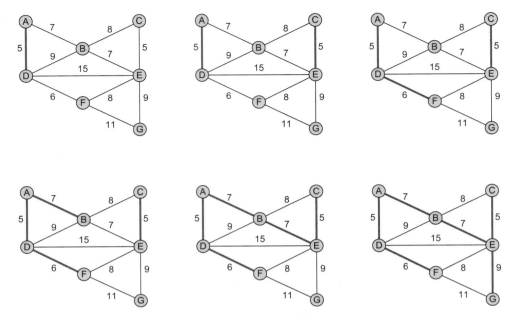

Figure 6.4   Iteration steps of Kruskal's algorithm to find a Minimum Spanning Tree. In each iteration, the whole graph is searched for the unused edge of lowest weight. But there's a catch: that edge can't form a cycle (as a *tree* is what is being sought).

Unlike the Travelling Salesman algorithm in the previous section, Kruskal's algorithm doesn't build up the tree by extending out an edge at a time from some growing tree. Rather, it does a global search throughout the graph to find the edge with the least weight to add to the set of edges that will eventually form a tree. The algorithm can be described like this:

1 Initialize the set of edges that will eventually comprise the resulting minimum spanning tree to be empty.
2 Find the edge of smallest weight throughout the whole graph that meets the following two conditions and add it to the result set:
   a The edge isn't already in the result set of edges.
   b The edge doesn't form a cycle with the edges already in the result set of edges.
3 Go to step 2, unless all vertices are already represented in the result set of edges.

The second condition (b) in step 2 is the tricky one. Finding a cycle is easy for a human to comprehend, but it's not immediately obvious how to describe it to a computer. There are a few approaches we could have taken. We could find the shortest path (for example, by invoking GraphX's built-in `ShortestPaths`, described in section 5.3) for every candidate edge (which is all or almost all of them in the beginning) and then discard from consideration those edges whose vertices already have a path between them. Another approach, which is the one taken in listing 6.6, is to call GraphX's built-in `connectedComponents()`, described in section 5.4. This gives vertex connectivity information across the whole graph in one fell swoop. If the two vertices of an edge belong to the same connected component of the result tree so far, then that edge is ineligible for consideration because adding it to the result set would create a cycle.

Listing 6.6   Minimum Spanning Tree

```
def minSpanningTree[VD:scala.reflect.ClassTag](g:Graph[VD,Double]) = {
  var g2 = g.mapEdges(e => (e.attr,false))

  for (i <- 1L to g.vertices.count-1) {
    val unavailableEdges =
      g2.outerJoinVertices(g2.subgraph(_.attr._2)
                             .connectedComponents
                             .vertices)((vid,vd,cid) => (vd,cid))
        .subgraph(et => et.srcAttr._2.getOrElse(-1) ==
                        et.dstAttr._2.getOrElse(-2))
        .edges
        .map(e => ((e.srcId,e.dstId),e.attr))

    type edgeType = Tuple2[Tuple2[VertexId,VertexId],Double]

    val smallestEdge =
      g2.edges
        .map(e => ((e.srcId,e.dstId),e.attr))
        .leftOuterJoin(unavailableEdges)
        .filter(x => !x._2._1._2 && x._2._2.isEmpty)
        .map(x => (x._1, x._2._1._1))
        .min()(new Ordering[edgeType]() {
          override def compare(a:edgeType, b:edgeType) = {
            val r = Ordering[Double].compare(a._2,b._2)
            if (r == 0)
              Ordering[Long].compare(a._1._1, b._1._1)
            else
              r
          }
        })

    g2 = g2.mapTriplets(et =>
      (et.attr._1, et.attr._2 || (et.srcId == smallestEdge._1._1
                               && et.dstId == smallestEdge._1._2)))
  }

  g2.subgraph(_.attr._2).mapEdges(_.attr._1)
}

minSpanningTree(myGraph).triplets.map(et =>
(et.srcAttr,et.dstAttr)).collect

Res2: Array[(String, String)] = Array((A,B), (A,D), (B,E), (C,E), (D,F),
(E,G))
```

SCALA TIP   Sometimes when using Scala generics it's necessary to declare the type parameters to be of `scala.reflect.ClassTag`. This is due to JVM type-erasure at runtime. In listing 6.6, the type VD is needed at runtime and not only at compile-time for the call to `subgraph()`.

In this implementation, the only type change we make to the graph during iteration is to add a Boolean to the Edge properties to indicate whether that edge is part of the result set of edges for the Spanning Tree.

All the tricky magic happens in the assignment to unavailableEdges. After first subsetting the graph to be those edges already in the growing result set of edges, we run it through connectedComponents(). We then take those component IDs and glom them onto the regular vertex data with outerJoinVertices(). Then we say that an edge is unavailable if its two vertices belong to the same connected component. Those component IDs could be conceptually null (in Scala-speak, Option[VertexId] could be None) due to the way outerJoinVertices() works. If a vertex isn't part of the growing result set of edges, then it's free and clear, and we prevent such edges from being declared unavailable by saying None is equivalent to a component ID of –1 or –2. –1 and –2 were intentionally chosen to be not only invalid vertexIds but also different from each other so that an edge with both vertices not already part of the growing result set of edges would be considered still available.

The computation of smallestEdge contains that conceptual join on edges that we said earlier in this chapter was messy because GraphX doesn't have an edge join built in. We'll convert the edges to a Tuple2[Tuple2[VertexId, VertexId], Tuple2 [Double, Boolean]] and then use the regular RDD leftOuterJoin() (not to be confused with the GraphX-specific join()s and outerJoin()s). leftOuterJoin() will treat the Tuple2[VertexId, VertexId] as a single entity and key off that when it performs the join. After the leftOuterJoin(), the data type has five parts and looks like figure 6.5.

After removing the edges unavailable for consideration, the subsequent map() then extracts only the two pieces of information we care about: the pair of VertexIds and the edge weight. The override def compare first compares the edge weights, and if those are equal, breaks the tie by comparing to see which VertexId is less. This is to make the execution deterministic and repeatable and to match the results in the

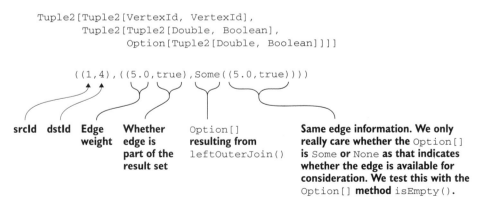

Figure 6.5   The data type after the leftOuterJoin() of listing 6.6.

Wikipedia example, because that is apparently how they broke ties. If you don't care about repeatability or matching Wikipedia (if you don't care about trying to make sure your program is matching that known working implementation), you can replace the `override def compare` body with `Ordering[Double].compare(a._2,b._2)`.

The return value of `minSpanningTree()` is the tree itself rather than the whole graph. The edge property type (`Edge attribute`) is restored to be the weight; the temporary Boolean is stripped off.

6.3.1 Deriving taxonomies with Word2Vec and Minimum Spanning Trees

One way to look at Minimum Spanning Trees is to see them as extracting (in some sense) the most important connections in the graph. By removing the less important edges we make the graph sparser, reducing it to its essentials. This section shows you how to use machine learning and graph processing to turn a simple list of unconnected terms—in this case, a list of animal names—into a connected taxonomy using Minimum Spanning Trees (MSTs).

MSTs can't do all the work, though; we'll also get some help from a natural language-processing tool called Word2Vec. Word2Vec lets us assign distances between each of our terms so that we can build a weighted graph of the connections between the terms. We can then run Minimum Spanning Tree on the graph to reveal the most important connections.

UNDERSTANDING WORD2VEC

Word2Vec is a natural language-processing algorithm that turns a text corpus (a collection of text documents) into a set of *n*-dimensional vectors that represent each distinct word in the corpus. Each word in the corpus is represented by a vector in the set. See figure 6.6.

What's useful about the vectors that Word2Vec generates is that words that are semantically similar tend to be close together. We can use a measure of similarity called *cosine similarity* to assign a number to how similar those words are. Cosine similarity

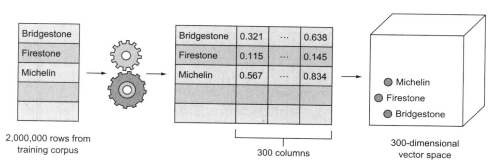

Figure 6.6   **Words are extracted from the training corpus and processed by the Word2Vec algorithm to produce an *n*-dimensional vector for each word—here, *n* is 300. Semantically similar words, such as *Michelin* and *Firestone*, are close together.**

ranges from 1 (similar) through 0 (not similar) to –1. We then turn cosine similarity into cosine distance by subtracting from 1:

```
cosine distance = 1 - cosine similarity
```

Now we have a measure where similar words have small distances between them and less similar words have larger distances.

   Models trained with Word2Vec usually require large amounts of data to be effective. Luckily there are already a number of well-regarded pre-trained models that can be used. For this task we'll use the model trained on a subset of Google News (100 billion words). Even though Spark's machine learning library, MLlib, contains an implementation of the Word2Vec algorithm, it doesn't yet have the functionality to load the binary format Google News model. Instead, we've pre-calculated cosine distance for every pair of names in the animal list and stored the results in a comma-separated variable file. The file, called animal_distances.txt, is included as part of the code download for this chapter. If you open up the file, you should see the following in the first few lines:

```
sea_otter,sea_otter,-0.000000
sea_otter,animal,0.638965
sea_otter,chicken,0.860217
sea_otter,dog,0.705229
sea_otter,aardvark,0.767667
sea_otter,albatross,0.770162
```

The file is in comma-separated format with three columns of data. Each row contains a single pair of terms and their cosine distance. There are around 224 different animal names in the list.

Creating the distances file

Because Spark MLlib doesn't yet have the ability to load Word2Vec models created by other implementations of Word2Vec, we use the Python library Gensim. If you want to use Word2Vec to generate the distance file yourself, you will need to follow the installation instructions at https://radimrehurek.com/gensim/install.html. Typically this involves using easy_install

```
easy_install -U gensim
```

or pip:

```
pip install --upgrade gensim
```

Then you will need to download the Google News model from the link on the page at https://code.google.com/p/word2vec/. Be warned: the file is several GBs in size.

Now we are ready to generate the distances. We start with a list of 200 animal terms that are in the file animal_terms.txt in the code download for this chapter:

```
from gensim.models import Word2Vec
model = Word2Vec.load_word2vec_format(
```

```
        'GoogleNews-vectors-negative300.bin',
        binary=True)
f = open('animal_terms.txt')
animals = f.read().splitlines()
animals = [x.lower() for x in animals if x.lower() in
            model.vocab.keys()]
f.close()
f = open('animal_distances.txt','w')
f.truncate()
for i in range(0, len(animals)):
  for j in range(i, len(animals)):
    f.write('%s,%s,%1.6f\n' %
        (animals[i], animals[j],
            1 - model.similarity(animals[i], animals[j])))
f.flush()
f.close()
```

The output is the file animal_distances.txt that is used to build the distances graph.

CREATING THE MINIMUM SPANNING TREE

We now use the list to build a graph of the connections between each animal based on the distances derived from the GoogleNews Word2Vec model.

> **DEFINITION** A complete graph is one where every vertex has an edge with every other vertex. The number of edges e in the graph as a function of the number of vertices v is $e = n(n-1)/2$

Each animal is a vertex, and the connections between animals are weighted edges. Each edge corresponds to the cosine distance between the vector representation of each animal. Because we generate an edge for every pair of animals, our graph is complete.

Listing 6.7 shows the code to build the graph and generate the Minimum Spanning Tree. We use the `toGexf()` method developed in chapter 4 to write the tree to a file that can be opened for visualization by Gephi. With more than 200 vertices, the tree is rather big, so we show a portion of the graph in figure 6.7.

Listing 6.7   Building the distances graph

animal_distances.txt has animal names in columns 0 and I, we choose column 0 and apply distinct method to ensure unique vertices.

```
val dist = sc.textFile("animal_distances.txt")
val verts = dist.map(_.split(",")(0)).distinct.
  map(x => (x.hashCode.toLong,x))
val edges = dist.map(x => x.split(",")).
  map(x => Edge(x(0).hashCode.toLong,
              x(1).hashCode.toLong,
              x(2).toDouble))
```

Calling hashCode and converting to Long is one way to allocate a VertexID to each vertex.

```
val distg = Graph(verts, edges)
val mst = minSpanningTree(distg)                    ⟵⎤  Call our Minimum Spanning
val pw = new java.io.PrintWriter("animal_taxonomy.gexf")    Tree algorithm!
pw.write(toGexf(mst))
pw.close
```

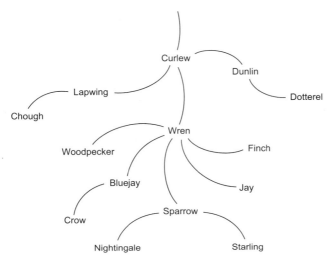

Figure 6.7   A section of the animal taxonomy Minimum Spanning Tree showing connections between birds.

This example shows how we can derive accurate semantic connections between a set of terms. We used an example of animal names, but a similar approach could be used for other areas with large corpuses of unstructured text, such as medical literature or reports of companies listed on global stock exchanges.

6.4   *Summary*

- Many of the classic graph algorithms don't lend themselves to implementation with Pregel. We looked at custom implementations of Shortest Paths with Weights, Travelling Salesman, and Minimum Spanning Tree.
- A Minimum Spanning Tree "sparsifies" a graph, reducing it to its essentials.
- Spark allows you to easily combine graph processing with other machine learning algorithms, as we showed in the creation of an animal taxonomy.

Machine learning

7

This chapter covers

- Machine learning using graphs
- Supervised learning: movie recommender system, spam detection
- Unsupervised learning: document clustering, image segmentation via clustering
- Semi-supervised learning: graph generation from numeric vectors
- Using Spark MLlib with GraphX

Machine learning is a subset of the broader field of artificial intelligence (AI) that deals with predicting data given some body of reference data, such as predicting whether you might like the film *The Empire Strikes Back* given that you liked the film *Star Wars*.

Even though it's a subset of AI, machine learning is an enormous topic. There are dozens of different categories of machine learning algorithms and hundreds of standard machine learning algorithms, covering many different use cases and employing varying techniques. Many of the algorithms use matrices as their primary data structure, but some use graphs instead. The MLlib component of Spark focuses on the matrix-based machine learning algorithms, though it does make use of GraphX for a couple of its algorithms. The overlap between MLlib and GraphX goes in the other direction, too: GraphX includes one machine learning algorithm, SVDPlusPlus, for recommender systems.

This chapter covers the only three (as of Spark 1.6) machine learning algorithms built on GraphX: SVDPlusPlus (Singular Value Decomposition) for product recommendations, LDA (Latent Dirichlet Allocation) for topic identification from a collection of documents, and Power Iteration Clustering (PIC) for general-purpose data clustering. The latter two are invoked through MLlib. We also describe how one of the matrix-based algorithms in MLlib can be applied to graphs. We show that using a graph representation of the input data can add to the predictive power of a standard machine learning algorithm. Finally, we show a custom algorithm for performing what is called *semi-supervised learning*, which in some ways is the most interesting application of graphs to machine learning.

The first section describes the usual first way to break up the huge subject of machine learning: into supervised, unsupervised, and semi-supervised learning. Subsequent sections show how to use individual algorithms for particular applications and scenarios. A deep understanding of machine learning would allow you to better select algorithms and tweak them and their parameters for different applications, but that is beyond the scope of this book. Peter Harrington's book *Machine Learning in Action* (Manning, 2012) is a good start for delving deeper. Kim Falk's book *Practical Recommender Systems* (Manning, 2016) provides a much deeper and more general treatment than the brief overview given here, in section 7.2, of a single recommender algorithm.

What is "artificial intelligence?"

The quest for human-level capability in computers has been going on since the 1950s. The exaggerated claims of success over the decades have led to fatigue regarding the term and several resulting "AI winters" where AI research funding and interest dried up. Early attempts at AI involved searching a state space or employing heuristics, statistics, or symbolic logic. These had limited success. Machine learning is concerned with the optimization of a problem. With this goal, which is more modest than emulating human-level intelligence, machine learning has seen success and widespread adoption in the era of Big Data. Due to the stigma associated with the term *AI*, those in the field of machine learning tend to avoid that term these days.

Even those who are trying to achieve human-level intelligence in machines today avoid the term AI. Instead, they prefer terms like *Artificial General Intelligence (AGI)* or *Artificial Superintelligence (ASI)*. It seems like these days AI refers only to 1970s-style approaches to AI. But in terms of academic definitions, machine learning is a subset of AI.

7.1   Supervised, unsupervised, and semi-supervised learning

In this section, we break up the subject of machine learning into three categories and in later sections we show examples of each. At first glance, machine learning can be broken into two broad categories: supervised learning and unsupervised learning. Later, some clever folks came up with ways to get the best of both worlds with semi-supervised learning.

Figure 7.1 illustrates the difference between supervised learning and unsupervised learning. In supervised learning we are provided with data on different things we want to predict; for example whether an image is of a cat or a dog. We call this *labeled* data because we are provided with a label—"cat" or "dog"—for each image and can train an algorithm to predict the label for a previously unseen image.

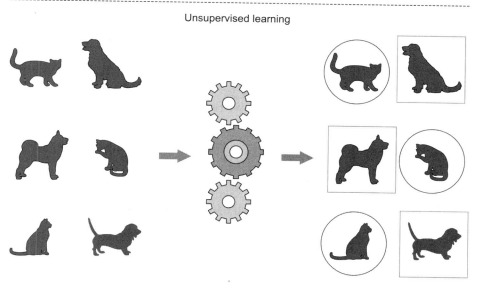

Figure 7.1   **Unsupervised learning clusters similar data together, but doesn't know how to attach any labels.**

By contrast, unsupervised learning is carried out where we don't know what the data contains; it groups similar things together, but we don't necessarily know what those groupings mean. Unsupervised learning is generally of this clustering type of application, but there are many different applications of supervised learning, including classification, time series prediction, and recommender systems.

For both supervised and unsupervised learning, the goal is to train a machine learning *model*. Once we have a trained model, we can use it to *predict* based on new incoming data. In figure 7.1, for the supervised learning model, the unknown image of a cat is predicted to have the label "cat." The model may or may not be correct all the time. The percentage of time a machine learning model is correct is called its *accuracy*. For the unsupervised learning model, the labels it will be able to output as predictions will be either red circles (perhaps labeled automatically by the algorithm as "Group 1") or blue squares (perhaps "Group 2") rather than a human-readable label like "cat" because the model was trained on unlabeled data.

The advantage of unsupervised learning is that unlabeled data is much easier and cheaper to come by. You can scrape it off the web in an automated fashion. Labeled data, in contrast, requires human labor.

The algorithms and applications discussed in this chapter can be broken up like this:

Supervised Learning
- Movie recommendation with SVDPlusPlus
- Web spam detection with LogisticRegressionWithSGD

Unsupervised Learning
- Topic grouping with LDA
- Graph construction from K-Nearest Neighbors
- Image segmentation with PIC

Semi-supervised Learning
- Labeling data with semi-supervised learning

7.2 *Recommend a movie: SVDPlusPlus*

The field of recommender systems is one of the most familiar applications of machine learning. If you're shopping for books or films, which ones might you like based on past purchase history? Or perhaps based on your similarity to other shoppers?

This section shows how to use the sole machine learning algorithm (as of Spark 1.6) contained entirely within GraphX, called SVDPlusPlus. Like all recommender system algorithms, SVDPlusPlus is a form of supervised learning.

Assume that we're tasked with developing a recommender system that recommends movies, and we have past ratings by users who rate movies they've watched on a scale from one to five stars. This can be expressed as a bipartite graph, as shown in figure 7.2, where the vertices on the left are the users, the vertices on the right are the movies, and the edges are the ratings. The dashed edge represents a prediction to be made: what rating would Pat give *Pride and Prejudice*?

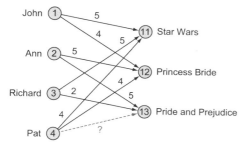

Figure 7.2 **Recommending movies. What is the estimate for how Pat will rate** *Pride and Prejudice?* **(Edge labels represent ratings of one to five stars, and vertex numbers are vertex IDs we'll use later instead of the text names.)**

An alternative representation of the problem is as an adjacency matrix. Generally, data for a recommender system forms a *sparse matrix*, as shown in figure 7.3, where most of the entries in the matrix have no data. Internally, SVDPlusPlus converts the input graph into a sparse matrix representation. A lot of the terminology surrounding SVDPlusPlus is in reference to the matrix representation as opposed to the graph representation.

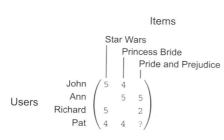

Figure 7.3 **Sparse matrix representation of the graph represented in figure 7.2. The matrix is called sparse because not every matrix position has a number. In our tiny example, there are only four positions missing numbers (including the one with the question mark), but in a typical large example of, say, a million users and a hundred thousand items, almost all the positions would be empty. Recommender systems, including SVDPlusPlus, often internally use the matrix representation of the graph.**

A recommender system is an example of supervised learning because we're given a bunch of data of known movie ratings and are asked to predict an unknown rating for a given pair of a user and an item (such as a movie). There are two major ways that machine learning researches have attacked this problem.

The first major approach is the straightforward and naïve approach: for the user in question, Pat, find other users with similar likes and then recommend to Pat what those other users like. This is initially how Netflix handled recommendations. It is sometimes called the *neighborhood approach* because it uses information from neighboring users in the graph. A shortcoming of this approach is that we may not find a good matching user, as in the case with Pat. It also ignores lurking information we might be able to glean about movies in general from other, possibly dissimilar, users.

The second major approach is to exploit *latent variables*, which avoid needing an exact user match. This may sound like an obscure term, but it's a simple concept, as illustrated in figure 7.4. With latent variables, each movie is identified with a vector that represents some characteristics of that movie. In our example with two latent variables, each movie is identified with a rank 2 vector (for our purposes this is a vector of length 2). Even though figure 7.4 draws *Star Wars* as being only Science

Fiction/Fantasy, in reality it is associated with a vector of length 2 that indicates the degree to which it is a Science Fiction/Fantasy movie and the degree to which it is a Romance movie. We would expect the first number to be high and the second number to be low, though probably not zero.

The reason we use the term *latent* is that these variables aren't contained directly in our input ratings data; the algorithm will "infer" that certain films have common characteristics from the pattern of user likes and dislikes.

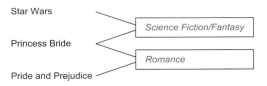

Figure 7.4 Although in our example we don't get genre information with our data, latent variables can automatically infer genre or something close to it. The algorithm doesn't know the actual label "Romance," but infers that *The Princess Bride* and *Pride and Prejudice* are similar in some unspecified way. We have suggested human-appropriate labels in this illustration, but there are no such labels, human-applied or otherwise, for latent variables. It is somewhat of a mystery how algorithms pick latent variables; it could be something other than what we would call genre—it could be something like "a Harrison Ford movie," a quirky sub-genre like "steampunk comedy," or an age-related issue like "rough language."

In this second major approach of using automatically identified latent variables, global information gets used. Even for users dissimilar from Pat, their likes and dislikes contribute to this latent variable information for each movie, and this is indirectly used when a recommendation is made for Pat. A weakness of this approach, though, is that it doesn't use local information as well as the first, naïve, approach. For example, if Pat's best friend has the exact same likes and dislikes as Pat, then we should recommend to Pat whatever movies Pat's best friend has watched that Pat hasn't watched. The first approach based on finding similar users would do this, but this second approach based on latent variables would not.

The SVD++ algorithm uses the latent variable approach but improves over previous such algorithms by going beyond the values of the ratings themselves and also finding a role for *implicit* information. Implicit information is provided by the fact that whether a user rates a movie at all, even if it is a low rating, has value in determining the characteristics of the movie. For example, a user may have given a low rating to *The Phantom Menace* compared to other science fiction movies. Nonetheless, the fact it has been rated at all suggests that it has something in common with other moves the user has rated

SVD++ was introduced in a 2008 paper called "Factorization Meets the Neighborhood: a Multifaceted Collaborative Filtering Model" by Yehuda Koren, and is linked from the Scaladocs for Spark GraphX SVDPlusPlus. Not only is it a readable paper, providing background on recommender system approaches, it also contains important definitions, concepts, and formulas because the Spark documentation on SVD-PlusPlus is so sparse. Besides introducing SVD++, the paper also describes an extension that further enhances the quality of the recommendations by combining information from neighboring users and items. With this extension, it uses all three techniques simultaneously: latent variables, implicit information, and neighborhood (again, the standard SVD++ algorithm is the latent variables together with the implicit information). We break down enough of the Koren paper here for you to be productive, but if you want to dig more deeply, you can look it up.

Listing 7.1 shows how to use the graph from figure 7.2 to train an SVDPlusPlus machine learning model. The input to the algorithm is an EdgeRDD that represents the graph rather than a Graph object itself. As usual, we run the algorithm by calling the `run()` method of the algorithm object (in this case `SVDPlusPlus`), and once it has run its course, we are returned two values that represent a model from which predictions can be made.

Listing 7.1 Invoking SVDPlusPlus with the data from figure 7.2

```scala
import org.apache.spark.graphx._

val edges = sc.makeRDD(Array(
  Edge(1L,11L,5.0),Edge(1L,12L,4.0),Edge(2L,12L,5.0),
  Edge(2L,13L,5.0),Edge(3L,11L,5.0),Edge(3L,13L,2.0),
  Edge(4L,11L,4.0),Edge(4L,12L,4.0)))
```
Construct EdgeRDD for graph in Figure 7.2

```scala
val conf = new lib.SVDPlusPlus.Conf(2,10,0,5,0.007,0.007,0.005,0.015)
```

```scala
val (g,mean) = lib.SVDPlusPlus.run(edges, conf)
```

Run SVD++ algorithm returning model—an enriched version of input graph and mean rating for dataset

Specify hyperparameters for algorithm (see table 7.1)

> **SCALA TIP**   Although Scala doesn't support *multiple return values* in a first-class way as, for example, Python does, Scala provides a special `val` declaration syntax to break up a tuple (such as one returned by a function) and assign its components to individual values (variable names).

The `Conf` parameters, along with recommended values, are broken out in table 7.1. The *biases* referenced in the table descriptions for `gamma1` and `gamma6` are specific to the SVD++ type algorithms and are described later in this section.

> **DEFINITION**   The four parameters γ_1, γ_2, λ_6, and λ_7 from the Koren paper (what GraphX `SVDPlusPlus.Conf` calls `gamma1`, `gamma2`, `gamma6`, and `gamma7`) are examples of machine learning *hyperparameters*. Some have suggested that that's a fancy word for "fudge factors." Hyperparameters are settings to the machine learning system that are set before training begins. Tuning hyperparameters is done empirically. Knowing how to set them in advance is difficult, so you have to take the advice of those who have used the algorithm on other applications or experiment on your own with your own application.

In this example, we have set rank to 2 under the premise that there are two genres for our three movies. Again, that means that in the algorithm's internal latent variable vectors for each movie, they will be of length 2, with the first number indicating degree of (perhaps) Science Fiction/Fantasy and the second number indicating (perhaps) Romance. With a much larger dataset there would be many more movies, and a typical setting for rank would be 10, 20, or even over 100.

Those are the input parameters. Listing 7.2 shows how to create a prediction from the model returned by SVDPlusPlus.run. It defines a function `pred()`, which takes as input the two model parameters along with the IDs for the user and the movie we want to predict. In this case we invoke the function to predict the rating Pat would give to *Pride and Prejudice* by passing in the ID for Pat and for the movie. In this case, the model predicts a rating of 3.95 stars.

Table 7.1 The `Conf` parameters

Parameter	Example	Description
Rank	2	Number of latent variables.
maxIters	10	Number of iterations to execute; the more iterations, the closer the machine learning model is able to converge to its ideal solution, and the more accurate its predictions will be.
minVal	0	Minimum rating (zero stars).
maxVal	5	Maximum rating (five stars).
gamma1	0.007	How quickly biases can change from one iteration to the next. γ_1 from the Koren paper, which recommends 0.007.
gamma2	0.007	How quickly latent variable vectors can change. γ_2 from the Koren paper, which recommends 0.007.
gamma6	0.005	Dampener on the biases, to keep them small. λ_6 from the Koren paper, meaning *lambda6* would have been a more appropriate variable name. Koren recommends 0.005.
gamma7	0.015	The degree to which the different latent variable vectors are permitted to interact. λ_7 from the Koren paper, meaning *lambda7* would have been a more appropriate variable name. Koren recommends 0.015.

Listing 7.2 `pred()` function and invoking it

```
def pred(g:Graph[(Array[Double], Array[Double], Double, Double),Double],
        mean:Double, u:Long, i:Long) = {
  val user = g.vertices.filter(_._1 == u).collect()(0)._2
  val item = g.vertices.filter(_._1 == i).collect()(0)._2
  mean + user._3 + item._3 +
    item._1.zip(user._2).map(x => x._1 * x._2).reduce(_ + _)
}
pred(g, mean, 4L, 13L)
```

SCALA TIP   The combination of `zip()`, `map()`, and `reduce()` is a Scala idiom to compute the dot product.

NOTE Part of the initialization of SVDPlusPlus uses a random number generator, so the exact prediction answers will vary every time SVDPlusPlus is executed on the same input data.

You can use the pred() from the listing as is. But if you want a deeper insight into how the model works, seeing how it's constructed is helpful. First we show the SVD++ formula from the Koren paper. Then we break down the return value from GraphX's SVDPlusPlus to see how it relates to the formula. Finally, we match up the variables in Koren's formula with the SVDPlusPlus return value to come up with the pred() function.

From the Koren paper, the prediction formula looks like this:

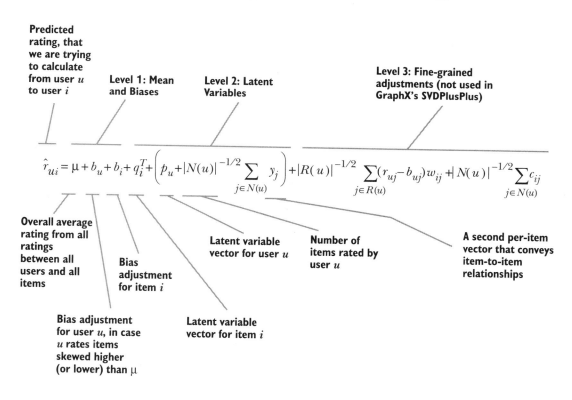

To make a prediction, we need to use the model returned from our invocation to SVDPlusPlus. As we saw in listing 7.1, SVDPlusPlus returned two values wrapped in a tuple: a graph and a Double value representing the mean rating value over the entire graph (that would be μ in the preceding formula). The edge attribute values of this graph are the same edge attribute values of the original graph passed into SVDPlusPlus—namely, the known user ratings. The vertices of this returned graph, though, are a complicated Tuple4:

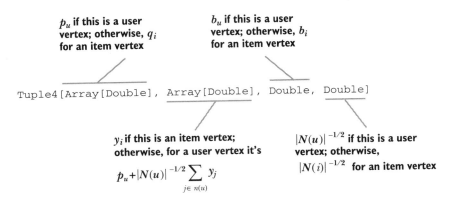

p_u if this is a user vertex; otherwise, q_i for an item vertex

b_u if this is a user vertex; otherwise, b_i for an item vertex

```
Tuple4[Array[Double], Array[Double], Double, Double]
```

y_i if this is an item vertex; otherwise, for a user vertex it's

$$p_u + |N(u)|^{-1/2} \sum_{j \in n(u)} y_j$$

$|N(u)|^{-1/2}$ if this is a user vertex; otherwise, $|N(i)|^{-1/2}$ for an item vertex

Now that we know the formula and what we get as output from GraphX's SVDPlus-Plus, we can see how to put it together to define a `pred()` function that calculates the predicted rating for user u and item i. The return value of `pred()` is the sum of the first four of the five elements of the Koren formula. The fifth is omitted because GraphX's SVDPlusPlus doesn't implement the "third level" of the algorithm, which is the fine-grained adjustments that take into account the neighborhood effects.

7.2.1   *Explanation of the Koren formula*

You can use `pred()` and be able to incorporate an SVDPlusPlus-based recommender system into your project. But if you would like further explanation of the Koren formula, the rest of this section describes it.

LEVEL 1: BIASES

The overall mean μ is over all known ratings. In our case, where movie ratings range from 0 to 5 stars, we would expect μ to be 2.5, but it's probably not exactly that because there is likely an overall bias up or down that users have when they rate; either users as a whole tend to rate high or they tend to rate low.

Similarly, each individual user has a bias. One particular user may be a curmudgeon and consistently rate everything low. Such a user would have a negative bias b_u that gets added to every rating that we predict for that user. Each movie also has an associated bias. If everyone hates a movie, then when we predict a rating for a user who has not yet rated it, we need to bring that predicted rating down. This is encoded in the bias variable b_i.

LEVEL 2: LATENT VARIABLES

Again, the number of latent variables is determined by the `Rank` parameter set in the `Conf` object. In the prediction formula, all the latent variables are in the vector p_u, which is of length `Rank`.

The rest of what is labeled as Level 2 in the prediction formula is related to what Koren calls *implicit feedback*, and specifically in this case which movies users bothered to rate. Koren explains that which movies a user bothers to rate (apart from the actual rating values) carries information that can be used to make more accurate predictions.

This information is carried by the variable y_j, and in the formula it's weighted by the inverse square root of the total number of items the user rated.

LEVEL 3: ITEM-TO-ITEM SIMILARITY

As mentioned, GraphX's SVD++ doesn't implement the third level, the neighborhood similarity approach. For neighborhood similarity, the Koren paper prefers user item-to-item similarity rather than user-to-user similarity. The w_{ij} weights in the first half of the third level of the prediction formula indicate how similar item i is to item j. The second half of the third level of the prediction formula takes into account implicit feedback in a manner similar to the implicit feedback term in level 2.

7.3   *Using GraphX With MLlib*

The MLlib component of Spark contains a number of machine learning algorithms. This section shows how to use two of those that use GraphX under the covers, as well as how to use one of the matrix-based MLlib supervised learning algorithms in conjunction with a graph.

Although SVDPlusPlus is the only machine learning algorithm wholly in the GraphX component of Spark, two other algorithms, Latent Dirichlet Allocation (LDA) and Power Iteration Clustering (PIC), were similarly built on top of GraphX, but it was ultimately decided that they would be part of MLlib rather than GraphX. We show an example of using LDA, which is unsupervised learning, for determining topics in a collection of documents. And we show an example of using PIC, also unsupervised learning, for segmenting an image, which is useful for computer vision.

Then, for a different application—that of detecting web spam—we show how another MLlib algorithm, LogisticRegressionWithSGD, which is not normally associated with graphs at all, can be used together with GraphX's PageRank to enhance web spam detection.

7.3.1   *Determine topics: Latent Dirichlet Allocation*

Suppose you have a large collection of text documents and you want to identify the topics covered by each document. That is what LDA can do, and in this subsection we assign topics to a collection of Reuters news wire items from the 1980s. LDA is unsupervised learning, where the topics aren't specified in advance but rather fall out from the clustering it performs.

MLlib's LDA is built on GraphX to realize computational efficiencies, even though it neither takes graphs as input nor outputs graphs. As its name suggests, LDA is based on latent variables. The latent variables in this case are "topics" automatically inferred by the LDA algorithm. These topics are characterized by words associated with the topic, but don't carry any explicit topic name. Typically, a human will examine the words for each topic and come up with a sensible name to attach to each topic. An example of this is shown in figure 7.5, where some such sensible names have been tacked on to each topic word list.

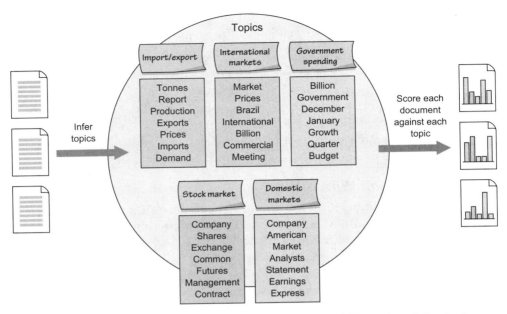

Figure 7.5 Latent Dirichlet Allocation. The topics are the latent variables and are determined automatically by the algorithm. The names of those topics shown in the thin strips are human-inferred and human-applied; the algorithm has no inherent capability to name the topics. Each document expresses each latent variable (topic) to a varying degree.

Once LDA identifies the topics, it scores each document against each topic. This is a basic principle and assumption behind LDA: that each document expresses to some extent all the topics simultaneously, not merely one or two.

EXAMPLE: CLASSIFY REUTERS WIRE NEWS ITEMS

LDA expects a collection of documents as input. As output it provides a list of topics (each with its own list of associated words), as well as how strongly each document is associated with each of those topics.

In this example, we download Reuters wire news items from 1987 and use LDA to infer the topics and tell us how each document scores in each of the topics. Listing 7.3 shows how to download this data from the University of California, Irvine's Knowledge Discovery in Databases Archive, and then how to clean this data using Linux/OSX shell commands. To do the cleaning, it uses a lot of tricks with tools like sed and tr. If you aren't familiar with these commands, you can seek out a book or web resource that explains them. The Reuters data is in the form of SGML, which is a kind of a predecessor to HTML. For each news item, we're interested in the text between the <BODY> and </BODY> tags. For convenient Spark processing of a text file, we want it to be one news item per line (so some of the resulting lines are fairly long).

Listing 7.3 Downloading and cleaning the Reuters wire news items

```
wget https://archive.ics.uci.edu/ml/machine-learning-databases/
    reuters21578-mld/reuters21578.tar.gz
tar -xzvf reuters21578.tar.gz reut2-000.sgm
cat reut2-000.sgm | tr '\n' ' ' | sed -e 's/<\/BODY>/\n/g' |
    sed -e 's/^.*<BODY>//' | tr -cd '[[:alpha:]] \n' >rcorpus
```

Although this accomplishes the brunt of the data-cleansing work, there is still some document prep work to be done. Spark's implementation of LDA expects documents to be in the form of *bags of words*, a common representation in machine learning. When creating a bag of words, we first filter out *stop words*, words that are so common they carry little specific meaning.

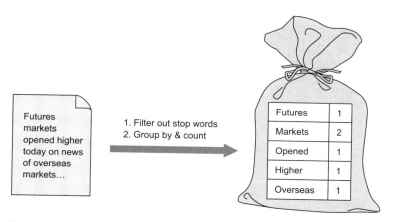

Figure 7.6   Bag of words representation of a document.

Having a good set of stop words is important for LDA so that it doesn't get distracted by irrelevant terms. However, in `bagsFromDocumentPerLine()` in listing 7.4, instead of a good set of stop words, we filtered out short words—those containing five characters or less—together with the word *Reuter*. We also eliminated variations in uppercase versus lowercase by mapping everything to lowercase.

Note also in `bagsFromDocumentPerLine()` that everything inside after the `split()` is a plain old Scala collection (not an RDD), so that, for example, the `groupBy()` is a Scala collection method as opposed to the similar `groupByKey()` method available on Spark RDDs.

In terms of what Spark's LDA expects as input, it's expecting not the raw Strings, but rather integer indices into a global vocabulary. We have to construct this global vocabulary, which is called `vocab` in the next listing. We made `vocab` local to the driver instead of keeping it as an RDD. You'll notice a `flatMap()` as part of the computation of `vocab`. This is a common functional programming operation, explained in the next sidebar.

Listing 7.4   Running LDA on the Reuters wire news items

```scala
import org.apache.spark.mllib.linalg._
import org.apache.spark.mllib.clustering._
import org.apache.spark.rdd._

def bagsFromDocumentPerLine(filename:String) =
  sc.textFile(filename)
    .map(_.split(" ")
        .filter(x => x.length > 5 && x.toLowerCase != "reuter")
        .map(_.toLowerCase)
        .groupBy(x => x)
        .toList
        .map(x => (x._1, x._2.size)))

val rddBags:RDD[List[Tuple2[String,Int]]] =
  bagsFromDocumentPerLine("rcorpus")

val vocab:Array[Tuple2[String,Long]] =
  rddBags.flatMap(x => x)
        .reduceByKey(_ + _)
        .map(_._1)
        .zipWithIndex
        .collect

def codeBags(rddBags:RDD[List[Tuple2[String,Int]]]) =
  rddBags.map(x => (x ++ vocab).groupBy(_._1)
                     .filter(_._2.size > 1)
                     .map(x => (x._2(1)._2.asInstanceOf[Long]
                                         .toInt,
                               x._2(0)._2.asInstanceOf[Int]
                                         .toDouble))
                     .toList)
        .zipWithIndex.map(x => (x._2, new SparseVector(
                                        vocab.size,
                               x._1.map(_._1).toArray,
                               x._1.map(_._2).toArray)
                           .asInstanceOf[Vector]))

val model = new LDA().setK(5).run(codeBags(rddBags))
```

SPARK TIP Spark defines something called `Vector` in the `org.apache`
`.spark.mllib.linalg` package, which has nothing to do with Java's `Vector` in
the `java.util` package. As the package name suggests, Spark's `Vector` is specific to MLlib. It is abstract and has two concrete implementations: `Dense-`
`Vector` and `SparseVector`.

During the computation of `vocab`, after the `flatmap`, we're left with a collection of
`Tuple2[String,Int]` items from all the documents mixed together, meaning there are
some duplicates. For example, there might be a `("commerce", 3)` and a `("commerce",`
`2)` in the RDD at that point after the `flatmap` because perhaps "commerce" appeared
three times in, say, document 5 and twice in document 12. We only want a unique list
of words, and we don't care about the counts, so we dump the counts and then do a
`distinct()`.

flatMap()

Although the name `flatMap()` originated with Scala, it has counterparts in other functional programming languages because it addresses a common problem. Whereas `map()` transforms every element of the input into an element of the output, `flatMap()` transforms every element into a sequence of zero, one, or many elements. Each of the sequences is then "flattened" into a single sequence. In many ways `flatMap()` is like a `map()` followed by a `flatten()` (though not precisely for some cases involving mixed data types). Spark provides its own `flatMap()` for RDDs, and its use in helping create a global vocabulary is illustrated here.

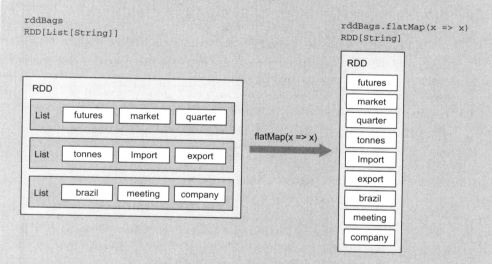

In this particular case, the `x => x` nullifies the map part of `flatMap()`, making it more like a `flatten()`. But although Scala has `flatten()`, Spark RDDs don't have a separate `flatten()`, and we have to use `flatMap(x=>x)` instead.

`flatMap()` is useful even for data that looks one-dimensional because the function you pass in as its parameter has the opportunity to convert each element into its own collection. For example, an alternative way to build up the vocabulary could be `sc.textFile("rcorpus").flatMap(_.split(" "))` because this would explode each document into individual words and then collapse that into a single list of words (representing all the documents combined), all in one fell swoop.

With `vocab` established, we can prepare the data to be in the format that Spark's LDA expects. `codeBags()` does two things: the first half converts from String vocabulary words to their corresponding `vocab` index values, and the second half converts to `SparseVector`, which is a format LDA can handle.

To convert to `vocab` index values, the first half of `codeBags()` conceptually does the equivalent of a SQL INNER JOIN or Spark RDD `join()`. But each element of rdd-Bags is merely a Scala List, which has no `join()`. We have to dance around this lack of a join capability in Scala by instead concatenating the two arrays with the ++ operator, doing a groupBy(), and filtering out all the groups that didn't pick something up from both lists.

To put everything into the format that Spark's LDA expects, the second half of codeBags() does two things: it converts the bags of words to SparseVectors and it assigns a document ID to each document using zipWithIndex().

Because our full global vocab has over 8,000 entries, we don't want to have to have a memory-consuming 8,000-element vector for each "document" (Reuters news story) in our collection. Each news story consists of a few dozen distinct words, so storing all those thousands of zeros (representing the words not in the document) would be a waste of memory. For that reason we prefer to use SparseVector over DenseVector.

In executing LDA, we specify that we want to classify the documents into five topics with setK(5). The return value of run() is a machine learning model, which has several methods that give us the information we're seeking: what words characterize each topic, and for each document, how much each topic represents it.

In examining the returned model, we first specify to describeTopics() that we want to see the top six words associated with each topic (recall that we specified five topics when we ran LDA):

```
model.describeTopics(6).map(_._1.map(vocab(_)._1))
res1: Array[Array[String]] = Array(
  Array(profit, company, billion, president, products, treasury),
  Array(market, japanese, billion, international, brazil, american),
  Array(billion, january, december, government, quarter, growth),
  Array(company, shares, exchange, common, interest, securities),
  Array(tonnes, prices, production, billion, exports, system))
```

Now, let's look at the topics for the first document. Because topicDistributions() scrambles the order of the documents, we have to use filter() to get to the document with document ID of zero to get to the first document:

```
model.asInstanceOf[DistributedLDAModel].topicDistributions
    .filter(_._1 == 0).collect
res2: Array[(Long, org.apache.spark.mllib.linalg.Vector)] =
    Array((0,[0.050547152608283755,0.05217337794656473,0.041732176735789286,
0.0418304122726957,0.8137168804366666]))
```

> **SPARK TIP** The typecast to DistributedLDAModel is necessary only due to a weakness in the Spark REPL. It would be unnecessary if you were writing code to be compiled.

The last topic resonates most strongly in this first document—it's at 0.81, whereas none of the other four topics breaks 0.10. What this first topic is about can be gleaned from the describeTopics() done previously: it's about import/export and commodities stories. Interestingly, if you look at the original story at the top of the reut2-000.sgm, you'll see it doesn't talk directly about import, export, or commodities, but rather about how weather patterns are affecting cocoa crops. The last topic is indeed the closest match, but it's not immediately obvious based on matching exact keywords. This is the result of the latent variables at work for us.

So far we've characterized the documents from the training set. But how about using this trained-up LDA model to predict topics for previously unseen documents? To do that, we must first convert our model from a `DistributedLDAModel`, which is stored across the cluster, to a `LocalLDAModel`, which is stored entirely within the driver, because the prediction function is available only on `LocalLDAModel`.

For a test document, we use a more recent Reuters story, "Monsanto seeks higher sales in Mexico, pending GMO corn decision" from October 27, 2015. If reuters.com doesn't change its CSS too much, these shell commands should isolate and extract the story text:

```
wget http://www.reuters.com/article/2015/10/28/
➥  mexico-monsanto-idUSL1N12S00D20151028 -O Mexico
cat Mexico | tr '\n' ' ' |
➥  sed -e 's/^.*midArticle_start">//;s/<script.*$//;s/<[^>]*>//g' |
➥  tr -cd '[[:alpha:]] \n' >Mexico2
```

Then to convert `model` to a `LocalLDAModel` and predict topics:

```
model.asInstanceOf[DistributedLDAModel].toLocal.topicDistributions(codeBags(b
    agsFromDocumentPerLine("Mexico2"))).collect
res3: Array[(Long, org.apache.spark.mllib.linalg.Vector)] = Array(
(0,[0.20745026733300995,0.1957256951092684,0.1664498204599232,
0.17574123052282312,0.25463298657497535]))
```

All these values are painfully close to 0.2, suggesting that our model, trained on 1980s Reuters stories, isn't that great at predicting for a 2015 Reuters story. Evidently vocabulary and topics have changed over the intervening 30 years. But the last topic is the highest at 0.25. The last topic is, again, about import/export, which this story is indeed about.

HOW LDA USES GRAPHS IN ITS IMPLEMENTATION

As our use of LDA has demonstrated, there's no indication that graphs are being used under the covers. If you'd like to know how using graphs can speed algorithm performance, this subsection discusses—at a high level, without delving deeply into the details—how Spark's LDA implementation uses graphs. For greater detail, see the 2009 paper "On Smoothing and Inference for Topic Models" by Asuncion et al.

As of Spark 1.6, its LDA can use one of two different algorithms: either the Expectation-Maximization (EM) algorithm, which is the default and is graph-based, or the Online Variational Bayes algorithm. We discuss EM here. EM is used to solve probabilistic equations when there are unknown or hidden variables, such as the latent variables in LDA's model. LDA establishes a system of probability equations, such as the probability that a particular word is in a particular topic and the probability that a particular word is in a particular document.

To solve this system of equations, the two major steps of EM, namely expectation and maximization, operate in a tick-tock fashion similar to how K-Means works, if you're familiar with that. In the expectation step, a guess or estimate is made for some of the variables. Then, in the maximization step, the resulting error is computed, and those estimated variables receive some correction. This process is run for a number of iterations and the guess made in the expectation step will get ever closer to the true probabilities.

What does this have to do with graphs?

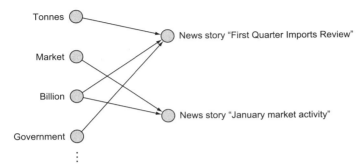

Figure 7.7   **Not every word in the corpus vocabulary is used in every document. A graph representation realizes computational efficiency.**

Although Expectation-Maximization, which solves a system of probabilistic equations, is not inherently a graph algorithm, Spark's implementation of LDA uses GraphX to realize computational efficiencies. It's similar to how Spark's implementation of SVD++, discussed in section 7.1, uses a graph instead of a sparse matrix. These efficiencies for EM arise in LDA because any given document uses only a tiny subset of the global corpus vocabulary. The idea is illustrated in figure 7.7. As a result, when computing summations, only the relevant terms are summed, and steps such as multiply-by-zero-and-add, which otherwise might be taken in a non-graph implementation, are skipped entirely.

LDA PARAMETERS

Table 7.2 lists the four major parameters to Spark's LDA, which have getters and setters available on the constructed LDA() object.

Table 7.2   **LDA Parameters**

Name	Default	Description
k	10	Number of topics.
maxIterations	20	Exact number of iterations to execute (that is, numIterations might have been a more descriptive name).
alpha	50/k + 1	Document concentration, should be > 1.0 for EM. Higher values correspond to documents represented by most or all of the topics.

Table 7.2　LDA Parameters *(continued)*

Name	Default	Description
beta	1.1	Topic concentration, must be > 1.0 for EM. Higher values correspond to topics represented by most or all of the words, while for a lower value topics will key off a few words.

The recommended values for alpha and beta come from the 2004 paper "Finding Scientific Topics" by Griffiths and Steyvers, with an additional +1 adjustment recommended by the aforementioned 2009 Asuncion paper.

7.3.2　*Detect spam: LogisticRegressionWithSGD*

We're sure most readers are familiar with spam email, but there are a number of other types of spam as well. In this section we consider *web spam*—web pages that contain similar types of content to those of spam emails, with the spammers using alternative techniques to try to trick us into browsing to their pages. Usually this involves manipulating search engine rankings so their pages are listed high up on a search results page. The success of this spamming attempt rests on the fact that the unsuspecting search engine user has a tendency to click on the first few links on the search engine page.

Typical techniques for achieving this high ranking involve *link farms*, clusters of apparently normal web pages controlled by spammers that happen to have links pointing to the spam web page. For this application of detecting spam web pages, instead of relying completely on graph processing, we'll combine PageRank with one of the general-purpose (non-graph-based) MLlib algorithms for supervised learning, LogisticRegressionWithSGD (Stochastic Gradient Descent).

A lot of the more straightforward spam detection approaches use only some kind of regression like LogisticRegressionWithSGD, with no assistance from a graph. This applies machine learning to the web pages as independent entities without considering their linked interconnections. Such a non-graph approach can't directly detect the link farms shown in figure 7.8.

Logistic Regression is similar to the more commonly known Linear Regression. In Linear Regression, the output, or *predicted*, value is a floating point number. In Logistic Regression, the predicted value is instead an integer that represents which of a small set of labels the example belongs to. In our case, we have two possible labels: "spam" and "not spam." In Logistic Regression (and Linear Regression), each example item (in our example, each web page) has a *feature vector*, which is a vector of floating point numbers, where each floating point number represents a feature. A *feature* is a machine learning term meaning a measure of some aspect of the example. In our case, we have three features: the number of times the word *free* occurs in the web page, the number of times the word *earn* occurs in the web page, and something called the *Truncated Page Rank* of the web page. In a full-fledged spam detector, there would be hundreds of spam "trigger words," but in our simple example we are using only two such trigger words: *free* and *earn*.

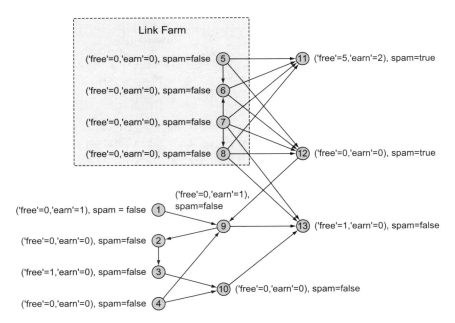

Figure 7.8 Web spam training data. Each vertex represents a web page, with the number of times the spam words *free* and *earn* occur, and a human-based determination of whether the page is spam. By augmenting the spam word data with PageRank data, link farms can be detected to assist in spam determination.

The term *Truncated Page Rank* comes from the 2006 paper "Link-Based Characterization and Detection of Web Spam" by Becchetti et al. The motivation is to detect link farms by removing the influence of the first immediate layer of vertices from a Page-Rank calculation to form this modified Page Rank calculation. The Becchetti paper describes taking snapshots of various iterations of the PageRank calculations, normalizing these values, and differencing them in order to come up with the Truncated Page Rank.

Here, we take an even simpler and more basic approach. We run PageRank twice—once with one iteration and another time with five iterations—and ratio these two PageRanks for each vertex. The motivation for this is that we expect a spam page to have a different topology—a difference in the structure of its link graph—compared to a normal page. We hope to capture this difference with our Truncated Page Rank feature.

Supervised learning, in general, needs a training set and a testing set. Our training set is in figure 7.8 and listing 7.5, and our testing set is in figure 7.9 and listing 7.9. To run our graph vertex data through `LogisticRegressionWithSGD`, we first have to put it into the format it expects, which is an RDD of `LabeledPoints`. A `LabeledPoint` is the feature vector together with its human-supplied label. Remember, in supervised learning, during training, we give the machine learning algorithm the answers. These labels are the answers. The hope is that if trained sufficiently, then when we present the trained machine learning model with new data, it can *predict* the label—that when presented with a web page it hasn't seen before, it should be able to determine whether it is a spam web page.

Listing 7.5 Constructing the training set graph of figure 7.8

```
import org.apache.spark.graphx._
import org.apache.spark.mllib.classification.LogisticRegressionWithSGD

val trainV = sc.makeRDD(Array((1L, (0,1,false)), (2L, (0,0,false)),
  (3L, (1,0,false)), (4L, (0,0,false)), (5L, (0,0,false)),
  (6L, (0,0,false)), (7L, (0,0,false)), (8L, (0,0,false)),
  (9L, (0,1,false)), (10L,(0,0,false)), (11L,(5,2,true)),
  (12L,(0,0,true)),  (13L,(1,0,false))))

val trainE = sc.makeRDD(Array(Edge(1L,9L,""), Edge(2L,3L,""),
  Edge(3L,10L,""), Edge(4L,9L,""), Edge(4L,10L,""), Edge(5L,6L,""),
  Edge(5L,11L,""), Edge(5L,12L,""), Edge(6L,11L,""), Edge(6L,12L,""),
  Edge(7L,8L,""), Edge(7L,11L,""), Edge(7L,12L,""), Edge(7L,13L,""),
  Edge(8L,11L,""), Edge(8L,12L,""), Edge(8L,13L,""), Edge(9L,2L,""),
  Edge(9L,13L,""), Edge(10L,13L,""), Edge(12L,9L,"")))

val trainG = Graph(trainV, trainE)
```

Our graph vertices from this listing have only two of the three features (count of "free" and count of "earn") together with the human-applied label ("true" or "false" in regards to whether it is spam). But the vertices are missing the third feature, namely the Truncated Page Rank. Listing 7.6 calculates the Truncated Page Rank and bundles it together with the rest of the vertex data into the `LabeledPoint` that `Logistic-RegressionWithSGD` expects. The `augment()` function we define there conducts a three-way join between three RDDs—the vertex data, the PageRank of one iteration, and the PageRank of five iterations—and boils it all down into a `LabeledPoint`, taking the ratio of the two PageRanks in the process. `LabaledPoint` requires the feature values to be in a `Vector`, and in this case we opt to go with `DenseVector` rather than `SparseVector` because our feature vectors have no holes—no missing values—and it's more convenient to list out all the feature values.

Listing 7.6 Preparing the data for Logistic Regression

```
import org.apache.spark.graphx.lib.PageRank
import org.apache.spark.mllib.linalg.DenseVector
import org.apache.spark.mllib.regression.LabeledPoint

def augment(g:Graph[Tuple3[Int,Int,Boolean],String]) =
  g.vertices.join(
    PageRank.run(trainG, 1).vertices.join(
      PageRank.run(trainG, 5).vertices
    ).map(x => (x._1,x._2._2/x._2._1))
  ).map(x => LabeledPoint(
    if (x._2._1._3) 1 else 0,
    new DenseVector(Array(x._2._1._1, x._2._1._2, x._2._2))))
```

NOTE Even though `LabeledPoint.label` is defined as a `Double`, Logistic Regression only expects whole numbers starting from zero: 0.0, 1.0, 2.0, and so on. `LabeledPoint` is also used in Spark's linear regression, and that's why its label is defined as a `Double`.

Now let's train up our Logistic Regression model, as shown in the following listing. Here, we arbitrarily chose to execute `LogisticRegressionWithSGD` with 10 iterations. In general, though, SGD can sometimes take hundreds of iterations to converge properly.

Listing 7.7 Training the Logistic Regression model

```
val trainSet = augment(trainG)
val model = LogisticRegressionWithSGD.train(trainSet, 10)
```

We now have a Logistic Regression model called `model`. Now what? Well, the most important thing the model gives us is a function called `predict()`, which takes a feature vector and returns what it thinks is the most suitable label. We could try some of the vertices out one at a time from our training set or test set. But what we usually do in machine learning is to try them *all* out at once. `perf()` in the following listing measures the performance, or the accuracy, of our model by comparing the human-applied labels to what `model.predict()` comes up with.

Listing 7.8 Measuring the performance of the Logistic Regression model

```
import org.apache.spark.rdd.RDD

def perf(s:RDD[LabeledPoint]) = 100 * (s.count -
  s.map(x => math.abs(model.predict(x.features)-x.label)).reduce(_ + _)) /
  s.count

perf(trainSet)
res3: Double = 92.3076923076923
```

Ideally, we might hope to get 100% or close to it when we run our training set through the model, but 92% isn't terrible. Running the training set through the model it was trained on is cheating, but it's a good sanity test to make sure we didn't do something completely wrong. Now let's run our test dataset, which is shown in figure 7.9 and in the next listing.

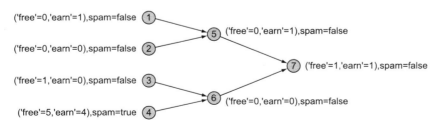

Figure 7.9 Test dataset

Listing 7.9 Constructing the test data graph and evaluating its performance

```
val testV = sc.makeRDD(Array((1L, (0,1,false)), (2L, (0,0,false)),
  (3L, (1,0,false)), (4L, (5,4,true)), (5L, (0,1,false)),
  (6L, (0,0,false)), (7L, (1,1,true))))

val testE = sc.makeRDD(Array(Edge(1L,5L,""), Edge(2L,5L,""),
  Edge(3L,6L,""), Edge(4L,6L,""), Edge(5L,7L,""), Edge(6L,7L,"")))

perf(augment(Graph(testV,testE)))
res4: Double = 85.71428571428571
```

On the test dataset, our trained model performed at 86%. Not nearly as high as is typically expected for machine learning, but not absolutely terrible. The reason our model isn't doing so well is due to the small number of vertices (web pages) in the training dataset, and to the small number of features—we should have hundreds of features corresponding to hundreds of spam trigger words. A decent size training set would have at minimum 100,000 example web pages. The performance of both the training and test datasets missed one label in each case, so there aren't even any other possible percentage numbers we could have hit short of hitting the full 100%—yet another symptom of running on such small data sizes.

7.3.3 *Image segmentation (for computer vision) using Power Iteration Clustering*

In section 7.3.1, you saw clustering of documents. In this section, we show how to cluster pixels in an image using unsupervised learning. Using this technique we can address a problem in computer vision called *image segmentation*. The idea is to try and assign one of a number of labels to each pixel in an image. Figure 7.10 shows the idea—we want to assign the labels "lion" and "background" to each pixel in the image on the left. One possible segmentation is shown in the image on the right. By clustering image pixels and then assigning to each cluster one of two (or a few) possible colors, the image can be segmented in a similar way to figure 7.10.

Figure 7.10 Original image (shown in black and white in this book) is on the left, and after segmentation on the right. The low resolution is to allow it to run on a single 4GB machine. The number of clusters has to be set in advance, and here the default of two was used.

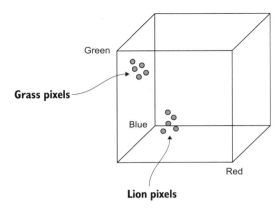

Figure 7.11 **The pixels are in a three-dimensional vector space—each vector has three numeric components (red intensity, green intensity, and blue intensity)—and the clustering algorithm finds the two clusters.**

To cluster, each pixel is represented as a position in the red/green/blue cube, as shown in figure 7.11, and the clustering algorithm finds the two clusters.

The clustering algorithm, called Power Iteration Clustering (PIC), is built into Spark MLlib even though it takes a GraphX `Graph` as its input. The graph it takes as input is expected to be completely connected (every vertex connected to every other vertex), where the edge weight represents a "distance" between the two vertex values.

In this case, we take as our feature vector (red, green, blue) and use a simple *cosine similarity* to be our similarity metric. We convert each pixel into a vector of length three. The 2010 paper, "Power Iteration Clustering" by Frank Lin and William Cohen, where PIC was introduced, recommends using cosine similarity.

Cosine similarity

One way to measure the similarity between two vectors A and B is called the *cosine similarity*. Conveniently, the cosine similarity is always in the range [−1,1] (because you take cos(θ) to be the similarity measure rather than θ), where 1 means A and B are most similar (equal) and −1 means A and B are most dissimilar (pointing in opposite directions). A value of 0, incidentally, means A and B are orthogonal (at a right angle to each other).

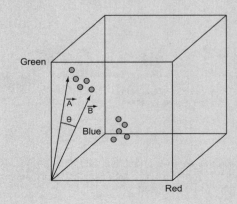

$$\cos(\theta) = \frac{A \cdot B}{\|A\| \|B\|} \text{ where } \|A\| = \sqrt{a_1^2 + a_2^2 + \ldots + a_n^2}$$

Now that you've seen finding similar pixels, you'll see the code that implements this. In the following code there is a lambda expression (an inline function) that turns out to be too complex for the Spark REPL to handle correctly, so we compile a standalone program usng sbt as described in chapter 3. We give the sbt file first in listing 7.10 and the Scala code in listing 7.11. Create a directory under your spark home directory called PIC and save the sbt file to this directory with a name like PIC.sbt. Then create the scala file (PIC.scala) under the directory structure PIC/src/main/scala. Compile and package the code using the command

```
sbt package
```

If successful, this will create a jar file under the directory structure PIC/target/scala-2.10. The program can be executed from the spark home directory with the following command:

```
bin/spark-submit PIC/target/scala-2.10 <jar file>
```

The code expects the input file (an image file 105053.jpg) to be in the same directory and creates a segmented image as output (out.png) like in figure 7.10. This image file is contained within the Berkeley Segmentation Data Set, which can be downloaded here:

```
wget  https://www.eecs.berkeley.edu/Research/Projects/CS/vision/bsds/
      ➥BSDS300-images.tgz
```

A lot of the code is using the Java image-handling APIs and attempting to minimize the memory footprint on the driver (instead preferring to use memory on the workers in the cluster). For example, the red, green, and blue values are expanded from the packed Int only after the Ints have been put into an RDD. On the other end, data is sorted and packed into Arrays while still in RDDs, prior to the collect(), which sends the data back to the driver.

But buried in listing 7.11 are two new concepts intertwined, and one of them is extremely subtle and tricky. The r.cartesian(r) performs a Cartersian product on the RDD r. That creates an RDD of Tuple2s representing every possible permutation of taking two values from r.

Cartesian product

If you have an RDD, say val myRDD:RDD[Int] = sc.make-RDD(Array(5,8,9)), which has three elements, then the Cartesian product of myRDD with itself has $3^2 = 9$ elements and is an RDD of Tuple2[Int,Int], as shown here:

9	(5,9)○	(8,9)○	(9,9)○
8	(5,8)○	(8,8)○	(9,8)○
5	(5,5)○	(8,5)○	(9,5)○
	5	8	9

We use this Cartesian product because we need to compute the similarity between every pixel with every other pixel.

Listing 7.10 PIC.sbt for image segmentation

```
scalaVersion := "2.10.5"
libraryDependencies += "org.apache.spark" %% "spark-core" % "1.6.0"
libraryDependencies += "org.apache.spark" % "spark-graphx_2.10" % "1.6.0"
libraryDependencies += "org.apache.spark" % "spark-mllib_2.10" % "1.6.0"
```

Listing 7.11 PIC.scala for image segmentation

```
import org.apache.spark.SparkContext
import org.apache.spark.SparkConf
import org.apache.spark.mllib.clustering.PowerIterationClustering
import org.apache.spark.graphx._

import java.awt.image.BufferedImage
import java.awt.image.DataBufferInt
import java.awt.Color
import java.io.File

import javax.imageio.ImageIO

object PIC {
  def main(args: Array[String]) {
    val sc = new SparkContext(new SparkConf().setMaster("local")
                                             .setAppName("PIC"))
    val im = ImageIO.read(new File("105053.jpg"))
    val ims = im.getScaledInstance(im.getWidth/8, im.getHeight/8,
                                   java.awt.Image.SCALE_AREA_AVERAGING)
    val width = ims.getWidth(null)
    val height = ims.getHeight(null)
    val bi = new BufferedImage(width, height, BufferedImage.TYPE_INT_RGB)
    bi.getGraphics.drawImage(ims, 0, 0, null)
    val r = sc.makeRDD(bi.getData.getDataBuffer
                      .asInstanceOf[DataBufferInt].getData)
          .zipWithIndex.cache
    val g = Graph.fromEdges(r.cartesian(r).cache.map(x => {
      def toVec(a:Tuple2[Int,Long]) = {
        val c = new Color(a._1)
        Array[Double](c.getRed, c.getGreen, c.getBlue)
      }
      def cosineSimilarity(u:Array[Double], v:Array[Double]) = {
        val d = Math.sqrt(u.map(a => a*a).sum * v.map(a => a*a).sum)
        if (d == 0.0) 0.0 else
        u.zip(v).map(a => a._1 * a._2).sum / d
      }
      Edge(x._1._2, x._2._2, cosineSimilarity(toVec(x._1), toVec(x._2)))
    }).filter(e => e.attr > 0.5), 0.0).cache
    val m = new PowerIterationClustering().run(g)
    val colors = Array(Color.white.getRGB, Color.black.getRGB)
    val bi2 = new BufferedImage(width, height, BufferedImage.TYPE_INT_RGB)
    m.assignments
```

```
    .map(a => (a.id/width, (a.id%width, colors(a.cluster)))))
    .groupByKey
    .map(a => (a._1, a._2.toList.sortBy(_._1).map(_._2).toArray))
    .collect
    .foreach(x => bi2.setRGB(0, x._1.toInt, width, 1, x._2, 0, width))
  ImageIO.write(bi2, "PNG", new File("out.png"));
  sc.stop
}
}
```

Now comes the extremely tricky part. We use `zipWithIndex()` to number the pixels to keep track of them. But we are careful and `cache()` right after the `zipWithIndex()`. If we didn't, there's a chance that Spark would end up performing the `zipWithIndex()` twice (because everything is lazy), with the second time coming up with a different ordering! In a comment to Jira ticket SPARK-3098, Matei Zaharia indicated that the randomness was by design to speed shuffle performance and that ordering within RDDs is not guaranteed.

> **SPARK TIP**   If an RDD is based on a `zipWithIndex()` and participates in a self-join (for example `join()` to itself or `cartesian()` to itself), then do a `cache()` after the `zipWithIndex()` but before the self-join in order to lock in the ordering of the RDD.

After the Cartesian product result is converted into an RDD of Edges, that RDD of Edges is reduced in size because we don't need all of them. We only keep around those Edges that have a similarity of 0.5 or higher. Besides reducing the size of the RDD so that PIC will run faster, another reason is that PIC requires that all similarities be zero or higher, so at the same time we're eliminating those Edges with a similarity of between −1 and 0 that would confuse the PIC algorithm.

PIC is a general-purpose clustering algorithm. Here we used it to cluster pixels with the ultimate goal of image segmentation. But PIC can be used for any clustering task, provided you have a way to measure similarity from any data element to another.

7.4   Poor man's training data: graph-based semi-supervised learning

Now that you've seen examples of both supervised learning and unsupervised learning, it's time to embark on semi-supervised learning, which combines the best of both worlds. Although supervised learning has the advantage of predicting human-understandable labels (because it was trained with labeled data), the disadvantage is the time required for a human to label all that training data. That's expensive. Because unsupervised learning is trained with unlabeled data, vastly larger training datasets are easier to come by.

The general approach behind semi-supervised learning is to first perform unsupervised learning on the unlabeled data. This provides some structure that can be applied to the labeled data. Then this enhanced labeled data can be trained using supervised learning to generate more powerful models.

In this section, we handle the situation where we have a bunch of data points in a multi-dimensional space, such as a 2-D plane, a 3-D cube, or a higher dimension. The axes of such a space could represent any variable: temperature, test scores, population, and so forth. The idea is that we're trying to attach class labels to points in this space under the assumption that similar points will be clustered together.

For example, in the case of a cable TV and internet provider, a 2-D plane could be constructed with axes for hours of television watched versus gigabytes of data transferred. We could then distinguish some categories—for example, heavy TV, heavy internet, and heavy users of both.

By generating a graph to fit these data points, boundaries between these classes of users can be determined. As it turns out, identifying these clusters of similar users will boost the power of our prediction algorithm when we apply it to new data points.

To implement this idea, we'll first implement a K-Nearest Neighbors graph construction algorithm (not to be confused with the K-Nearest Neighbors algorithm for computing a prediction, which is different and not covered in this book), which will serve as our unsupervised learning piece, and apply it to a dataset, the vast majority of which is unlabeled. Then we'll implement a simple label propagation algorithm that propagates the labels to surrounding unlabeled vertices. Finally, we'll implement a simple `knnPredict()` function that when given a new data point, predicts which class (label) it belongs to.

> **NOTE** Many machine learning algorithms are prefixed with the letter *K*. Generally this refers to a parameter in the model which is conventionally named K and needs to be chosen by the user. The actual meaning of K depends on each specific algorithm, although there are classes of algorithm that all use K in a similar way. For example, in the clustering algorithms, K-Means and K-Medians, K is the number of clusters that we're asking the algorithm to generate. In K-Nearest Neighbors algorithms, we infer something about a point by looking at a number of the most similar points. In this case, we have to choose K, the number of most similar points.

Figure 7.12 shows the starting condition, and figure 7.13 shows what it looks like after both the K-Nearest Neighbors and semi-supervised learning label propagation algorithms have run. These horseshoe-shaped clusters of data are the classic counterexample of where the K-Means algorithm fails—another type of clustering algorithm (not related at all to K-Nearest-Neighbors). K-Means is focused on finding centers of clusters and gets confused by long, stringy chains of points. But because this approach of using K-Nearest Neighbors for graph construction can follow such chains, it doesn't get confused by this type of data.

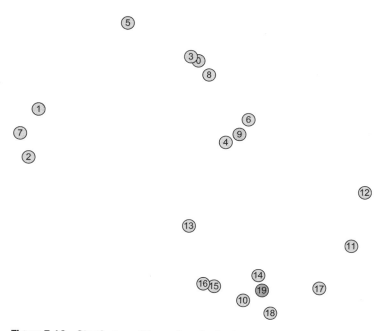

Figure 7.12 Starting condition: a bunch of points in two-dimensional space, almost all of them unlabeled, with the exception of two labeled points

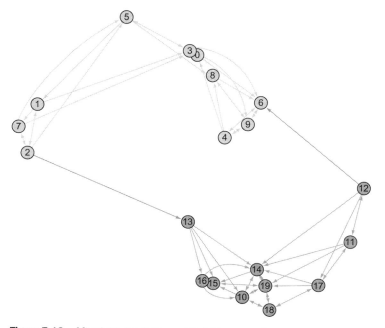

Figure 7.13 After both the K-Nearest Neighbors graph construction algorithm and the semi-supervised learning label propagation algorithm have run

7.4.1   K-Nearest Neighbors graph construction

Spark does not (as of version 1.6) contain an implementation for the K-Nearest Neighbors algorithm. That's the subject of Jira ticket SPARK-2335.

Conceptually, finding the K-Nearest Neighbors is trivially simple. For every point, find its K-Nearest Neighbors out of all the other points and extend edges to those points. This naïve, brute-force approach is shown in listing 7.12.

Listing 7.12   Brute force K-Nearest Neighbors

```
import org.apache.spark.graphx._

case class knnVertex(classNum:Option[Int],
                     pos:Array[Double]) extends Serializable {
  def dist(that:knnVertex) = math.sqrt(
    pos.zip(that.pos).map(x => (x._1-x._2)*(x._1-x._2)).reduce(_ + _))
}
def knnGraph(a:Seq[knnVertex], k:Int) = {
  val a2 = a.zipWithIndex.map(x => (x._2.toLong, x._1)).toArray
  val v = sc.makeRDD(a2)
  val e = v.map(v1 => (v1._1, a2.map(v2 => (v2._1, v1._2.dist(v2._2)))
                                 .sortWith((e,f) => e._2 < f._2)
                                 .slice(1,k+1)
                                 .map(_._1)))
          .flatMap(x => x._2.map(vid2 =>
            Edge(x._1, vid2,
                 1 / (1+a2(vid2.toInt)._2.dist(a2(x._1.toInt)._2)))))
  Graph(v,e)
}
```

The problem is performance. For each of the *n* points, *n* distances have to be computed, and then these *n* distances have to be sorted, at a cost of $n \log n$. That's $n^2 \log n$. All those various K-Nearest Neighbor algorithms are attempting to solve the problem more efficiently. But because it's a non-polynomial problem (no algorithm can be constructed to solve it in any reasonable amount of time), they all come up with approximate solutions. We look at such an approximate approach, and one suited to Spark's distributed processing, later in this subsection.

But first look at listing 7.12. If you'd like to try it out, listing 7.13 will generate the data shown in figure 7.14, and listing 7.14 is a special export to the Gephi .gexf file format tailored to our knnVertex that outputs color and position tags. Listing 7.15 executes the algorithm and the export to .gexf. Here we choose k=4 for K-Nearest Neighborhood. 3 or 4 are typical values for k.

Listing 7.13   Generate example data

```
import scala.util.Random

Random.setSeed(17L)
val n = 10
val a = (1 to n*2).map(i => {
  val x = Random.nextDouble;
  if (i <= n)
```

```
        knnVertex(if (i % n == 0) Some(0) else None, Array(x*50,
          20 + (math.sin(x*math.Pi) + Random.nextDouble / 2) * 25))
      else
        knnVertex(if (i % n == 0) Some(1) else None, Array(x*50 + 25,
          30 - (math.sin(x*math.Pi) + Random.nextDouble / 2) * 25))
})
```

The core of listing 7.12 is in the computation of e, which is an RDD of Edges that we pass into `Graph()` to create the return value graph. And within this computation, we can see the n^2 nature of the computation. There is an outer `RDD.map()` (performed on v, the RDD of vertices) and an inner `Array.map()` (performed on a2, the Array version of v). For each vertex, we compute and sort all the distances and pick off the k with shortest distance (we ignore index 0, because that's the same vertex as itself with distance zero). When we construct the actual `Edge()` at the end, we use the Edge attribute to store the inverse of the distance. This will be used in the semi-supervised learning label propagation but isn't needed for K-Nearest Neighbors itself.

The use of `flatMap()` in listing 7.12 is a non-trivial use of it: it is effectively doing both a `map()` (to transform each collection of distant vertices into a collection of Edges) and a `flatten()` (to make a single collection of Edges out of the collection of collections of Edges).

Listing 7.14 Custom export (with layout) to Gephi .gexf for knnVertex-based graphs

```
import java.awt.Color
def toGexfWithViz(g:Graph[knnVertex,Double], scale:Double) = {
  val colors = Array(Color.red, Color.blue, Color.yellow, Color.pink,
                     Color.magenta, Color.green, Color.darkGray)
  "<?xml version=\"1.0\" encoding=\"UTF-8\"?>\n" +
  "<gexf xmlns=\"http://www.gexf.net/1.2draft\" " +
        "xmlns:viz=\"http://www.gexf.net/1.1draft/viz\" " +
        "version=\"1.2\">\n" +
  "  <graph mode=\"static\" defaultedgetype=\"directed\">\n" +
  "    <nodes>\n" +
  g.vertices.map(v =>
    "      <node id=\"" + v._1 + "\" label=\"" + v._1 + "\">\n" +
    "        <viz:position x=\"" + v._2.pos(0) * scale +
          "\" y=\"" + v._2.pos(1) * scale + "\" />\n" +
    (if (v._2.classNum.isDefined)
    "        <viz:color r=\"" + colors(v._2.classNum.get).getRed +
          "\" g=\"" + colors(v._2.classNum.get).getGreen +
          "\" b=\"" + colors(v._2.classNum.get).getBlue + "\" />\n"
    else "") +
    "      </node>\n").collect.mkString +
  "    </nodes>\n" +
  "    <edges>\n" +
  g.edges.map(e => "      <edge source=\"" + e.srcId +
                "\" target=\"" + e.dstId + "\" label=\"" + e.attr +
                "\" />\n").collect.mkString +
  "    </edges>\n" +
  "  </graph>\n" +
  "</gexf>"
}
```

Listing 7.15   Execute K-Nearest Neighbors on the example data and export to .gexf

```
val g = knnGraph(a, 4)

val pw = new java.io.PrintWriter("knn.gexf")
pw.write(toGexfWithViz(g,10))
pw.close
```

TOWARD A DISTRIBUTED K-NEAREST NEIGHBORS ALGORITHM

Of the various approximate K-Nearest Neighbors graph construction algorithms out there, most are geared toward conventional serial processing rather than distributed parallel processing. A notable exception that does do distributed processing is from the 2012 Microsoft Research paper, "Scalable k-NN graph construction for visual descriptors" by Wang et al.

That paper includes a lot of optimizations for distributed computing, but here we'll take and implement one of their many ideas and ignore the rest. It won't do their paper justice, but it'll put us on a path toward a more practical K-Nearest Neighbors implementation for Spark.

The first key insight from the Wang paper, and the only one we adapt, is to break the space up into grids and perform the brute-force K-Nearest Neighbor graph construction algorithm on each cell in the grid. In figure 7.14, the space is variously broken up into 3x3 grids (in the first of the two dividings, the last grids have zero width or height). If we then say m=3, the complexity is $cm^2(n/m^2)(n/m^2)\log(n/m^2) = c(n/m)^2\log(n/m^2)$, where c is the number of different grids we use.

This is the simple approach we'll take. Again, the full algorithm described in the Wang paper is much more sophisticated, such as its use of Principal Component Analysis (PCA) to determine the grid orientation (breaking the space up into parallelograms

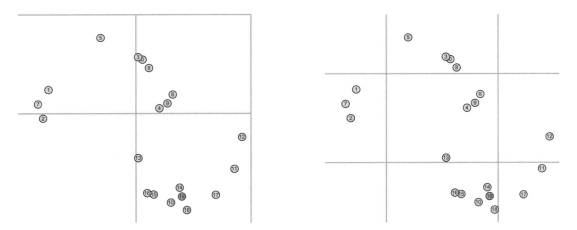

Figure 7.14   Distributed K-Nearest Neighbor graph construction. Divide the space into grids and perform brute-force K-Nearest Neighbor graph construction within each grid cell. To avoid missing edges that would cross a cell boundary, vary the grid and run again, and take the union of the two edge sets.

instead of squares), using many random grids, and coalescing directed edges into undirected edges.

For implementing in Spark, we want to map each grid cell onto a separate executor (task). This can be done by paying attention to Spark RDD partitioning.

Listing 7.16 uses `groupByKey()` to shuffle the data to partitions, as shown in figure 7.14, and then uses `mapPartitions()` to do the brute-force K-Nearest Neighborhood edge generation within each cell. `mapPartitions()` allows us to capture up front (into the variable `af`) that full subset of vertices inside that grid cell—say there are d vertices in the grid cell—and then compute the d^2 distances and complete the K-Nearest Neighborhood edge generation.

RDD Partitioning (and mapPartitions())

At a fundamental level, RDDs are distributed datasets, and how Spark decides to distribute the data among the nodes in the cluster depends on the RDD's *partitioner*. The default partitioner is the `HashPartitioner`, which hashes the key in `Tuple2 [K,V]` key/value pairs, sending RDD data elements with equal keys to the same node. This assumes the RDD is composed of key-value pairs in the first place (like those that `PairRDDFunctions` operate on). But if it's a plain, old RDD with no keys, then Spark makes up random keys before running it through the `HashPartitioner`.

As described in section 9.3, GraphX adds another layer of abstraction to partitioning. But under the covers, GraphX is merely controlling partitioning via `HashPartitioner` and setting hidden keys to ensure `HashPartitioner` puts RDD elements where it wants it to.

But when making a copy of the edges RDD or vertices RDD—recall that RDDs are immutable, and any operations done on them make copies—we may opt to apply our own partitioning for performance or algorithmic purposes. A convenient side effect of `groupByKey()` is that data is shuffled and repartitioned by key. This can sometimes obviate having to create a *custom partitioner*, which involves subclassing `Partitioner` and overriding member functions.

Partitioning is something that happens behind the scenes, and we normally don't need to worry about it. But if we want to specify exactly where data goes, either for performance or algorithmic purposes, then we need to pay attention. An important means of making good use of partitions is through the `mapPartitions()` function.

`mapPartitions()` lets you deal with all the data in a partition in the form of a Scala collection. This lets you do any expensive setup and teardown—such as creating a database cursor or instantiating and initializing a parser object—once in each executor before that executor goes to work on its portion of the RDD. If you were to try to do this using RDD's `map()`, that expensive operation would be done once per data element instead of once per partition.

The result of executing this approximate K-Nearest Neighborhood graph generation algorithm on the example data, followed by executing the semi-supervised learning label propagation algorithm described in the next subsection, is shown in figure 7.15.

Listing 7.16   Distributed, approximate K-Nearest Neighborhood graph generation

```
def knnGraphApprox(a:Seq[knnVertex], k:Int) = {
  val a2 = a.zipWithIndex.map(x => (x._2.toLong, x._1)).toArray
  val v = sc.makeRDD(a2)
  val n = 3
  val minMax =
    v.map(x => (x._2.pos(0), x._2.pos(0), x._2.pos(1), x._2.pos(1)))
     .reduce((a,b) => (math.min(a._1,b._1), math.max(a._2,b._2),
                       math.min(a._3,b._3), math.max(a._4,b._4)))
  val xRange = minMax._2 - minMax._1
  val yRange = minMax._4 - minMax._3

  def calcEdges(offset: Double) =
    v.map(x => (math.floor((x._2.pos(0) - minMax._1)
                          / xRange * (n-1) + offset) * n
              + math.floor((x._2.pos(1) - minMax._3)
                          / yRange * (n-1) + offset),
                x))
     .groupByKey(n*n)
     .mapPartitions(ap => {
       val af = ap.flatMap(_._2).toList
       af.map(v1 => (v1._1, af.map(v2 => (v2._1, v1._2.dist(v2._2)))
                           .toArray
                           .sortWith((e,f) => e._2 < f._2)
                           .slice(1,k+1)
                           .map(_._1)))
         .flatMap(x => x._2.map(vid2 => Edge(x._1, vid2,
            1 / (1+a2(vid2.toInt)._2.dist(a2(x._1.toInt)._2)))))
         .iterator
     })

  val e = calcEdges(0.0).union(calcEdges(0.5))
                        .distinct
                        .map(x => (x.srcId,x))
                        .groupByKey
                        .map(x => x._2.toArray
                                  .sortWith((e,f) => e.attr > f.attr)
                                  .take(k))
                        .flatMap(x => x)

  Graph(v,e)
}
```

SPARK TIP   The RDD function union(), unlike SQL UNION, doesn't eliminate duplicates. You have to call distinct() right afterward if you want unique values in your resulting RDD.

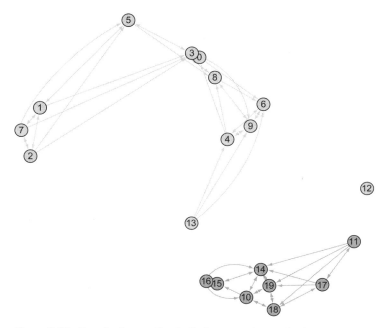

Figure 7.15 Result of executing both the approximate distributed K-Nearest Neighborhood algorithm and the semi-supervised learning label propagation algorithm from the next section. There are only about two-thirds as many edges in this one. Compared to the exact result shown in figure 7.13, one vertex, number 13, was misclassified, and another vertex, number 12, wasn't classified at all. But the benefit of the approximate result is that it does it with distributed computing and can be performed on large graphs.

Note that in order to get the `groupByKey()` to partition and shuffle the way we expect it to, we had to use its optional parameter to specify the number of partitions. If we didn't, then `groupByKey()` might combine some of the small partitions into one if they're small. Because it affects our algorithm, in this case we want to insist on the larger number of partitions. We specify the maximum it could be (n*n), and if there happen to be fewer (if some of the grid cells are empty), `groupByKey()` will use as many partitions as keys that exist.

Also note that due to the preceding, the parameter passed into the function we supply to `mapPartitions()` is technically not for a single key. It's a collection containing multiple keys. Because we assume we're getting a single key for the partition, we start off with a `flatMap()` on that parameter to eliminate that extra level of nesting.

When we calculate e at the end, the set of edges, we `union()` the two sets of edges from the two possible grids shown in figure 7.14. Because that may result in more than k edges for any given vertex, we trim that list down with the `groupByKey()`, `map()`, `flatMap()` sequence of function calls. The comparator in the `sortWith()` is a greater-than rather than the usual less-than because the edge attributes are the reciprocals of the distances rather than the distances themselves.

7.4.2   *Semi-supervised learning label propagation*

What we have done so far is extract some structure from all the points in our dataset without worrying about what label we're going to apply to them. Figure 7.16 shows the structure we've built up. Our two labeled points are colored—vertex 9 (light red) and vertex 19 (dark blue)—but most of our points have no labels associated with them and remain medium grey. We resolve this now by implementing a label propagation algorithm to assign a label to all those grey vertices. We then show how this fully labeled model can be used to predict the label for new unlabeled data point.

Now we're ready to implement the label propagation, which is in listing 7.17. We discussed Spark's built-in label propagation algorithm in chapter 5, where we explained how the algorithm takes a dataset of already labeled vertices and attempts to identify and label communities through a label-consensus process.

By contrast, what we present in this chapter is a means of propagating labels from a few known labeled vertices to a much larger selection of unlabeled vertices by using the graph structure built by our unsupervised learning. It also takes into account edge distances, weighting nearby vertices more heavily. The result is an algorithm that almost always converges.

The algorithm can be described as follows:

1 For each edge emanating from a labeled vertex, send that vertex's label together with the edge weight (the reciprocal of the edge length) to both the source and destination of the edge.

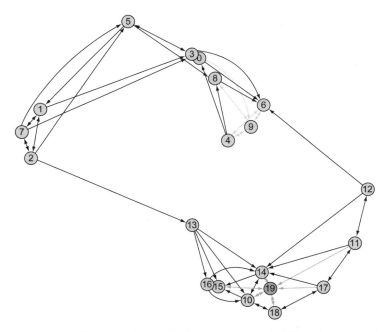

Figure 7.16   The graph that results from applying our distributed, approximate, unsupervised learning algorithm. Now there is structure, but unlabeled vertices remain unlabeled.

2 For each vertex, add up the scores on a by-class (by-label) basis. If the vertex is not one of the vertices with a pre-known, fixed label, then assign the winning class (label) to the vertex.

3 If no vertices changed labels, or if maxIterations is reached, then terminate.

We use aggregateMessages() (together with joinVertices()) rather than Pregel() because the terminating condition in Pregel() is when no messages are sent any longer. Here, we always send a labeled vertex's label back to itself to ensure that permanently labeled vertices can retain their label. We can't use Pregel() in this code.

Note that the gist of this algorithm is that it treats the graph as an undirected graph. The actual implementation treats source and destination slightly differently in its attempt to ensure that permanently labeled vertices never switch their label, but conceptually labels can travel in either direction along the edge.

Figure 7.17 on page 163 illustrates iteration by iteration the application of this algorithm to the perfect K-Nearest Neighborhood graph from figures 7.12 and 7.13.

> **SCALA TIP** The operator -> is shorthand for establishing a key-value pair in a Scala HashMap. For those familiar with PHP, this is similar to PHP's array initialization using =>.

Listing 7.17 Semi-supervised learning label propagation

```
import scala.collection.mutable.HashMap
def semiSupervisedLabelPropagation(g:Graph[knnVertex,Double],
                                   maxIterations:Int = 0) = {
  val maxIter = if (maxIterations == 0) g.vertices.count / 2
                else maxIterations

  var g2 = g.mapVertices((vid,vd) => (vd.classNum.isDefined, vd))
  var isChanged = true
  var i = 0

  do {
    val newV =
      g2.aggregateMessages[Tuple2[Option[Int],HashMap[Int,Double]]](
        ctx => {
          ctx.sendToSrc((ctx.srcAttr._2.classNum,
                         if (ctx.dstAttr._2.classNum.isDefined)
                           HashMap(ctx.dstAttr._2.classNum.get->ctx.attr)
                         else
                           HashMap[Int,Double]()))
          if (ctx.srcAttr._2.classNum.isDefined)
            ctx.sendToDst((None,
                           HashMap(ctx.srcAttr._2.classNum.get->ctx.attr)))
        },
        (a1, a2) => {
          if (a1._1.isDefined)
            (a1._1, HashMap[Int,Double]())
          else if (a2._1.isDefined)
            (a2._1, HashMap[Int,Double]())
          else
```

```
        (None, a1._2 ++ a2._2.map{
          case (k,v) => k -> (v + a1._2.getOrElse(k,0.0)) })
      }
    )
  val newVClassVoted = newV.map(x => (x._1,
    if (x._2._1.isDefined)
      x._2._1
    else if (x._2._2.size > 0)
      Some(x._2._2.toArray.sortWith((a,b) => a._2 > b._2)(0)._1)
    else None
  ))

  isChanged = g2.vertices.join(newVClassVoted)
                   .map(x => x._2._1._2.classNum != x._2._2)
                   .reduce(_ || _)
  g2 = g2.joinVertices(newVClassVoted)((vid, vd1, u) =>
    (vd1._1, knnVertex(u, vd1._2.pos)))
  i += 1
} while (i < maxIter && isChanged)

g2.mapVertices((vid,vd) => vd._2)
}
```

PREDICTION

Now that the graph is trained up for semi-supervised learning, we can use it now to "predict" labels. Given a point with (x,y) coordinates, to which class (label) does it belong? Listing 7.18 contains code for a dead-simple prediction function. It finds the closest labeled vertex (regardless of whether it was originally labeled or got its label as a result of the propagation) and returns that value. Technically, this is implementing K-Nearest Neighbors prediction (not to be confused with K-Nearest Neighbors graph construction) with k=1.

Listing 7.19 shows invoking this simple knnPredict() on a model produced by listing 7.17's semiSupervisedLabelPropagation().

Listing 7.18   Prediction function to use the semi-supervised learned graph

```
def knnPredict[E](g:Graph[knnVertex,E],pos:Array[Double]) =
  g.vertices
    .filter(_._2.classNum.isDefined)
    .map(x => (x._2.classNum.get, x._2.dist(knnVertex(None,pos))))
    .min()(new Ordering[Tuple2[Int,Double]] {
      override def compare(a:Tuple2[Int,Double],
                           b:Tuple2[Int,Double]): Int =
        a._2.compare(b._2)
    })
    ._1
```

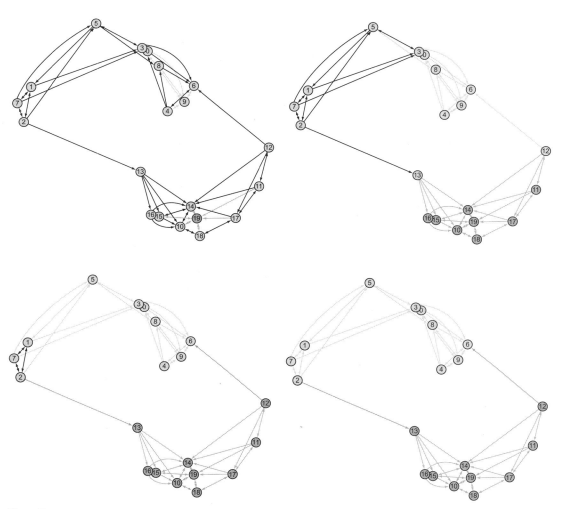

Figure 7.17 Iterations of semi-supervised learning label propagation applied to the perfect K-Nearest Neighbors example

Listing 7.19   Execute semi-supervised learning label propagation and use it to predict a class (label) for a particular (x,y) coordinate of (30.0,30.0)

```
val gs = semiSupervisedLabelPropagation(g)
knnPredict(gs, Array(30.0,30.0))
res5: Int = 0
```

7.5   *Summary*

- All three major types of machine learning can be done with GraphX: supervised, unsupervised, and semi-supervised.
- The subject of machine learning is vast, and GraphX and MLlib provide a select set of algorithms.
- GraphX's SVDPlusPlus can be used to build a recommender system, a form of supervised learning.
- MLlib's Latent Dirichlet Allocation, a form of unsupervised learning that uses GraphX under the covers, can be used to assign topics to documents.
- MLlib's Logistic Regression, a matrix-based form of supervised learning that doesn't use graphs at all, can be used in conjunction with PageRank to detect web spam.
- MLlib's Power Iteration Clustering, another form of unsupervised learning but which takes a graph as input, can be used to segment an image for computer vision.
- Neither GraphX nor MLlib has semi-supervised learning built in, but an example of semi-supervised learning can be achieved via a combination of K-Nearest Neighbors graph construction and an intuitive label propagation.

Machine learning is an advanced subject—the most advanced in this book. The next chapter covers some more standard graph algorithms along with some of their applications, which are somewhat along the lines of chapter 6, but more contemporary than the old classics from chapter 6.

Part 3

Over the arc

Part 3 covers the missing pieces and documentation. In chapter 8, you'll see algorithms you might expect to be part of the GraphX API but that aren't as of Spark 1.6. From reading standard RDF format graph data to merging graphs, the algorithms in chapter 8 plug some of those holes.

Chapter 8 also covers how to use IndexedRDD, which is like the HashMap of RDDs. We go through an example showing how it can speed up performance.

Finally, you'll see an example of identifying likely missing data from Wikipedia using ideas from graph *isomorphisms*—finding pieces of graphs that are similar to each other.

Chapter 9 is all about putting GraphX into production and doing debugging and performance tuning. It steps you through tools like DAG Visualization and the History Server, and provides a concrete set of tools like caching, checkpointing, and serializer tuning to improve the performance of your Spark GraphX application.

In chapter 10, you'll see how to use languages other than Scala. The combination of Apache Zeppelin and d3.js lets you visualize graphs inline in a notebook, an interactive shell that can show graphics inline. The ability to see graphs immediately without having to write out a separate file is powerful, provided you don't need to fine-tune the rendering parameters. We also cover how to use Spark Job Server, which almost lets you treat GraphX as a database instead of a graph processing system. Finally, a library from GitHub called GraphFrames allows convenient and high-performance querying through the languages SQL and Cypher.

The missing algorithms

8

This chapter covers

- Reading RDF files
- Merging graphs
- Filtering out isolated vertices
- Using IndexedRDD for performance gains
- Taking a simplistic approach to finding graph isomorphisms
- Computing the global clustering coefficient

You've seen examples of reading graph data from edge list files in earlier chapters. RDF is another important file format used for many existing file formats. This chapter shows you how to read in this file format and use this knowledge to make use of the YAGO3 dataset.

Aside from the classic graph algorithms from chapter 6, there are other slightly more modern algorithms that one comes to expect in a graph database or graph processing system. Some of these are missing—not implemented yet (or at least not commonly available in either the official Apache Spark distribution as of Spark 1.6 or even from spark-packages.org).

In this chapter, you'll see how to implement some of these algorithms. You'll also see how to use IndexedRDD for performance gains. IndexedRDD was originally written by one of the main GraphX code contributors but never merged into the Apache Spark distribution.

8.1 Missing basic graph operations

This section lays the groundwork for the next, which is about reading RDF files. Before reading RDF files, though, we need to look at a couple of basic graph operations that GraphX doesn't provide (as of Spark 1.6). The first is taking subgraphs in a common sense fashion, and the second is merging two graphs together.

8.1.1 Common sense subgraphs

When we introduced GraphX's `subgraph()` in a sidebar in section 5.2, we indicated that it would leave an isolated vertex whenever you filtered out all that vertex's edges (see figure 8.1). That can be inconvenient. Often you know which edges you want to keep and which you want to filter out, and you don't want to have to figure out which vertices need to stay for the edges you want to keep.

The next listing provides a function to filter out those singleton (isolated) vertices after you've executed `subgraph()` with a function to filter edges. We'll use this function in section 8.3 on simplistic graph isomorphisms.

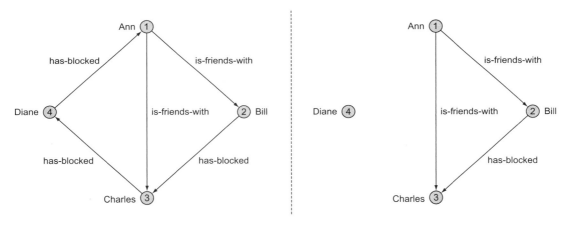

Figure 8.1 If you use GraphX's `subgraph()` to keep only the is-friends-with edges, it leaves straggler vertices like Diane (on the right).

Listing 8.1 Delete isolated vertices: handy for after having called `subgraph()`

```
import scala.reflect.ClassTag

def removeSingletons[VD:ClassTag,ED:ClassTag](g:Graph[VD,ED]) =
  Graph(g.triplets.map(et => (et.srcId,et.srcAttr))
                  .union(g.triplets.map(et => (et.dstId,et.dstAttr)))
                  .distinct,
        g.edges)
```

To remove the singletons, this listing uses the fact that the vertices in the information returned by `triplets()` all participate in edges—any singleton vertices have no edges and so won't be returned by `triplets()`. It gets all the source vertices from `triplets()` and `union()`s that with all the destination vertices from a second invocation of `triplets()`. Then with a `distinct()` set of vertices, it returns a new Graph constructed with those vertices and the original set of edges.

The following listing shows the function in action on the graphs from figure 8.1. The output shows the vertices for the original subgraph, including the singleton vertex for Diane, followed by the vertices for the graph after running `removeSingletons`.

> **Listing 8.2 The `removeSingletons` function in action**

```
val vertices = sc.makeRDD(Seq(
(1L, "Ann"), (2L, "Bill"), (3L, "Charles"), (4L, "Dianne")))
val edges = sc.makeRDD(Seq(
Edge(1L,2L, "is-friends-with"),Edge(1L,3L, "is-friends-with"),
Edge(4L,1L, "has-blocked"),Edge(2L,3L, "has-blocked"),
Edge(3L,4L, "has-blocked")))
val originalGraph = Graph(vertices, edges)
val subgraph = originalGraph.subgraph(et => et.attr == "is-friends-with")

// show vertices of subgraph - includes Dianne
subgraph.vertices.foreach(println)

// now call removeSingletons and show the resulting vertices
removeSingletons(subgraph).vertices.foreach(println)
```

The vertices for the original graph, `subgraph`, should look like this, Diane included:

```
(4,Dianne)
(3,Charles)
(2,Bill)
(1,Ann)
```

After `removeSingletons`, the result looks like this:

```
(3,Charles)
(2,Bill)
(1,Ann)
```

8.1.2 Merge two graphs

If you have two graphs with vertex type of `String`, it's sometimes useful to merge two such graphs on common vertex names, as shown in figure 8.2. *Merging* means treating equally named vertices from the two graphs as the same vertex and merging the adjacent edges together for those vertices. All the other vertices and edges that are unique to one graph or the other are also brought in. This is useful if you have two graphs constructed from two different data sources and you want to make one big graph out of them to do further analysis.

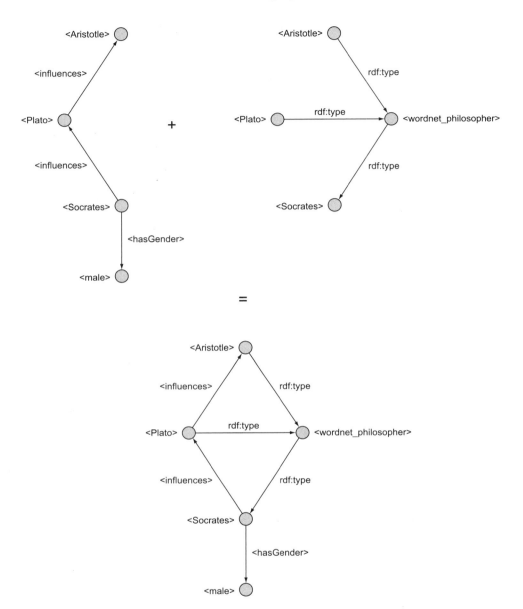

Figure 8.2   Merging two graphs together based on commonly named vertices is a useful operation that isn't built into GraphX (as of Spark 1.6).

The next listing shows how it can be done. The function takes two graphs that we want to merge and returns a single graph with any common vertices merged.

Listing 8.3 Merge two graphs into one

```
import org.apache.spark.graphx._

def mergeGraphs(g1:Graph[String,String], g2:Graph[String,String]) = {
  val v = g1.vertices.map(_._2).union(g2.vertices.map(_._2)).distinct
                    .zipWithIndex
  def edgesWithNewVertexIds(g:Graph[String,String]) =
    g.triplets
      .map(et => (et.srcAttr, (et.attr,et.dstAttr)))
      .join(v)
      .map(x => (x._2._1._2, (x._2._2,x._2._1._1)))
      .join(v)
      .map(x => new Edge(x._2._1._1,x._2._2,x._2._1._2))
  Graph(v.map(_.swap),
        edgesWithNewVertexIds(g1).union(edgesWithNewVertexIds(g2)))
}
```

First, it constructs a common vertex dictionary in v. The procedure is to generate an RDD of the vertex attributes for the first input graph using the code g1.vertices .map(_._2). We then do the same for the second input graph. The two RDDs are concatenated with a union, and we take a distinct to generate an RDD with a unique set of vertex attributes from across the graph. Finally, we generate new IDs for each vertex using zipWithIndex. For our example in figure 8.2, it would look something like this:

```
(Plato, 0)
(Aristotle, 1)
(wordnet_philosophers, 2)
(Socrates, 3)
(male,4)
```

The nested function edgesWithNewVertexIds() translates a graph's set of edges to the new vertexIds in v, and this is used on both input graphs g1 and g2. The ultimate return value is a graph with the translated edges from both g1 and g2 (along with the vertices from v).

The following listing shows the function in action on the graphs from figure 8.2. The output from running this code will be a list of all the vertices and their connections in the merged graph.

Listing 8.4 Using mergeGraphs on the philosopher graphs

```
val philosophers = Graph(
sc.makeRDD(Seq(
    (1L, "Aristotle"),(2L,"Plato"),(3L,"Socrates"),(4L,"male"))),
sc.makeRDD(Seq(
    Edge(2L,1L,"Influences"),
    Edge(3L,2L,"Influences"),
    Edge(3L,4L,"hasGender"))))
```

```
val rdfGraph = Graph(
    sc.makeRDD(Seq(
        (1L,"wordnet_philosophers"),(2L,"Aristotle"),
        (3L,"Plato"),(4L,"Socrates"))),
    sc.makeRDD(Seq(
        Edge(2L,1L,"rdf:type"),
        Edge(3L,1L,"rdf:type"),
        Edge(4L,1L,"rdf:type")))))

val combined = mergeGraphs(philosophers, rdfGraph)

combined.triplets.foreach(
        t => println(s"${t.srcAttr} --- ${t.attr} ---> ${t.dstAttr}"))
```

The output should look like this:

```
Socrates --- Influences ---> Plato
Plato --- Influences ---> Aristotle
Socrates --- hasGender ---> male
Plato --- rdf:type ---> wordnet_philosophers
Aristotle --- rdf:type ---> wordnet_philosophers
Socrates --- rdf:type ---> wordnet_philosophers
```

> **SCALA TIP** Scala provides syntactic sugar of "${myVar}" to avoid writing out long string concatenations for formatted output.

8.2   *Reading RDF graph files*

Although GraphX has the power to represent property graphs, there is quite a bit of graph data out there that's represented only in terms of triples. A *triple* consists of a *subject*, *predicate*, and *object*. In terms of GraphX, the subject and object are vertex String properties, and the predicate is an edge property. There are various standard file formats to store triples, such as RDF (Resource Description Framework) and N3 (Notation 3).

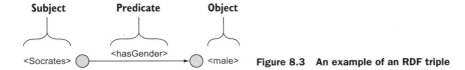

Figure 8.3   An example of an RDF triple

One well-known set of RDF data is YAGO3 (Yet Another Great Ontology) from the Max Planck Institute in Germany. YAGO3 is derived from Wikipedia, WordNet, DBPedia, GeoNames, and other sources and is an attempt to create a universal kitchen-sink ontology. The full YAGO3 data set encompasses over 500 million triples consuming 90 GB, and a miniscule subset is shown in figure 8.3. There are many varied uses of YAGO3 involving some sort of natural language processing and finding relationships between concepts expressed in text. Section 8.3 shows a simplistic use of YAGO3—finding missing or inconsistent data in Wikipedia—which is possible because YAGO3 is derived largely from Wikipedia.

8.2.1 Matching vertices and constructing the graph

In this subsection, we show a basic technique for reading an RDF file. YAGO3 is available for download as a few dozen .tsv files (tab-separated files). Here are a couple of example lines from the file yagoFacts.tsv:

```
<id_10silts_1sv_1rii7g7>   <Plato>   <influences>   <Aristotle>
<id_10silts_p3m_zkjp59>   <Plato>   <hasGender>   <male>
```

The first column is an ID that we'll ignore. The second column is the subject, the third the predicate, and the fourth the object. Notice that there are no vertex IDs. The main task when reading an RDF file is to generate vertex IDs from the vertex names.

In the next, a vertex dictionary is first created in v. Then through a complex sequence of join()s and map()s, the vertex names are translated into vertex IDs using v. In the final map(), an Edge instance is constructed for each computed triple.

Listing 8.5 Read a tab-separated RDF file

```
def readRdf(sc:org.apache.spark.SparkContext, filename:String) = {
  val r = sc.textFile(filename).map(_.split("\t"))
  val v = r.map(_(1)).union(r.map(_(3))).distinct.zipWithIndex
  Graph(v.map(_.swap)
        r.map(x => (x(1),(x(2),x(3))))
         .join(v)
         .map(x => (x._2._1._2,(x._2._2,x._2._1._1)))
         .join(v)
         .map(x => new Edge(x._2._1._1, x._2._2, x._2._1._2)))
}
```

Create dictionary of unique vertices using similar approach used in mergeGraphs function

Another mergeGraphs trick—turn vertex-name-to-ID RDD into a VertexRDD by swapping pair elements

Because it can be difficult to mentally keep track of anonymous Scala tuples nested three-deep, figure 8.4 illustrates the motion of the data.

`r.map(x => (x(1),(x(2),x(3))))`	(SubjectName, (Predicate, ObjectName))
`.join(v)`	(SubjectName, ((Predicate, ObjectName), SubjectId))
`.map(x => (x._2._1._2,(x._2._2,x._2._1._1)))`	(ObjectName, (SubjectId, Predicate))
`.join(v)`	(ObjectName, ((SubjectId, Predicate), ObjectId))
`.map(x => new Edge(x._2._1._1, x._2._2, x._2._1._2)))`	Edge(SubjectId, Predicate, ObjectId)

Figure 8.4 Data flow representation of listing 8.5. First the Predicate (source) vertex string name is translated to a vertex ID and then the Object (destination) vertex is. Finally an Edge() is constructed with these two vertex IDs plus the original edge String attribute.

As an example of using `readRdf()`, download the file from YAGO3 called yago-Types.tsv:

```
wget http://resources.mpi-inf.mpg.de/yago-naga/yago/download/
    yago/yagoTypes.tsv.7z
```

Then decompress the .7z file format. The specifics will vary for your particular OS, but for CentOS (which is the OS of the Cloudera QuickStart VM recommended in appendix A), it would be the following:

```
wget http://packages.sw.be/rpmforge-release/
    rpmforge-release-0.5.2-2.el6.rf.i686.rpm
sudo rpm -ivh rpmforge-release-0.5.2-2.el6.rf.i686.rpm
sudo yum install p7zip
7za e yagoTypes.tsv.7z
```

Now, yagoTypes.tsv is a 1.5 GB file, and if you're running the Spark REPL locally, it only defaults to allocating 500 MB in the JVM. Therefore, for performance (and to have it succeed), you'll want to launch the Spark REPL with the `--driver-memory` option for more memory, as well as with the `--driver-cores` option to use all the cores on your machine (4 is shown next for an Intel i5 processor, but go ahead and bump that up to 8 if, for example, you know you have an Intel i7 processor):

```
./spark-shell --driver-memory 2g --driver-cores 4
```

Once you're in the Spark REPL, after entering in the code for `readRdf()`, it's just

```
val gTypes = readRdf(sc, "yagoTypes.tsv")
```

You can then download another one of the YAGO3 files:

```
wget http://resources.mpi-inf.mpg.de/yago-naga/yago/download/
    yago/yagoSimpleTaxonomy.tsv.7z
```

Now you can use the `mergeGraphs()` in the Spark REPL to read in this second file and merge it with the first:

```
val gSimpleTaxonomy = readRdf(sc, "yagoSimpleTaxonomy.tsv")
val gMerged = mergeGraphs(gTypes, gSimpleTaxonomy)
```

Finally, download the yagoFacts file:

```
wget http://resources.mpi-inf.mpg.de/yago-naga/yago/download/
    yago/yagoFacts.tsv.7z
```

8.2.2 *Improving performance with IndexedRDD, the RDD HashMap*

You may have noticed that the performance of reading these larger YAGO3 files is not too peppy. There's a way to speed it up, perhaps by 30%, by using IndexedRDD, a library developed by AMPlab and available from spark-packages.org.

As of Spark 1.6, IndexedRDD is not part of the Apache Spark distribution. Ankur Dave, one of the original major contributors to GraphX, developed IndexedRDD in 2014 (around the time of the Spark 1.0 release) as a way to improve GraphX performance. Jira ticket SPARK-2365, which is to merge IndexedRDD into the official Apache Spark distribution, has not yet been targeted for any particular future release of Spark.

IndexedRDDs have two major features over regular RDDs. First, as the name suggests, they're indexed and act similar to HashMaps from Java and other languages. Second, they're mutable. It is this mutability that makes them particularly attractive for incorporation into GraphX, as at present any small change to a graph necessitates creating a whole new graph. The indexing makes IndexedRDDs particularly attractive to the Spark SQL component of Spark. But integrating IndexedRDD into Spark so deeply would require a lot of testing because it changes the fundamental assumption of RDD immutability, which Spark uses to manage RDD lineages, laziness, checkpoints, and other core features of Spark.

When we wrote that IndexedRDDs act like HashMaps, that wasn't quite right. They're better because, as shown in figure 8.5, under the covers they use search *tries* (a specific kind of search tree) instead of a hash map. The linear scans that worker nodes perform for conventional RDDs are fine for `map()`s on the entire collection of data items in an RDD, but not so great for `join()`s.

As listing 8.5 contains two `join()`s, we can improve the performance by converting to use IndexedRDDs instead. The improved version is shown in listing 8.6. IndexedRDD's have an `innerJoin()` function instead of `join()` as in conventional RDDs. IndexedRDD's `innerJoin()` takes a second parameter list with one parameter—namely, a function to perform a map operation. We can't make use of this map convenience because we want to discard the key we're joining on (the subject name or object name), and IndexedRDD forces the key back on to its return result. To make `innerJoin()` act like the `join()` we're familiar with, we need to pass in the function `(id, a, b) => (a, b)` because that's what `join()` produces for the value portion of the key-value pairs it generates.

You may have noticed that we structured this listing as a standalone program rather than a code snippet that you can enter into the Spark REPL. There's a reason for that. We need to bring in IndexedRDD as an external Jar, and adding an external Jar to the command line when launching the Spark REPL can be tricky and tedious when that Jar depends on other Jars. It's easier to use a dependency manager such as Apache Ivy (which is built into sbt) or Maven, and to then build an assembly Jar (also known as a *fat Jar*, or Jar with dependencies). Maven should be familiar to Java programmers, and here we use Maven rather than sbt because its assembly plug-in doesn't require tweaking or external configuration. Listing 8.7 has the pom.xml file, which should go into a directory ~/readrdf, and listing 8.6 should go into a file ~/readrdf/src/main/scala /readrdf.scala.

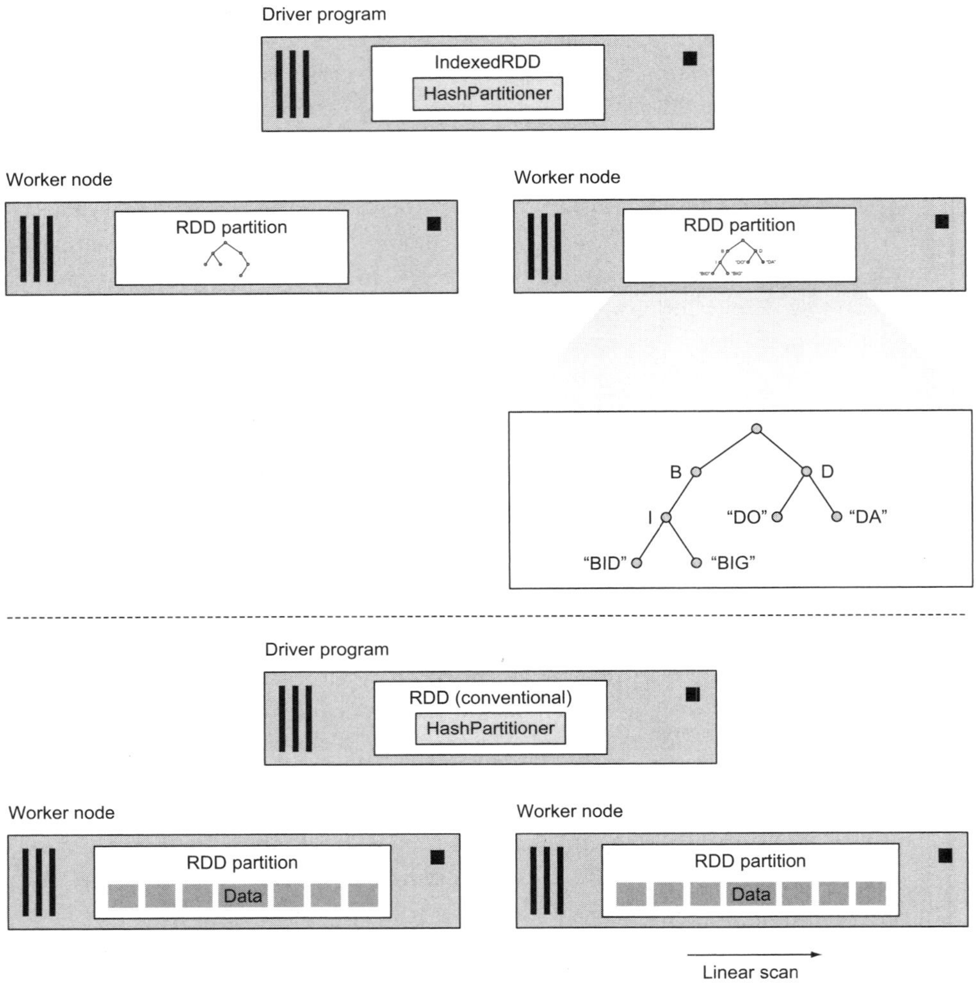

Figure 8.5   To find one particular data item by key in an RDD is a two-step process. First, the Spark driver uses the RDD's HashPartitioner to identify which worker/partition the data item is in, and then the worker node finds the data item in the RDD partition that it is on. The difference between an IndexedRDD and a conventional RDD is in this second step. For an IndexedRDD, the worker node uses a search try, and for a conventional RDD, the worker node performs a linear scan. Note that even though search tries are a kind of graph, IndexedRDD uses a custom, efficient, non-distributed implementation and doesn't use distributed GraphX Graphs to implement them.

Listing 8.6   Read a tab-separated RDF file, performance improved with IndexedRDD

```
import org.apache.spark.graphx._
import org.apache.spark.{SparkContext, SparkConf}

import edu.berkeley.cs.amplab.spark.indexedrdd.IndexedRDD
import edu.berkeley.cs.amplab.spark.indexedrdd.IndexedRDD._
```

```
object readrdf {
  def readRdfIndexed(sc:SparkContext, filename:String) = {
    val r = sc.textFile(filename).map(_.split("\t"))
    val v = IndexedRDD(r.map(_(1)).union(r.map(_(3))).distinct
                        .zipWithIndex)
    Graph(v.map(_.swap),
          IndexedRDD(IndexedRDD(r.map(x => (x(1),(x(2),x(3)))))
            .innerJoin(v)((id, a, b) => (a,b))
            .map(x => (x._2._1._2,(x._2._2,x._2._1._1))))
            .innerJoin(v)((id, a, b) => (a,b))
            .map(x => new Edge(x._2._1._1, x._2._2, x._2._1._2)))
  }

  def main(args: Array[String]) {
    val sc = new SparkContext(
      new SparkConf().setMaster("local").setAppName("readrdf"))
    val t0 = System.currentTimeMillis
    val r = readRdfIndexed(sc, args(0))
    println("#edges=" + r.edges.count +
            " #vertices=" + r.vertices.count)
    val t1 = System.currentTimeMillis
    println("Elapsed: " + ((t1-t0) / 1000) + "sec")
    sc.stop
  }
}
```

Force Spark to evaluate the lazy graph.

If Maven isn't already installed (it comes preinstalled on the Cloudera QuickStart VM recommended in appendix A), use your favorite search engine to find instructions on how to install it for your particular OS. Once it's installed, compile with the following:

```
cd ~/readrdf
mvn clean package
```

To launch the compiled program, change to the Spark bin directory (from which you normally launch `spark-shell`) and use `spark-submit` instead:

```
./spark-submit --class readrdf --master local[4] --driver-memory 2g
➥ ~/readrdf/target/graphx-readrdf-1.0-SNAPSHOT-jar-with-dependencies.jar
➥ yagoTypes.tsv
```

The input RDF file

Using IndexedRDD improves the runtime performance by about 30% in this example. You can compare it yourself by dropping in the original `readRdf()` function from listing 8.5 into the `readrdf` object in listing 8.6 and calling that from `main()` instead of `readRdfIndexed()`, as shown in the following listing.

Listing 8.7   Listing 8.7 pom.xml for listing 8.6

```
<project xmlns="http://maven.apache.org/POM/4.0.0"
    xmlns:xsi="http://www.w3.org/2001/XMLSchema-instance"
    xsi:schemaLocation="http://maven.apache.org/POM/4.0.0
    http://maven.apache.org/maven-v4_0_0.xsd">
  <modelVersion>4.0.0</modelVersion>
  <groupId>com.manning</groupId>
```

```
<artifactId>graphx-readrdf</artifactId>
<version>1.0-SNAPSHOT</version>
<packaging>jar</packaging>

<repositories>
  <repository>
    <id>SparkPackagesRepo</id>
    <url>http://dl.bintray.com/spark-packages/maven/</url>
  </repository>
</repositories>

<dependencies>
  <dependency>
    <groupId>org.apache.spark</groupId>
    <artifactId>spark-core_2.10</artifactId>
    <version>1.5.0</version>
  </dependency>
  <dependency>
    <groupId>org.apache.spark</groupId>
    <artifactId>spark-graphx_2.10</artifactId>
    <version>1.6.0</version>
  </dependency>
  <dependency>
    <groupId>amplab</groupId>
    <artifactId>spark-indexedrdd</artifactId>
    <version>0.3</version>
  </dependency>
  <dependency>
    <groupId>org.scala-lang</groupId>
    <artifactId>scala-library</artifactId>
    <version>2.10.5</version>
  </dependency>
</dependencies>

<build>
  <plugins>
    <plugin>
      <groupId>org.scala-tools</groupId>
      <artifactId>maven-scala-plugin</artifactId>
      <version>2.15.0</version>
      <executions>
        <execution>
          <goals>
            <goal>compile</goal>
            <goal>testCompile</goal>
          </goals>
        </execution>
      </executions>
    </plugin>
    <plugin>
      <artifactId>maven-assembly-plugin</artifactId>
      <version>2.5.5</version>
      <configuration>
        <descriptorRefs>
          <descriptorRef>jar-with-dependencies</descriptorRef>
        </descriptorRefs>
```

```
    </configuration>
    <executions>
      <execution>
        <phase>package</phase>
        <goals>
          <goal>single</goal>
        </goals>
      </execution>
    </executions>
  </plugin>
 </plugins>
 </build>
</project>
```

8.3   *Poor man's graph isomorphism: finding missing Wikipedia infobox items*

One of the most interesting uses of graphs is for finding graph isomorphisms, which identify two portions of a graph that are similar in structure to each other and then use that to infer something about the second portion by using information from the first portion.

For example, figure 8.6 illustrates an example from YAGO-like data.

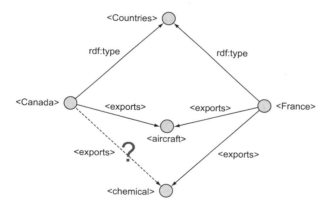

Figure 8.6   **The subgraph formed by the three vertices <France>, <Countries>, and <aircraft> is said to be *isomorphic* to the subgraph formed by the three vertices <Canada>, <Countries>, and <aircraft>. Not only are the edges in the same locations, but the edge attributes are the same. From this, could we infer that Canada also exports chemicals?**

YAGO data is notoriously incomplete because it's derived from Wikipedia, which depends on volunteer human editors, who devote an amount of time that varies by how interesting a topic, or even a particular item within a topic, is. We could use graph isomorphisms to detect inconsistencies within YAGO data.

First some background about how YAGO uses Wikipedia data. The YAGO graph edges that denote classification, the rdf:type edges, come from the Categories at the bottom of a Wikipedia page. These are accumulated into the yagoTypes.tsv file. The YAGO graph edges that denote facts such as "<exports>" and "<isLocatedIn>" come from the Infobox in the upper right corner of a Wikipedia page. These are accumulated into the yagoFacts.tsv file.

On a Wikipedia page, both the Categories and the Infobox are manually edited by volunteer human editors and are subject to a high level of inconsistency.

Graph isomorphisms are powerful, but implementing such an algorithm is beyond the scope of this book. Instead, we're going to cheat. Instead of looking for arbitrary graph structures (of arbitrary size), we're going to look only for "<exports>" edges and guess which other "<exports>" edges might be missing. We're taking advantage of the fact that the subject of "<exports>" is almost certainly a country, so we don't need to look for the edge that points up to "<Countries>". We're also taking advantage of the fact that the object of "<exports>" is almost certainly a product type. By looking only for "<exports>" edges, it's like we're getting some matching of larger subgraphs for free.

Notice also that by looking only for "<exports>" edges, we're in effect looking at a bipartite graph, from countries to products (see chapter 3 for more on bipartite graphs). The fact that we have a bipartite graph suggests the use of a recommender engine, and here we'll use SVDPlusPlus that was covered in chapter 7.

Our approach is to create the bipartite graph by subsetting only the "<exports>" edges out of the full YAGO graph and then train an SVDPlusPlus machine learning model on that. We'll find out the highest recommendation from this model, and that will suggest some information that might be missing from Wikipedia. The data flow we use, shown in figure 8.7, encompasses the next four code listings.

This example uses the Spark REPL launched with increased memory. We don't need to use `spark-submit` and Maven. First, as shown in listing 8.8, we read YAGO, create the bipartite graph, and use that as input to SVDPlusPlus to create the machine learning model. Because SVDPlusPlus expects a "rating" value (for example, one to four stars for a movie review), we assign a value of 1.0 for each rating. The absence of an "<exports>" edge is an implicit 0.0 rating.

Listing 8.8   Train SVDPlusPlus model on "<exports>" edges from YAGO

```
val gf = readRdf(sc, "yagoFacts.tsv").subgraph(_.attr == "<exports>")
val e = gf.edges.map(e => Edge(e.srcId, e.dstId, 1.0))
val (gs,mean) = lib.SVDPlusPlus.run(e,
     new lib.SVDPlusPlus.Conf(2,10,0,5,0.007,0.007,0.005,0.015))
```

Next, we need a list of all possible exports, which we compute from all countries' exports combined together (we're not considering exports that no country in the world exports yet). In this example we're only going to look for potential missing exports for a single country, Canada. The next listing generates an RDD, `vr`, that contains all the possible exports that Canada doesn't already export (which are removed by `subtractByKey()` where "subtract" refers to a set operation). Note that this listing relies on `removeSingletons()` from listing 8.1.

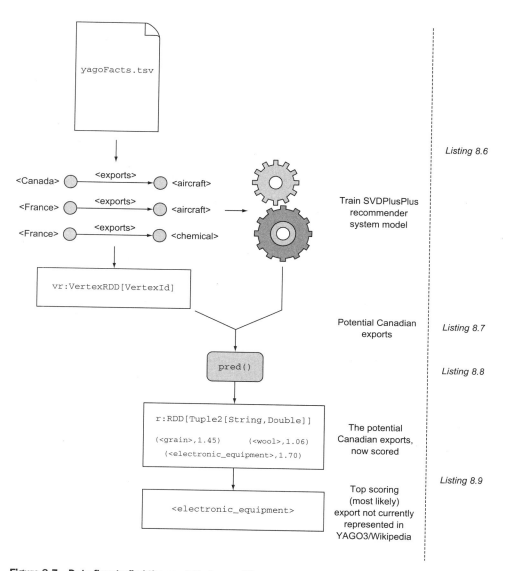

Figure 8.7   Data flow to find the most likely possible export from Canada that wasn't in Wikipedia when YAGO3 took a snapshot of it

Listing 8.9   Compute `vr`, the list of potentially missing exports for Canada

```
val gc = removeSingletons(gf.subgraph(et => et.srcAttr == "<Canada>"))
val vr = e.map(x => (x.dstId,""))
          .distinct
          .subtractByKey(gc.vertices)
          .map(_._1)
```

The idea is to run every item from vr through the SVDPlusPlus model we've created. Recall that the SVDPlusPlus model consists of two values, a graph and a double value (representing the mean), and that in chapter 7 we provided a pred() function to predict the "rating given by Canada" for every possible export. One would naturally think to call vr.map() where the function passed into the map calls pred(). But we can't pass gs, computed in listing 8.6, into vr.map().

> **SPARK TIP** The function passed into a map() can't reference a Graph or even an RDD. The reason is that to initiate a map() on the Spark cluster, Spark creates a closure (discussed in chapter 3), which means Spark ships all needed local variable data to the cluster along with the command to perform the map(). Spark won't bundle an RDD into a closure. Alternatives include a) converting the RDD to an Array in a local variable and relying on Spark to bundle that into a closure, b) using the Spark broadcast variable feature to broadcast such an array to the cluster in advance, or c) using a join(), if applicable, to create a single RDD out of the two RDDs (the one map() is being called on, and the one used by the function passed into map()).

Instead, the next listing provides a replacement for the pred() from chapter 7. This pred() takes a plain old Scala Map rather than a Graph as its parameter. The companion function vertexMap() converts the graph output from SVDPlusPlus into such a Scala map.

Listing 8.10   `map()`-friendly SVDPlusPlus prediction function and helper

```
def pred(v:Map[VertexId, (Array[Double], Array[Double], Double, Double)],
         mean:Double, u:Long, i:Long) = {
  val user = v.getOrElse(u, (Array(0.0), Array(0.0), 0.0, 0.0))
  val item = v.getOrElse(i, (Array(0.0), Array(0.0), 0.0, 0.0))
  mean + user._3 + item._3 +
  item._1.zip(user._2).map(x => x._1*x._2).reduce(_ + _)
}

def vertexMap(g:Graph[(Array[Double], Array[Double],
                  Double, Double),Double]) =
  g.vertices.collect.map(v => v._1 -> v._2).toMap
```

The following listing computes the most recommended export from Canada that might be valid yet missing from Wikipedia.

Listing 8.11   Find most likely Canadian export not in Wikipedia

```
val vm = vertexMap(gs)
val cid = gf.vertices.filter(_._2 == "<Canada>").first._1
val r = vr.map(v => (v,pred(vm,mean,cid,v)))

val maxKey = r.max()(new Ordering[Tuple2[VertexId, Double]]() {
  override def compare(x: (VertexId, Double), y: (VertexId, Double)): Int =
     Ordering[Double].compare(x._2, y._2)
})._1
```

```
gf.vertices.filter(_._1 == maxKey).collect

res0: Array[(org.apache.spark.graphx.VertexId, String)] =
 Array((1721488,<wordnet_electronic_equipment_103278248>))
```

The top recommendation for a missing edge in Wikipedia (based on the YAGO data) for a Canadian export is "electronic equipment." Anecdotally, we know the Canadian company Research In Motion exports Blackberry devices. But to look at it statistically, first take a look at the full list of exports that YAGO does have for Canada:

```
grep "<exports>" yagoFacts.tsv | grep "<Canada>"
<id_1wrx1wu_dv6_1pgb7a4>  <Canada> <exports> <wordnet_aluminum_114627820>
<id_1wrx1wu_dv6_j2l8e6>   <Canada> <exports> <wordnet_electricity_111449907>
<id_1wrx1wu_dv6_t6wmo1>   <Canada> <exports> <wordnet_lumber_114943580>
<id_1wrx1wu_dv6_jhowo0>   <Canada> <exports> <wordnet_natural_gas_114960090>
<id_1wrx1wu_dv6_s9bzqx>   <Canada> <exports> <wordnet_aircraft_102686568>
<id_1wrx1wu_dv6_12fzkgg>  <Canada> <exports> <wordnet_plastic_114592610>
```

Then, according to www.worldstopexports.com/canadas-top-exports/2502, the top 10 should be as follows:

1 *Oil*—US$128,926,515,000 (27.2% of total exports)
2 *Vehicles*—$59,753,479,000 (12.6%)
3 *Machines, engines, pumps*—$32,600,025,000 (6.9%)
4 *Gems, precious metals, coins*—$21,518,760,000 (4.5%)
5 *Electronic equipment*—$13,639,592,000 (2.9%)
6 *Plastics*—$13,192,128,000 (2.8%)
7 *Wood*—$12,686,263,000 (2.7%)
8 *Aircraft, spacecraft*—$12,409,459,000 (2.6%)
9 *Aluminum*—$8,865,363,000 (1.9%)
10 *Cereals*—$8,774,059,000 (1.8%)

The YAGO data was correct in listing aluminum, aircraft, wood, and plastics, yet failed to mention aircraft, which was above all of those.

This was a single recommendation. In reality, instead of looking for only maxKey, as in listing 8.11, a threshold for the predicted rating should be chosen, and all recommended edges above that threshold should be examined.

Note also that by using SVDPlusPlus as a poor man's graph isomorphism detector, a major benefit was realized unrelated to graph isomorphisms. As discussed in chapter 7, SVDPlusPlus models latent variables, meaning SVDPlusPlus is inferring some kind of virtual graph nodes that aren't in the graph. To see how that played out in this example with Canada and electronic equipment, grepping reveals that the only other country YAGO has for exporting electronic equipment is Liechtenstein. Then grepping for Liechtenstein's exports, the only other one listed is "<hardware>", which isn't even listed as one of Canada's exports. It seems SVDPlusPlus must have created a latent variable that says hardware is similar to lumber, and therefore Canada's exports must be similar to Liechtenstein's.

8.4   *Global clustering coefficient: compare connectedness*

In chapter 5 you saw GraphX's built-in Triangle Count as a way to measure connectedness. Another way to measure connectedness, the global clustering coefficient, is better in that it always returns a number between 0 and 1, making it possible to compare the connectedness of different sized graphs. For example, to compare the connectedness in a social network of Yale graduates versus Harvard graduates, you could directly compare the global clustering coefficients, even though those two sets would have a different number of graduates. A downside of the global clustering coefficient compared to, say, the Triangle Count, is that computing the global clustering coefficient is more computationally intensive. The global clustering coefficient is not to be confused with the related local clustering coefficient.

The global clustering coefficient is defined like this:

$$\frac{\text{\# of closed triplets}}{\text{total \# of triplets (open or closed)}}$$

A *triplet* in this case is a set of three vertices that have two or three edges among them. If there are three edges, then it's a triangle, and this is called a *closed triplet*. If there are only two edges, then it's called an *open triplet*. Triplets are counted for each vertex and then added all together; this means that a triangle will count as three closed triplets because each of the three vertices will have one closed triplet associated with it. This is illustrated in figure 8.8.

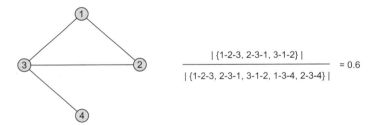

$$\frac{|\{1\text{-}2\text{-}3,\ 2\text{-}3\text{-}1,\ 3\text{-}1\text{-}2\}|}{|\{1\text{-}2\text{-}3,\ 2\text{-}3\text{-}1,\ 3\text{-}1\text{-}2,\ 1\text{-}3\text{-}4,\ 2\text{-}3\text{-}4\}|} = 0.6$$

Figure 8.8   Example of computing the global clustering coefficient. There are three closed triplets associated with the one triangle: one closed triplet associated with vertex 1, one with vertex 2, and one with vertex 3. There are two open triplets associated with vertex 3, namely 1-3-4 and 2-3-4.

Listing 8.12 defines a function `clusteringCoefficient` that takes a `Graph` object as input and returns the global clustering coefficient. To compute the global clustering coefficient in GraphX, we use a single iteration of `aggregateMessages()` to allow each vertex to compile a complete list of all its neighboring vertices.

Listing 8.12 Global clustering coefficient

```
import scala.reflect.ClassTag
def clusteringCoefficient[VD:ClassTag,ED:ClassTag](g:Graph[VD,ED]) = {
  val numTriplets =
    g.aggregateMessages[Set[VertexId]](
        et => { et.sendToSrc(Set(et.dstId));
                et.sendToDst(Set(et.srcId)) },
        (a,b) => a ++ b) // #A
      .map(x => {val s = (x._2 - x._1).size; s*(s-1) / 2})
      .reduce(_ + _)

  if (numTriplets == 0) 0.0 else
    g.triangleCount.vertices.map(_._2).reduce(_ + _) /
      numTriplets.toFloat
}
```

> **aggregateMessages function generates a VertexRDD, where each vertex contains a set of the IDs of vertices it shares an edge with.**

Here we use a Scala `Set`, which is similar to sets in other languages (they automatically eliminate duplicates, which has the effect of automatically filtering out parallel edges for us). In the function we pass into `aggregateMessages()` for the `mergeMsg` parameter, we use the `Set` operator named `++`, which performs a set union. As a final bit of filtering, we exclude loop edges (edges that start and end with the same vertex) because we don't want to count these as triplets. We do this with the `x._2 - x._1` expression, where the minus (`-`) is a `Set` function to perform set differencing. That expression removes the `vertexId` of (`x._1`) from the set of neighboring vertices (`x._2`).

Once we have a set of neighboring vertices for each vertex, computing the total number of triplets (open and closed) for that vertex is a simple combinatoric combination of "n choose 2":

$$\binom{n}{2} = \frac{n!}{2!(n-2)!} = \frac{n(n-1)}{2}$$

For the denominator, we use GraphX's built-in Triangle Count. That counts triangles on a per-vertex basis, and when we sum up all those triangles with `reduce(_ + _)`, it ends up counting each triangle three times—which is exactly what we need for the global clustering coefficient formula.

As an example, download the anonymized Facebook data from the Stanford Network Analysis Project:

```
cd ~/Downloads
wget https://snap.stanford.edu/data/facebook.tar.gz
tar xzvf facebook.tar.gz
```

Of the many data sets, we use the first one, set 0 (listing 8.13). The 0.edges file is in a format that can be read directly using GraphX's `GraphLoader`. By reviewing the 0.feat-names file, we see that feature 77 is gender, so we extract that and convert it to a Boolean as we read the file 0.feat with `sc.textFile`.

Listing 8.13   Example using the global clustering coefficient

```
import org.apache.spark.graphx._
val g = GraphLoader.edgeListFile(sc, System.getProperty("user.home") +
  "/Downloads/facebook/0.edges")
val feat = sc.textFile(System.getProperty("user.home") +
  "/Downloads/facebook/0.feat").map(x =>
  (x.split(" ")(0).toLong, x.split(" ")(78).toInt == 1))
val g2 = g.outerJoinVertices(feat)((vid,vd,u) => u.get)

clusteringCoefficient(g2)
res1: Double = 0.8517387509346008

clusteringCoefficient(g2.subgraph(_ => true, (vid,vd) => vd))
res2: Double = 0.8881188035011292

clusteringCoefficient(g2.subgraph(_ => true, (vid,vd) => !vd))
res3: Double = 0.8304622173309326
```

There's a difference in the connectedness between all the males in this anonymized Facebook data versus between all the females. Because even the gender data was anonymized, we don't know the real-life meaning of gender=1 versus gender=0.

8.5   Summary

- A number of algorithms one might expect from a graph processing system aren't present in GraphX.
- GraphX's subgraph() leaves isolated vertices, but we showed code to clean them up.
- Merging graphs is useful when a graph, such as YAGO3, comes broken up in multiple smaller graphs.
- RDF is a standard file format, and we showed code to parse and match the vertex names to construct a GraphX graph.
- Graph isomorphisms are a powerful way to find relationships and derive value from "kitchen sink" type graphs like YAGO3. Using a recommender system is a cheap way to identify some simple graph isomorphisms.
- The global clustering coefficient measures connectedness, similar to GraphX's built-in Triangle Count, but in a way that returns a normalized value between 0 and 1. This makes it easier to compare connectedness between graphs of different sizes.

Performance
and monitoring

This chapter covers

- Monitoring Spark applications
- Performance-related configuration options
- Tuning your application for maximum performance
- Using graph partitioning to boost large-scale processing

Most of the examples we've looked at so far have been small-scale. They would run on one machine and complete their processing without requiring a large amount of computing resources. But one of the key reasons to use Apache Spark is to take advantage of its distributed processing model. Spark's ability to distribute data and processing across a cluster of many machines is the key to its capacity to run the type of processing we've discussed on large datasets.

Once you have a cluster with plenty of resources and have installed Apache Spark, getting your Spark application to run on a large dataset is still likely to require some planning, configuration, and possibly some troubleshooting. In this chapter, we take you through the steps necessary to run your application successfully and discuss where to go for troubleshooting information if things don't go according to plan. In the course of this we'll provide you with a deeper understanding of the Spark processing model, which will be essential to knowing which of the many configuration "knobs" need twiddling.

9.1 Monitoring your Spark application

You've sourced and explored your data, written and tested your code, and now you want to run your graph algorithm on real-world Big Data. How do you ensure that your application runs as quickly as possible—or even runs at all?

Spark comes with an array of different APIs and configuration settings that you can use to extract the maximum performance. Before spending too much time attempting to tune Spark and your application, it's essential to have a clear understanding of how Spark runs your application.

Monitoring is an essential aspect of understanding the performance of Spark applications and is a key tool for troubleshooting issues. Spark provides a number of user interfaces that allow you to track what's going on in your application. First we explore a few core concepts that you need to get under your belt, and then we dive into the various monitoring tools provided by Spark.

9.1.1 How Spark runs your application

What happens when a Spark driver program executes an action such as `count` or `reduce` or writes the output of a graph's RDDs to disk (for example, when using one of our graph output routines from chapter 4)? This section discusses in detail how Spark executes some simple jobs and how we can see what's happening under the hood using Spark's monitoring tools. Later on we'll use this knowledge to understand what Spark is doing to execute large jobs that are run on Spark. The skills learned in this section will be essential for choosing the correct tuning options when diagnosing and troubleshooting your application.

Figure 9.1 shows an example of a job that reads in a text file, filters out lines with a particular word, and then displays the lines in lowercase. In so doing we'll create a chain of three RDDs and then call an action (`collect`) on the final RDD. The Spark driver will analyze the chain of RDDs required to generate the output and create a job that "contains" the operations that will be performed on the worker nodes.

A job consists of one or more stages, which are collections of operations to be performed on the data. Recall that the data in an RDD is split up into partitions that are operated on by different worker nodes in the cluster. A stage is created to contain a sequence of operations that can be executed on the data within each partition without the need to access data in other partitions. In our example of a map and a filter, we need one stage because the transformations `filter` and `map` are applied in isolation to each element of the initial RDD, as shown in figure 9.1.

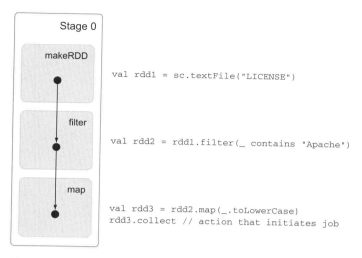

```
val rdd1 = sc.textFile("LICENSE")




val rdd2 = rdd1.filter(_ contains "Apache")




val rdd3 = rdd2.map(_.toLowerCase)
rdd3.collect // action that initiates job
```

Figure 9.1   A job involving filter and map operations only requires a single stage. Each operation is performed in isolation on each element of the initial RDD.

For many jobs though, the data needs to be shuffled across partitions to achieve the desired result. One example is `groupByKey`. Elements with the same key may be spread across a number of partitions. To group them by key we need all elements with the same key to end up together in the same partition. Spark will split the processing before and after the shuffle into two different stages.

> **DEFINITION**   When the processing must be split across multiple stages like this, the point in the data flow where the split occurs is called the *shuffle boundary*. Transformations that give rise to shuffles are called *wide* transformations (in comparison to *narrow* transformations that don't).

An example is shown in figure 9.2 and in the following listing.

Listing 9.1   Transformations that require multiple stages

```
val rdd = sc.makeRDD(1 to 10000)
rdd
  .filter(_ % 4 == 0)
  .map(Math.sqrt(_))
  .map(el => (el.toInt,el))
  .groupByKey
  .collect
```

"1 to 10000": Scala-based way to generate collection of integers in a particular range

"Narrow" transformations only operate on data within a partition.

groupByKey: a "wide" transformation, elements to be gathered from across different partitions via "shuffle"

The `groupByKey` forces Spark to create two stages. For more complex code there can be a large number of stages to produce a single result.

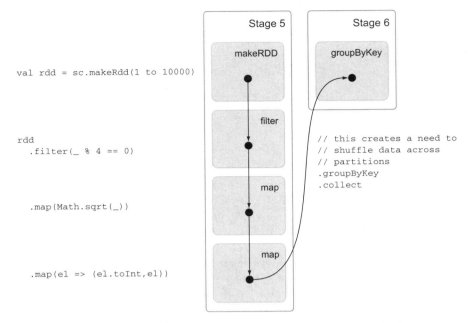

```
val rdd = sc.makeRdd(1 to 10000)

rdd
  .filter(_ % 4 == 0)

  .map(Math.sqrt(_))

  .map(el => (el.toInt,el))
```

```
// this creates a need to
// shuffle data across
// partitions
.groupByKey
.collect
```

Figure 9.2   Operations such as `groupByKey` that require data to be examined across partitions cause a shuffle to take place across stage boundaries.

As figures 9.1 and 9.2 show, each stage is a collection of one or more operations—or to give their official name, *tasks*.

> **DEFINITION**   A *task* is the smallest unit of work in Spark. A task represents work that is scheduled for processing on one of the Spark worker nodes.

Consider, for example, the Spark job in listing 9.1 and assume it operates on data in four partitions. When the first stage is executed, the processing is carried out in four tasks distributed across the worker nodes. When a worker node executes a task, it applies the stage operations (in this case, map and filter operations) to its subset of the data. The task outputs are then supplied to the next stage—in this case, a group-ByKey. Usually this means the data must be *shuffled*—written to disk and then read over the network so that data elements that must be processed together exist on the same worker node.

Because the processing on the data is confined to that defined by a stage (and therefore doesn't require data from any other partition), processing of tasks can be carried out in parallel.

EXECUTORS: WHERE THE WORK HAPPENS

We've talked about tasks being executed on worker nodes, but we need to discuss one more concept that relates to how worker nodes execute tasks.

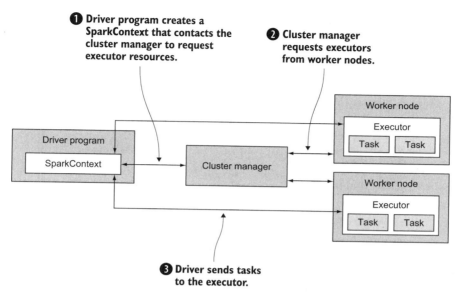

1 Driver program creates a SparkContext that contacts the cluster manager to request executor resources.

2 Cluster manager requests executors from worker nodes.

3 Driver sends tasks to the executor.

Figure 9.3 The driver program creates the `SparkContext` that negotiates with the cluster manager to create executors on the worker nodes. The `SparkContext` contains a job scheduler (not shown) that distributes tasks to the executors.

An *executor* is a process started on a worker node that will run for the lifetime of the application. The executor's job is to run tasks submitted by the application. Each executor is dedicated to one particular application, so if you have two or more applications running, you will have multiple executors running on the same worker node.

Each Spark application requests a number of executors from the cluster manager when it starts up (see figure 9.3). The executors' primary role is to receive and process the tasks given to them by the job scheduler running in the driver program that created the `SparkContext`. When the Spark application is finished, the executors are no longer needed.

When the `SparkContext` is created, it will be configured with a target number of resources (CPU cores and memory) to use. When the `SparkContext` negotiates the creation of executors with the cluster manager, it will request enough executors to provide the target resources. Section 9.2 looks at the options for configuring and tuning cluster resources.

9.1.2 *Understanding your application runtime with Spark monitoring*

Spark provides a number of tools that can be used to understand how Spark executed a completed job or even to examine the progress of an in-flight job. This section looks at some of the key features of the Application UI, a web-based monitoring app that will become your go-to tool for diagnosing application problems.

APPLICATION UI

When a `SparkContext` is created in your application, it creates a web UI to display the various elements of the application. By default, the web server will be created on port 4040, but if an application is already running on that port it will try successive ports (4041, 4042, and so on).

Note that `spark-shell` creates a `SparkContext` for you automatically, so the application UI is available as soon as the shell is open. When you compile and build your own application (demonstrated in chapter 3), you are responsible for creating a `SparkContext`; in this case, the Application UI is only available after you've created the `SparkContext`.

Let's rerun our first GraphX program from chapter 2 and see what information the application UI gives us. The program used the CitHep-Th.txt file located in the same directory where we ran the program:

```
scala> import org.apache.spark.graphx._
import org.apache.spark.graphx._

scala> val graph = GraphLoader.edgeListFile (sc, "Cit-HepTh.txt")
graph: org.apache.spark.graphx.Graph[Int,Int] =
    org.apache.spark.graphx.impl.GraphImpl@16120270

scala> graph.inDegrees.reduce((a,b) => if (a._2 > b._2) a else b)
res0: (org.apache.spark.graphx.VertexId, Int) = (9711200,2414)
```

When you navigate to the application UI (for example, http://<yourhost>:4040), you will be taken initially to a screen with five tabs:

- Jobs
- Stages
- Storage
- Environment
- Executors

In this section we look at what information the Jobs, Stages, and Environment screens display, including the incredibly useful Event Timeline and DAG Visualization graphical tools. (The Storage and Executors screens are covered in subsequent sections.) The screen defaults to the Jobs tab. After you've run the program, you should see something similar to figure 9.4.

The Jobs tab displays a list of all the jobs that have been run during the lifetime of the application. A number of attributes are displayed for each job, as shown in table 9.1.

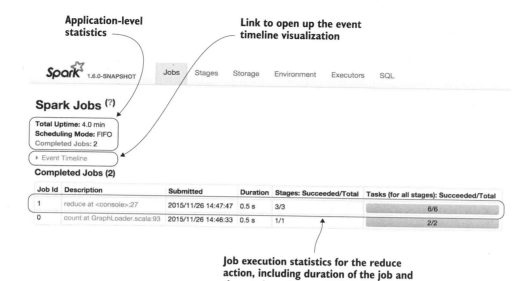

Figure 9.4 The Jobs tab lists all the actions that have been (or are being) executed in the application. The screenshot shows information about timings and duration for two jobs that have been run. The columns are described in more detail in table 9.1.

Table 9.1 Attributes of the Job list screen

Attribute	Description
Job ID	The first job is assigned the ID of 0 and then is incremented for each successive job.
Description	Each job is identified by a combination of the action being executed and the source code location.
Submitted	The time the job was submitted.
Duration	The time the job took to complete.
Stages	The total number of stages needed to complete the job and the number successfully run. For a successfully completed job, both these measures will be the same, but for a running job you can get an idea of how close the job is to completion.
Tasks	Each Stage is composed of a number of tasks. This column gives a graphical representation of the total number of tasks in all stages for the job and how many have completed.

In figure 9.4 you can see that the `reduce` action took 0.5 seconds to complete and involved 3 stages with a total of 6 tasks. But what is the `count` action in Job 0—where did that come from? It turns out this comes from a quirk of the implementation of the `GraphLoader.fromEdgeFile` method. Lets restart the `spark-shell` and construct the graph ourselves by creating an `EdgeRDD` from the Cit-HepTh.txt file and passing this to `Graph.fromEdges`:

Ignore lines that don't have two numbers.

Ignore comment lines in input file starting with #.

Each line should be two numbers separated by tab.

Turn each line into an GraphX Edge—returns an EdgeRDD.

```
import org.apache.spark.graphx._
val edgelist = sc.textFile("Cit-HepTh.txt")
val edges = edgelist
            .filter(!_.startsWith("#"))
            .map(_.split("\\s"))
            .filter(_.size > 1)
            .map(line => Edge(line(0).toLong, line(1).toLong, 1))
val g = Graph.fromEdges (edges, 1)
g.inDegrees.reduce((a,b) => if (a._2 > b._2) a else b)
```

This code explicitly reads the input file and constructs the same graph as `GraphLoader.edgeListFile`. If you look at the Jobs tab in the application UI (figure 9.5), you should now see one job for the reduce action. This is because unlike `edge-ListFile`, we don't throw in a count of the edges.

As you can see already, the application UI is a great way to investigate what is happening with your application.

Lets go back to our original example that had two jobs and see what information Spark provides about the Stages that the job creates. You could click the Stages tab to see all the Stages created by the application, but to be honest when you have a lot of jobs being executed in your application, the Stages tab can get a little cluttered. Usually when you're debugging or tuning an application, you're interested in what's happening for each individual job and what's happening to the stages and tasks that make

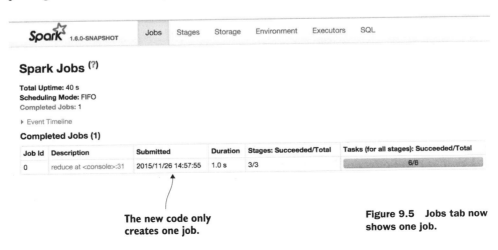

The new code only creates one job.

Figure 9.5   Jobs tab now shows one job.

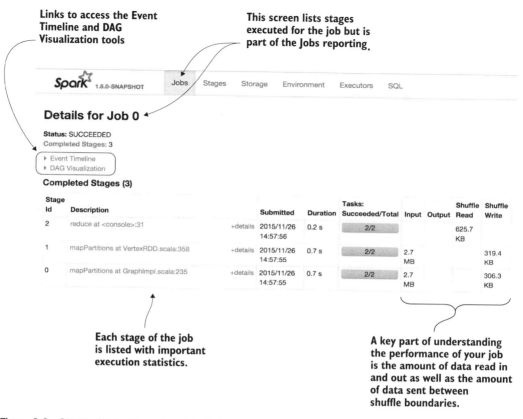

Figure 9.6   Stages list for the reduce job. Note the tab strip still has "Jobs" highlighted.

up that job. If we go back to the Jobs tab and click the `reduce at <console>:x` link, the Application UI displays a Stages view for that job, as shown in figure 9.6.

The "Details for Job x" screen lists all the stages for the selected job. The attributes of each Stage are shown in table 9.2.

Table 9.2   Attributes of the Stages list screen

Attribute	Description
Stage ID	The first stage is assigned the ID of 0 and then is incremented for each successive stage created by the `SparkContext`.
Description	Each stage is named for the action that initiated the job (such as reduce or count) or the transformation that generated a shuffle boundary.
Submitted	The time the stage was scheduled for processing by the Scheduler.
Duration	The elapsed time to process the stage.

Table 9.2   Attributes of the Stages list screen *(continued)*

Attribute	Description
Tasks	This column gives a graphical representation of the total number of tasks for the stage and how many have completed.
Input	Amount of data read in by all the tasks in the stage.
Output	Amount of data written by all the tasks in the stage.
Shuffle Read	The amount of shuffle data read from preceding stages in the DAG.
Shuffle Write	Amount of shuffle data delivered for subsequent stages.

This view lets you concentrate on what's happening for a single action. You can get some insight into the parallelism of the action using the Submitted and Duration columns. But things would be much easier with a visual display of when Stages and Tasks are executed, something Spark provides with the Event Timeline and DAG Visualizations, which are discussed in the following sections.

VISUALIZE JOB EXECUTION WITH EVENT TIMELINE

Although raw numbers for times and durations can be useful for understanding how your application is being run, nothing beats a good visual display of the data. This is especially true when your application increases in complexity and your datasets become bigger.

If you're running Spark 1.4 or later, you can take advantage of two new visualization features:

- Event Timeline
- DAG Visualization

We look at Event Timeline in this section and DAG Visualization in the next.

The Event Timeline is available in each of the jobs, stages, and tasks and shows slightly different information in each one. Figure 9.7 shows the jobs timeline. It gives a general overview of when executors were started for your application and in the section below a timeline of when jobs are run.

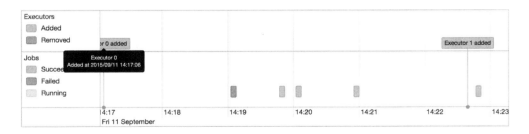

Figure 9.7   The Jobs timeline: a second executor is started at around 14:22. Four jobs are run on one executor; one job was run after the second executor had been started.

When you click a Job to view the Stages that have run, you'll see a timeline for the Stages. This view is particularly useful for understanding the runtime relationship between Stages—which ones will be run in parallel and which must wait for earlier Stages to complete.

Figure 9.8 shows the Stages timeline for our first GraphX program. Notice that the two stages that load and create the Edge and Vertex RDDs are run in parallel, but the reduce Stage must wait for completion of these earlier Stages before starting to execute.

It should also be apparent that the Vertex RDD Stage takes longer to execute than the Edge RDD Stage (labelled as `mapPartitions at GraphImpl.scala` in the timeline). If you're trying to tune the runtime for the job, improving the efficiency of the Edge RDD Stage is unlikely to have an impact on the overall runtime—`mapPartitions at VertexRDD.scala` and `reduce` are the critical sections of code in this particular example.

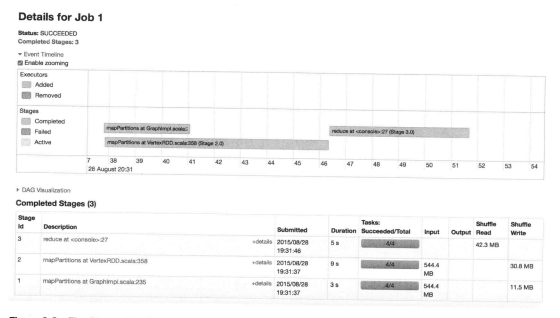

Figure 9.8 The Stages timeline shows you which stages Spark can run in parallel.

Clicking a stage link takes you to the Stage details page that displays metrics for all the tasks that make up the Stage. It includes a timeline showing when tasks were processed by executors.

A key design goal for Spark applications is to try to ensure the maximum amount of parallelism is achieved for your job. After all, you want all those CPUs and memory you've paid for to be utilized.

Figures 9.9 to 9.11 show the timelines for different executions of the same task. In each case, the application was configured to request a different number of CPU cores from the cluster.

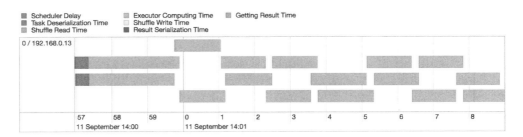

Figure 9.9   Stage details event timeline showing the timeline of task execution. Notice that only two tasks are ever executed in parallel.

You would expect to see that as the number of CPU cores increases, the level of parallelism increases. In situations where you expect an application to be running faster than it is, it's useful to look at the actual level of parallelism that you get as shown through the tasks event timeline. You can then easily measure the impact of configuration or code changes that you apply during tuning, some of which are discussed in the following sections.

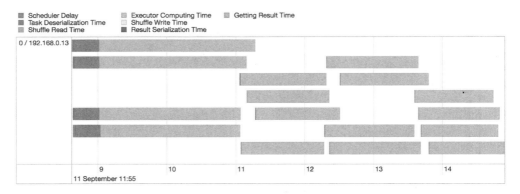

Figure 9.10   Stage details event timeline over four cores—parallelism has increased to use all the cores.

In figure 9.10, four cores are available to the application, so there are almost always four tasks running in parallel. In figure 9.11, the same idea is repeated with six cores running six tasks in parallel.

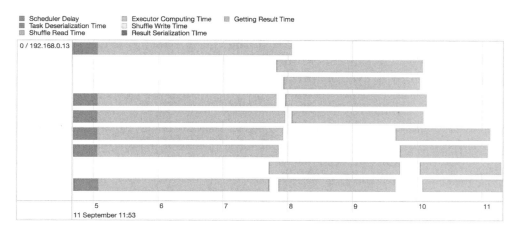

Figure 9.11   Stage details event timeline over six cores.

One more thing to note is that the display helpfully color-codes the task timeline bars to distinguish different types of activity or wait time associated with the task:

- *Scheduler Delay*—Before a task can be processed by an executor, the scheduler must send it the code to execute. This is the time to ship the task across the network from the scheduler to the executor and then to get the result back.

- *Task Deserialization Time*—The time the executor spent deserializing the code before it can start execution.

- *Shuffle Read Time*—The time waiting on network transfers if the task needed to read shuffled data from a previous stage.

- *Executor Computing Time*—The time spent executing the task code, including reading from HDFS or other data sources.

- *Shuffle Write Time*—The time to write out shuffle data to be read by the next stage.

- *Result Serialization Time*—The time taken for the executor to serialize any results before sending back to the driver code.

- *Getting Result Time*—The time taken to ship the results back to the driver code.

DAG VISUALIZATION

We've already seen that RDDs are chained together by transformations and that calling an action method on an RDD invokes a Spark job that reads in data from parent RDDs and applies the transformations to produce a result. It's natural for Spark code to contain a large number of chained RDDs, often with a fairly complex structure. Understanding how this structure plays out at runtime can be a challenge—which is where the DAG Visualization tool comes in handy.

Each RDD in the chain is derived from one or more parent RDDs, so we can think of the RDD as a vertex in a graph; the connection between a parent and child RDD can be thought of as an edge. The resulting graph is directed because parent RDDs can only pass data onto child RDDs; data can't flow in the opposite direction. Ultimately, a number of "root" RDDs generate the initial data, either from filesystems or other data sources such as databases or streaming data sources such as Kafka.

Finally this "execution" graph is *acyclic* (meaning no cycles in the graph) because we never have a situation where an RDD earlier in the chain has a parent that is further down the chain. The term used for such structures is *directed acyclic graph* (DAG).

The DAG Visualization feature—which is available for the whole job, and also for a specific stage—provides a neat graphical display of the RDDs and their connections. You've already seen examples of the display in figures 9.1 and 9.2. Another example is shown in figure 9.12.

The visualization of the DAG for a Spark job is useful for seeing the overall flow of a job and gives a quick visual indication of where RDD caching, a key performance technique, is taking place. Section 9.3 covers caching in more detail.

The visualization of a single stage is most useful for identifying the data sources for the root RDDs. In the case of file-based data, it provides an indication of the path to the underlying data.

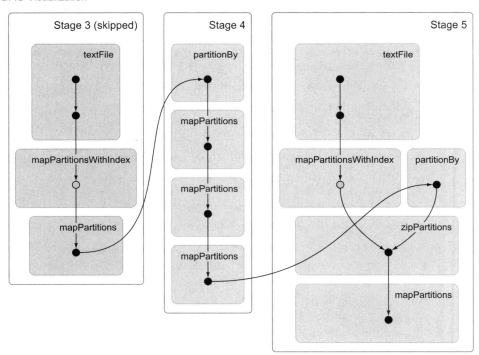

Figure 9.12   DAG visualization for an example Spark job. Notice that RDDs that have been cached have their stage marked "skipped"—Spark will read the RDD data from a cache rather than recalculate the RDD.

ENVIRONMENT TAB

The Environment screen (figure 9.13) provides a list of the various properties and classpath entries that have been set for the *driver* program. These can be useful for diagnosing issues where you want to be sure what a particular property has been set to. Note that if you're running `spark-shell` or `spark-submit` locally (you've set `master` to `local` or `local[n]`), then a single executor is created for you inside your driver JVM; in this case, the properties exposed by the Environment tab are also shared by the executor.

In all other cases, executors will be created in other JVMs, likely on other machines. Each worker will create a web UI to provide information on the executors it manages. Therefore, you will need to use the Worker node UIs to examine a specific executor's environment information.

9.1.3 History server

The Application UI lives and dies with the `SparkContext` created by the application. Once the application that created the `SparkContext` finishes (or you call `Spark-Context.stop`), the Application UI is no longer available. This means you won't be

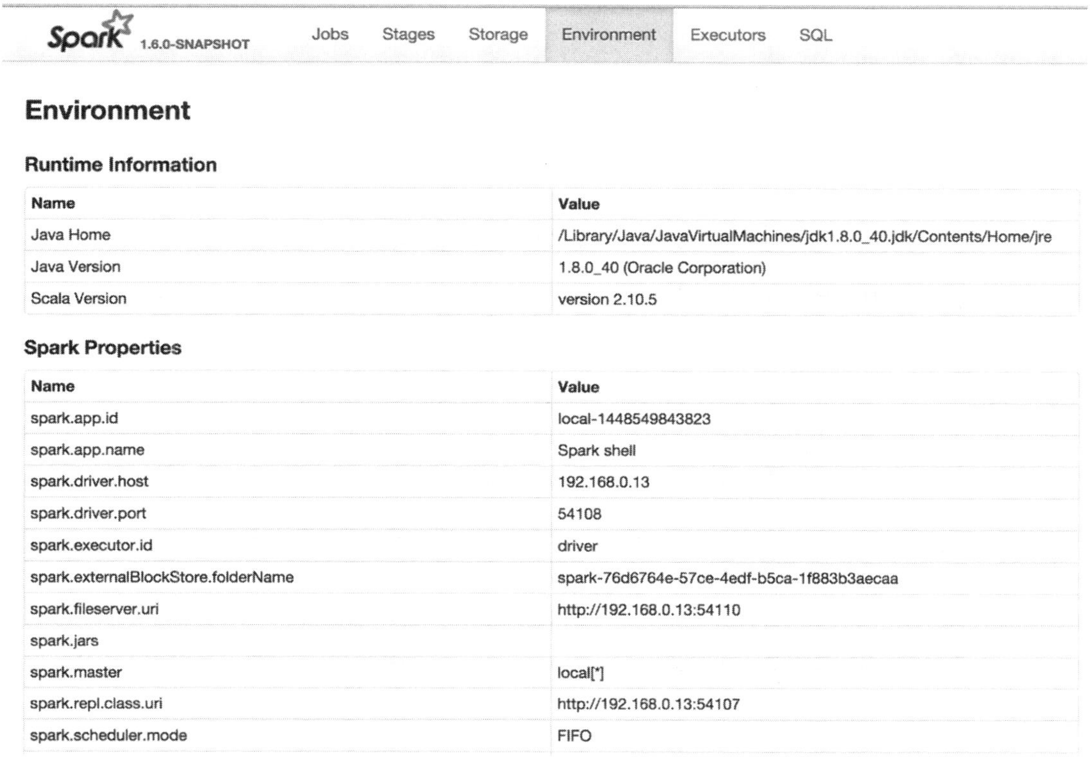

Spark 1.6.0-SNAPSHOT   Jobs   Stages   Storage   Environment   Executors   SQL

Environment

Runtime Information

Name	Value
Java Home	/Library/Java/JavaVirtualMachines/jdk1.8.0_40.jdk/Contents/Home/jre
Java Version	1.8.0_40 (Oracle Corporation)
Scala Version	version 2.10.5

Spark Properties

Name	Value
spark.app.id	local-1448549843823
spark.app.name	Spark shell
spark.driver.host	192.168.0.13
spark.driver.port	54108
spark.executor.id	driver
spark.externalBlockStore.folderName	spark-76d6764e-57ce-4edf-b5ca-1f883b3aecaa
spark.fileserver.uri	http://192.168.0.13:54110
spark.jars	
spark.master	local[*]
spark.repl.class.uri	http://192.168.0.13:54107
spark.scheduler.mode	FIFO

Figure 9.13   The Spark Environment tab (accessed from the Environment tab at the top of the browser screen)

able to diagnose issues after the application ends or compare execution history across a number of runs. This problem is addressed by the history server.

The *history server* is a long-lived web application that monitors a directory for event logs created by multiple Spark applications and reconstructs the application metrics and the associated UI. The history server UI for the application will be exactly the same as if you had looked at the Application UI before the `SparkContext` disappeared.

To use this feature you first need to decide where you will run the history server. The easiest way is to run it on the same machine that your driver program runs on. You then need to ensure that a directory is created for applications to log events to. By default, the directory is /tmp/spark-events, so go ahead and create the directory path.

Once the directory is set up, the history server can be started using the following command (issued from the SPARK_HOME directory):

```
./sbin/start-history-server.sh
```

This starts a web server listening on port 18080.

You need to ensure that `spark.events.enabled` is set to `true` for all Spark applications you're running. One way to do that is to append `--conf "spark.eventLog.enabled=true"` to the `spark-shell` or `spark-submit` command line, like this:

```
spark-shell --conf "spark.eventLog.enabled=true"
```

This will cause the application to log events to the default directory /tmp/spark-events. When the Spark application closes, the events will remain in the event logging directory. To see the application in the history server, open a web browser and point it to the history server address and port (for example, http://localhost:18080 if you browse from the machine where you started the history server).

The initial screen (see figure 9.14) shows a list of all completed applications logged to the events directory.

Clicking a link takes you to the Application UI for that application as if the application's `SparkContext` were still running. From this point, you can investigate the application as shown in the previous sections describing the Application UI.

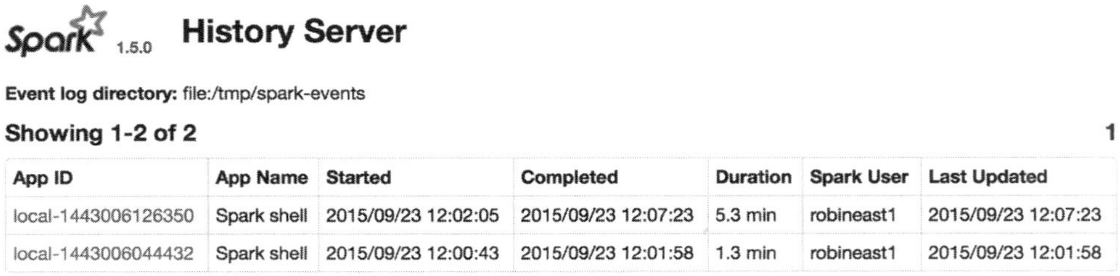

Spark 1.5.0 **History Server**

Event log directory: file:/tmp/spark-events

Showing 1-2 of 2   1

App ID	App Name	Started	Completed	Duration	Spark User	Last Updated
local-1443006126350	Spark shell	2015/09/23 12:02:05	2015/09/23 12:07:23	5.3 min	robineast1	2015/09/23 12:07:23
local-1443006044432	Spark shell	2015/09/23 12:00:43	2015/09/23 12:01:58	1.3 min	robineast1	2015/09/23 12:01:58

Figure 9.14   Spark history server UI containing two complete Spark applications

To write logs to another directory outside the /tmp directory, add the following configuration option to spark-shell:

```
--conf "spark.eventLog.dir=/logs/test-events"
```

Then start the history server like this:

```
./sbin/start-history-server.sh /logs/test-events
```

To write logs to HDFS (as a distributed Big Data storage layer, it's an obvious choice for storing application logs), use the prefix `hdfs:///` (for example, `hdfs:///logs/spark-events`).

> **TIP** If you configure `spark-shell` (or `spark-submit`) to write logs to a directory that doesn't exist, you'll get a `NullPointerException` in the `SparkContext` initialization, causing the application to fail. If you find your Spark application won't start up after configuring event logging, check to make sure the directory has been created.

9.2 Configuring Spark

The primary aim of a parallel processing system like Spark is to utilize the processing power—the CPU cores—as fully as possible while ensuring that sufficient memory is available to each executor. If there's only one user of the system at any one time, this is relatively easy to achieve. But if cluster resources must be shared with other users, a bit more work and planning is involved. This section covers the configuration options available to achieve these goals.

Spark can be deployed into three different cluster environments:

- Standalone
- Mesos
- YARN

We concentrate on the standalone cluster manager that comes as part of the Spark application. If your target environment is Mesos or YARN, much of the configuration is similar, but you'll need to work with your cluster administrator to identify the relevant configuration.

> **NOTE** The phrase *cluster manager* is used in the Spark documentation as a generic reference to the service (or set of services) that provide cluster resources to your application. When using the standalone cluster manager, the service that negotiates cluster resources is referred to as the *Spark Master*—you can use these two phrases interchangeably.

Out of the box, if you run `bin/spark-shell` with no other parameters, you get a nonclustered environment, where both the driver and a single executor run within the same Java Virtual Machine (JVM). By default, this setup will have 512 MB of memory and will allocate all the CPU cores of your machine to Spark. These resources are shared between the driver and the executor.

Though this setup works fine for small datasets and for initial exploratory work, if you're working with large datasets you'll want to run your jobs on a multi-node cluster. Spark clusters can range from a handful of machines up to hundreds or even thousands of machines for a large cluster. Each machine in the cluster will usually run a single worker JVM process that can spawn one or more executor JVMs on the same machine. As we've already seen, it is the executors that carry out your requests.

To utilize the Spark cluster, you start your driver program (spark-submit or spark-shell) as usual but supply a cluster URL as follows (where <master-host> is the name of the machine running the Spark Master):

```
bin/spark-shell --master spark://<master-host>:7077
```

The Spark Master will negotiate cluster resources (in the form of executor processes) from the worker nodes. Without any further parameters on the command line, this will start executors on each worker node, taking all the CPU cores on the machine and allocating 1 GB of RAM to each executor. Because we would normally want to allocate as much memory as there is available on each worker node (after all, that's one of the primary advantages of using Spark), we can add an extra parameter to specify the memory we want for each executor. Let's assume our worker nodes have 32 GB each. We can allocate 31 GB on each machine (Spark reserves 1 GB for the OS) using the --executor-memory parameter:

```
spark-shell --master spark://<master-host>:7077 --executor-memory 31g
```

Figure 9.15 shows this configuration for a four-node cluster.

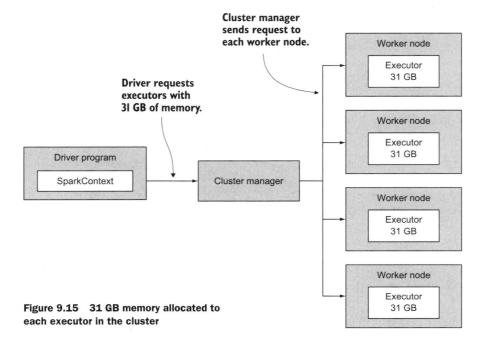

Figure 9.15 31 GB memory allocated to each executor in the cluster

We don't recommend having large JVM heap sizes—say, greater than 64 GB—because large garbage collection times start to become a problem. In many cases, the machines being used in production Spark clusters have memory sizes of 256 GB, 512 GB, or more. To prevent executor heap sizes greater than 64 GB, you need a number of smaller executors on each machine. You can achieve that using appropriate settings for `--executor-memory` and `--executor-cores`.

Suppose you have worker machines with 256 GB of memory and 24 CPU cores. Ideally, we want four executors on each machine with each executor limited to 63 GB memory and six CPU cores:

```
spark-shell --master spark://<master-host>:7077 --executor-memory 63g
    --executor-cores 6
```

Figure 9.16 shows this new configuration. Note that we gave 63 GB of memory to each executor, not 64 GB; Spark only allows a maximum 255 GB to be allocated on each machine (256 GB less 1 GB for the OS).

> **SPARK TIP**   When configuring the memory and cores for your executors, it's useful to use the Master and Worker UIs typically on ports 8080 and 8081 respectively. These will give details of the memory and cores available for the cluster and each of the executors respectively.

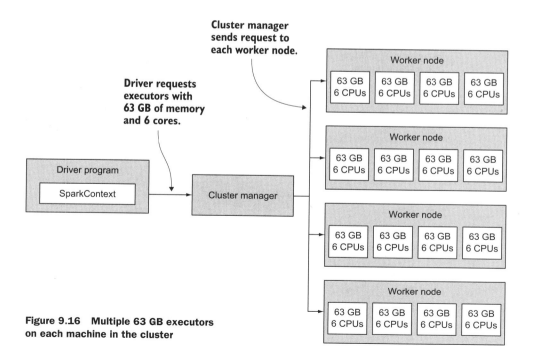

Figure 9.16   Multiple 63 GB executors on each machine in the cluster

9.2.1   *Utilizing all CPU cores*

Now that we have our cluster configured to make the maximum amount of CPU and memory resources available, we still need to ensure that we make full use of them. The next section covers memory usage, looking at caching and persistence. This section looks at maximizing CPU usage.

Using the parameters to `spark-shell` or `spark-submit`, we can ensure that memory and CPUs are available on the cluster for our application. But that doesn't guarantee that all the available memory or CPUs will be used.

As you've seen, Spark processes a stage by processing each partition separately. In fact, only one executor can work on a single partition, so if the number of partitions is less than the number of executors, the stage won't take advantage of the full resources available. Figure 9.17 shows an example.

> **TIP**   You can call `RDD.partitions.size` to find out how many partitions your RDD has.

In this case, a large number of vertices and edges will be packed into a single Spark partition. One way to resolve this problem is to use the `repartition` method on the RDD to supply a recommended new number of partitions:

```
val rdd = …
rdd.repartition(20)
```

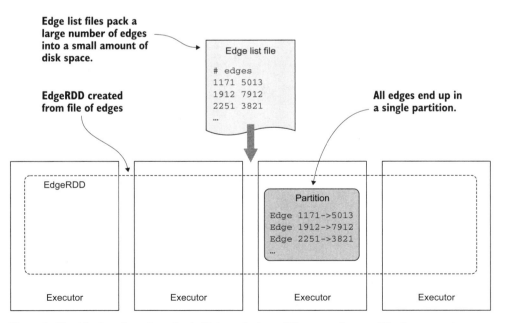

Figure 9.17   All edges have been loaded into a single partition, so only one of the four executors will process the resulting graph.

What determines the number of partitions? You've seen that RDDs are built into a chain of processing by transformations; the number of partitions for a RDD is based on the number of partitions in its parent RDD.

Eventually we reach an RDD without a parent. These are typically RDDs created from file or database storage. In the case of reading from HDFS, the number of partitions will be determined by the size for each HDFS block.

As a general rule, you want to ensure that you have at least as many partitions as cores. In fact, having two or three times as many partitions as cores is usually fine, due to Spark's low scheduling latency compared to Hadoop.

9.3 Spark performance tuning

Up to now, the discussion has concentrated on how Spark executes application code and how to configure Spark to efficiently utilize the computing resources available. But in order to make the best use of Spark's features, you should consider a number of tuning techniques. This section takes you through each one, describing when the technique should be used and giving the steps necessary to implement it.

9.3.1 Speeding up Spark with caching and persistence

We've already covered how Spark uses the notion of an RDD to embody a dataset. In addition, we've discussed the fundamentals of how Spark implements a chain of computations over an RDD: transformations are embedded in a chain of RDDs but only evaluated when an action is called. At this point, datasets are loaded from storage or databases, computations are performed, and results are returned. What happens if we repeatedly call actions on the RDD?

RDD PERSISTENCE

By default, an RDD doesn't retain the values it has computed. Instead, if another action is called on the chain of RDDs, the entire chain is recomputed. In some cases, this is fine. But for many machine learning and graph processing tasks, it's a problem. The algorithm will usually be iterative, executing many times on the same RDD, often resulting in time wasted continually reloading the data and repeating computations. Even worse, the algorithm will often proceed by building ever-longer chains of RDDs.

It seems like we need a way to make use of all the memory available across the cluster to store the results of RDDs. This is the purpose of caching (one type of persistence supported by Spark).

You can cache an RDD into memory by calling the `cache` method on the RDD object. The following code when executed in the `spark-shell` counts the number of lines in the file and then displays the contents of the file:

```
val filename = "..."
val rdd1 = sc.textFile(filename).cache
rdd1.count
rdd1.collect
```

Without the `cache` method, the file is read from storage when each action is called, resulting in the file being read twice. By calling the `cache` method, the first action (count) causes the RDD to keep the values it has calculated in memory. The RDD then uses the cached values for calculating the second action (`collect`).

Even if we build new RDDs by transformation of the cached RDD, the cached values will still be used. The following code will display all the comment lines (lines starting with #):

```
val rdd2 = rdd1.filter(_.startsWith("#"))
rdd2.collect
```

Because `rdd2` is derived from the cached `rdd1`, it shouldn't be necessary to reread the file from storage because `rdd1` has already cached its values in memory.

> **NOTE** The cache method acts as a flag to say the RDD should be cached but doesn't cause the RDD to be cached at that point. Caching occurs the next time the RDD is computed.

PERSISTENCE LEVELS

As mentioned, caching is one type of persistence. Table 9.3 shows some of the other persistence levels supported by Spark.

Table 9.3   Common persistence levels supported by Spark

Level	Description
MEMORY_ONLY	Store the RDD as Java objects in the JVM. If the RDD doesn't fit in memory, some partitions won't be cached and will be recomputed on the fly each time they're needed. This is the default storage level.
MEMORY_AND_DISK	Store the RDD as Java objects in the JVM. If the RDD doesn't fit in memory, store the partitions that don't fit on disk and read them from disk as needed.
MEMORY_ONLY_SER	Store the RDD as serialized Java objects. Usually more space-efficient than unserialized objects but more CPU-intensive to read and write.
MEMORY_AND_DISK_SER	Similar to MEMORY_ONLY_SER storage level, the RDD is stored as serialized Java objects, but if the RDD doesn't fit in memory, some partitions are evicted from memory and written to disk to be read as needed.
DISK_ONLY	Store the RDD partitions on disk rather than in memory. Useful if RDDs are much larger than available memory, and reading from source will be more time-consuming than reading from local disk.

Each of the persistence methods is represented by one of the `StorageLevel` objects defined by the singleton object `StorageLevel`. For example, calling `rdd.persist(StorageLevel.MEMORY_AND_DISK)` sets up the RDD for memory and disk caching. The cache method itself is implemented as a call to `rdd.persist(StorageLevel.MEMORY_ONLY)`. Section 3.3 covers MEMORY_ONLY_SER and MEMORY_AND_DISK_SER in more detail.

NOTE Additional persistence levels MEMORY_ONLY2, MEMORY_AND_DISK2, and so on are available that will replicate the RDD to other cluster nodes to provide fault-tolerance. That takes us beyond the scope of this book, but if interested you should consult a book such as *Spark in Action* by Petar Zečević and Marko Bonaći (Manning, 2016) that deals with Spark fault-tolerance in more depth.

GRAPH PERSISTENCE

You've seen that Spark constructs a `Graph` object from RDDs of vertices and edges. Whenever we call operations on the `Graph` object, such as `mapVertices` or `aggregate-Messages`, the `Graph` operates on the underlying RDDs.

The `Graph` class provides `cache` and `persist` convenience methods that call the `persist` methods of the underlying vertex and edge RDDs.

UNPERSIST AT THE RIGHT TIME

Though it may seem that caching is something so good it should be used everywhere, too much of a good thing can leave you wanting less of it.

As you cache more and more RDDs, the memory available will decrease. Eventually Spark will start evicting partitions from the cache (using a least-recently-used algorithm). You could let Spark do the job on its own, but by caching more objects than you need, excessive JVM garbage collection times become unavoidable. That's why it's usually desirable to call the `unpersist` method on the RDD when caching is no longer needed.

For iterative algorithms, this often results in the following method-calling pattern inside the algorithm loop:

- Call `cache` or `persist` on the `Graph`.
- Materialize the `Graph` by calling an action, which results in the underlying RDDs being cached..
- Execute the rest of the algorithm body.
- `unpersist` the RDD at the end of the loop.

You'll see an example of this in the next section on checkpointing.

TIP One of the benefits of using the Pregel API is that it deals with caching and uncaching for you.

WHEN NOT TO USE CACHING

Just because you can cache an RDD in memory doesn't mean you should blindly do so. Depending on how many times the dataset is accessed and the amount of work involved in doing so, recomputation can be faster than the price paid by the increased memory pressure.

It should go without saying that if you only read a dataset once, there's no point in caching it as this will make your job slower, especially if you use the serialized persistence options.

9.3.2 *Checkpointing*

A common pattern in graph algorithms is to update the graph with new data calculated during each iteration. What this means in practice is that the chain of Vertex and/or Edge RDDs that constitute the graph becomes longer and longer.

> **DEFINITION**   When an RDD is formed from a chain of ancestor RDDs, we say the path from the RDD to the root RDD is its lineage.

The next listing shows an example of this. It's a simple algorithm that generates a new set of vertices and updates the graph. The algorithm runs for a fixed number of iterations as controlled by the variable `iterations`.

Listing 9.2   A simple iterative graph update algorithm

```
val iterations = 500
var g = Graph.fromEdges (sc.makeRDD(
        Seq(Edge(1L,3L,1),Edge(2L,4L,1),Edge(3L,4L,1))),1)
for (i <- 1 to iterations) {
   println("Iteration: " + i)
   val newGraph: Graph[Int, Int] =
       g.mapVertices ((vid,vd)  => (vd * i)/17)
       g = g.outerJoinVertices[Int, Int](newGraph.vertices) {
                  (vid, vd, newData) => newData.getOrElse(0)
       }
}
g.vertices.collect.foreach(println)
```

Each call to `joinVertices` in this code adds a new RDD to the chain of Vertex RDDs.

Clearly we need to use caching to ensure that we don't have to recalculate the chain of RDDs on each iteration, but this doesn't change the fact that we have an ever-lengthening list of object references, from each RDD to its parent.

One consequence of this is that if we run a large number of iterations, we'll eventually hit a `StackOverflowError` in the code. A typical example is obtained if `iterations` is set to 500 in the code we ran.

Checkpointing is a feature provided by RDDs and inherited by `Graph`, designed to address the problem of long RDD lineages. The next listing demonstrates how to set up and call checkpointing. The code will now successfully run, outputting vertices for the resulting graph.

Listing 9.3   A simple iterative graph update algorithm with checkpointing

```
sc.setCheckpointDir("/tmp/spark-checkpoint")
var updateCount = 0
val checkpointInterval = 50
```

Call is necessary, otherwise no subsequent checkpoint call has any effect.

Record how many updates have occurred …

… because we will only checkpoint every 50 updates.

```
def update(newData: Graph[Int, Int]): Unit = {
  newData.persist()
  updateCount += 1
  if (updateCount % checkpointInterval == 0) {
    newData.checkpoint()
  }
}

val iterations = 500
var g = Graph.fromEdges (sc.makeRDD(Seq(Edge(1L,3L,1),
                        Edge(2L,4L,1),Edge(3L,4L,1))),1)
update(g)
g.vertices.count
for (i <- 1 to iterations) {
  println("Iteration: " + i)
  val newGraph: Graph[Int, Int] =
                g.mapVertices ((vid,vd) => (vd * i)/17)
  g = g.outerJoinVertices[Int, Int](newGraph.vertices) {
  (vid, vd, newData) => newData.getOrElse(0) }
  update(g)
  g.vertices.count
}
g.vertices.collect.foreach(println)
```

update method called every time graph is updated, caching and checkpointing as necessary.

Call update method after every update to graph and then materialize— otherwise nothing is cached or checkpointed.

Marking an RDD for checkpointing will result in the RDD being saved to a file inside a checkpoint directory, and the connection to the chain of parent RDDs being cut. Marking a Graph for checkpointing will result in the underlying Vertex and Edge RDDs being checkpointed.

You can set the checkpoint directory by calling `SparkContext.setCheckpointDir` and specifying a path on shared storage, such as HDFS.

As the listing shows, you must call `checkpoint` before any action is called on the RDD. Because checkpointing is a relatively costly activity (after all, we are writing the graph to disk), it's generally a good idea to only checkpoint as often as necessary to avoid errors—often this can be as infrequently as once every 100 or so iterations.

NOTE   One option to speed up checkpointing is to checkpoint to Tachyon instead of to a standard file system. Tachyon, from AMPLab, is a "memory centric fault-tolerant distributed file system, which enables file sharing at memory-speed across cluster frameworks, such as Spark."

9.3.3   *Reducing memory pressure with serialization*

Memory pressures are often one of the prime causes of poor performance and failures in Spark applications. Generally these problems manifest themselves as frequent, time-consuming JVM garbage collections and "Out of Memory" errors. Checkpointing won't help here because it doesn't relieve memory pressure. Instead, one of the first things you should think about is persisting your Graph objects using serialization.

DEFINITION   *Data serialization* is about transforming the JVM representation of object instances into a byte-stream representation that can be used to transport the object across the network to another JVM process. The object can then be "deserialized" from the byte-stream representation back into an object instance in the other JVM. Spark uses serialization for network transfers and also for caching objects in memory.

Using serialization means using the following serialization StorageLevels in the `persist` method:

- StorageLevel.MEMORY_ONLY_SER
- StorageLevel.MEMORY_AND_DISK_SER

Using serialization saves space at the expense of an increase in CPU necessary to serialize and deserialize objects.

USING KRYO SERIALIZER

The default serializer used in Spark is the `JavaSerializer`, which uses the standard but rather inefficient Java serialization framework. In general, it's better to use the Kryo serializer. Kryo is an open source Java serialization framework that provides fast and efficient serialization.

You can configure Spark to use the Kryo serializer by setting the `spark.serializer` parameter to `org.apache.spark.serializer.KryoSerializer`. One way to do this is on the command line, like this:

```
spark-shell --conf
    "spark.serializer=org.apache.spark.serializer.KryoSerializer"
```

This can become tedious for repeated use. An alternative is to create a conf directory and add a file called spark-defaults.conf. Put any spark parameters (like `spark.serializer`) in this file using standard properties file syntax (using a hard tab to separate the property name from the property value):

```
spark.serializer  org.apache.spark.serializer.KryoSerializer
```

For best performance, Kryo requires you to register classes with the serializer—otherwise, class names are written out with the serialized object bytes, leading to less-efficient serialization. Spark provides automatic registration for classes used by the Spark framework, but if you define custom classes in your application, those classes will need to be registered manually by calling `SparkConf.registerKryoClasses`. The following listing shows how to do this for a custom class, `Person`.

Define a custom Person class.

Listing 9.4   Using Kryo

```
import org.apache.spark.storage.StorageLevel

case class Person(name: String, age: Int)

val conf = new SparkConf()
conf.set("spark.serializer",

    "org.apache.spark.serializer.KryoSerializer")
```

To set Spark configuration parameters we need a SparkConf object passed to SparkContext.

Configuration required to use the Kryo serializer

```
conf.registerKryoClasses(Array(classOf[Person]))
val sc = new SparkContext (conf)
val rdd = sc.makeRDD(1 to 1000000).
        map(el => Person("John Smith", 42))
rdd.persist(StorageLevel.MEMORY_ONLY_SER)
rdd.count
```

> Registers custom class with Kryo—more than one class can be specified in the array.

CHECKING THE SIZE OF YOUR RDDS

When you tune your application, you'll often find that you need to know how big your RDDs are. This can be tricky because the size of objects in a file or database often has little relation to how much memory the object will take up.

One useful trick is to cache the RDD in memory and then use the Storage tab of the Application UI to record the size of the RDD. This idea also comes in handy when trying to measure the impact of configuring serialization.

9.4   *Graph partitioning*

Chapter 1 mentions partitioning strategy as being one of the advantages of GraphX—how it can do vertex cuts (partition edges into groups) instead of the more straightforward sharding of edge cuts (partition vertices into groups). But when you first construct a graph, either with `Graph.apply()` (invoked with the syntax `Graph()`) or the `GraphLoader`, the graph is "unpartitioned." `EdgeRDD` and `VertexRDD` have their own standard RDD partitioning, but the graph as a whole isn't partitioned in any logical fashion.

This can lead to poor performance; moreover, some methods such as `groupEdges()` and `triangleCount()` require the graph to be partitioned to work correctly.

Partitioning is accomplished via the `partitionBy()` method, and it takes one of the `PartitionStrategy`s as a parameter. To see the list of available `Partition-Strategy`s in the API docs, look at the object `PartitionStrategy` as opposed to the class/type `PartitionStrategy`. The four partitioning strategies (shown in figure 9.18) are as follows:

- `RandomVertexCut`—Usually the best strategy unless you have a reason to use one of the others. It's one of the two that uses vertex cut instead of edge cut. It optimally balances workload but is blind to communication costs.

- `CanonicalRandomVertexCut`—Same as `RandomVertexCut` except duplicate edges between any pair of vertices are assured to be in the same partition. But if your graph doesn't have any such duplicate edges, it can hurt performance when an algorithm needs to access the attribute of an edge that is on the perimeter of a partition.

- `EdgePartition1D`—Ensures that all edges for a vertex are on the same partition.

- `EdgePartition2D`—Takes the edge adjacency matrix and divides it up into tiles. It has the downside that it is designed to work on a number of partitions that is a perfect square (4, 9, 16, and so forth). If the number of partitions is not a perfect square, it rounds up to the nearest perfect square and allocates on the smaller number of partitions, resulting in a workload imbalance.

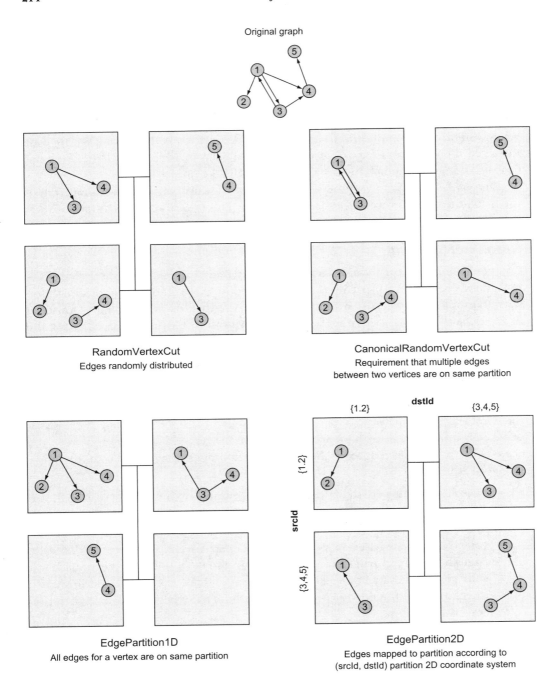

Figure 9.18 **The four different `PartitionStrategy` options showing how an example graph might be spread across four partitions**

Because vertices are partitioned independently of edges, there is no guarantee that an edge's two vertices will be available in the same partition (in fact, it is highly unlikely). Usually, Spark has to serialize edges and vertices to make `EdgeTriplets`. The `PartitionStrategy`, which affects only edges, allows a trade-off between load balancing (the two random strategies) and efficient access of groups of neighboring edges (the two edge partition strategies).

9.5   *Summary*

- All Spark applications operate as a series of *jobs* that are split into *stages*. Each *stage* creates executable *tasks* that perform processing on one partition of an RDD.

- Familiarity with the Spark Application UI is essential to understanding how your application is performing. The Jobs listing and detail screens provide raw stats for time and duration of jobs, stages, and tasks. The Event Timeline provides a visual insight into application performance.

- Tuning options include caching, checkpointing, serialization, and partitioning.

- Caching is a valuable tool when the same data is being queried repeatedly. By caching the data in memory, Spark avoids having to recreate the data from source each time it needs it. Different caching levels give you control over where the data is cached (in memory or on disk) and also whether cached data is serialized.

- Serialization provides better use of memory at the cost of additional CPU time when the data is accessed. Spark's default serializer is `JavaSerializer`, which uses the inefficient Java serialization framework. For fast and efficient serialization, we recommend you use the open source `KryoSerializer` instead.

- Certain data access patterns in Spark can create long chains of RDDs, resulting in `StackOverflowErrors`. This often occurs in iterative algorithms where a graph is repeatedly updated. To avoid this situation, you should checkpoint regularly. But you need to trade off the cost of checkpointing, so typically *regularly* means every 50 to 100 iterations.

Other languages and tools

So far we've done only Scala, and for visualization we've used only Gephi. In this chapter, you'll see how to use other languages supported by Spark. Although Spark supports other languages, their support from GraphX is limited at best. You'll also see how to visualize graphs using d3.js and Apache Zeppelin, which is notebook software similar to Mathematica, IPython Notebook, and Jupyter. A notebook has the advantage of combining a REPL-like interactive interface with visualization in one place.

Throughout this book we've repeated that GraphX is not a graph database. Well, with the addition of the external tool Spark Job Server, which adds a REST interface to Spark, one can almost have a (very) lightweight database using GraphX.

Finally, you'll see how to use the library GraphFrames, developed by some of the same people who developed GraphX, which makes querying graphs easier and faster than with GraphX.

10.1 Using languages other than Scala with GraphX

Although Scala is the native language of Spark, there are various reasons why one may want to use one of the other languages supported by Spark: personal preference, team or corporate preference, security, compatibility with preferred libraries, to name a few. As of the Spark 1.6 release, it's possible to use GraphX with Java 7 and Java 8, but there are no APIs provided for Python or R, and the APIs for Java are not easy to use. A true Java-friendly API for GraphX is the subject of Jira ticket SPARK-3665, which is not targeted for a particular release (as of Spark 1.6). There are several reasons why you might want to use Java with GraphX, but ease of use is not one of them. If you're considering using Java with GraphX because you're more familiar with Java than Scala, you'll want to rethink that decision. You have to write ten times as much code for Java as for Scala, a lot of it with obscure constructs. Plus, there is no REPL that comes with Java.

There are two other reasons to use Java that might make sense:

- Corporate mandate
- Compatibility with byte code tools such as Fortify that don't work as well with the myriad of .class byte code files generated by Scala

The first section on Java 7 covers all the intricacies of working with Java and GraphX. The lambda capabilities of Java 8 don't help very much with GraphX, and the section on Java 8 covers the limited places where Java 8 lambdas help. The last section provides details on the possibility of Python and R bindings being added to GraphX, but in short, they're not part of Apache Spark as of Spark 1.6.

10.1.1 Using GraphX with Java 7

In this section, we take the edge count example from section 4.2.3 and convert it to Java. Because Java doesn't come with a REPL, we need a pom.xml file for Maven, and we start with that.

The pom.xml in listing 10.1 is not surprising. There's one little nicety hidden in the inclusion of the `exec-maven-plugin`, and that's `cleanupDaemonThreads` being set to true. This allows the program to be executed with `mvn exec:java` and Maven won't complain about remaining Spark threads hanging around after shutdown.

Listing 10.1 pom.xml

```xml
<?xml version="1.0" encoding="UTF-8"?>
<project xmlns="http://maven.apache.org/POM/4.0.0"
    xmlns:xsi="http://www.w3.org/2001/XMLSchema-instance"
    xsi:schemaLocation="http://maven.apache.org/POM/4.0.0
                    http://maven.apache.org/xsd/maven-4.0.0.xsd">
  <modelVersion>4.0.0</modelVersion>
```

```
<groupId>com.manning</groupId>
<artifactId>graphx-propagate-edge-count</artifactId>
<version>1.0-SNAPSHOT</version>

<dependencies>
  <dependency>
    <groupId>org.apache.spark</groupId>
    <artifactId>spark-core_2.10</artifactId>
    <version>1.5.1</version>
  </dependency>
  <dependency>
    <groupId>org.apache.spark</groupId>
    <artifactId>spark-graphx_2.10</artifactId>
    <version>1.5.1</version>
  </dependency>
</dependencies>

<build>
  <plugins>
    <plugin>
      <groupId>org.codehaus.mojo</groupId>
      <artifactId>exec-maven-plugin</artifactId>
      <version>1.2.1</version>
      <executions>
        <execution>
          <goals>
            <goal>java</goal>
          </goals>
        </execution>
      </executions>
      <configuration>
        <mainClass>EdgeCount</mainClass>
        <cleanupDaemonThreads>false</cleanupDaemonThreads>
      </configuration>
    </plugin>
  </plugins>
</build>

</project>
```

The first thing you'll notice about the Java code in listing 10.2 is its length. Some of it is from the large number of imports needed to handle the Java/Scala interoperability, and some of it is from the more verbose syntax for constructing the example myVertices and myEdges. But there's also quite a bit of complicated code to handle the lambdas. The lambdas associated with the Spark Core calls map() and reduce() toward the end of the propagateEdgeCount() function aren't too bad. That's because the developers behind Apache Spark spent a lot of time making writing lambdas in Java for Spark Core as easy as possible. They didn't do so for GraphX.

The lambdas for Spark Core are instances of o.a.s.api.java.Function (where o.a.s. is an abbreviation for org.apache.spark), o.a.s.api.java.Function2, and so on, where Function is a lambda taking one parameter, Function2 is a lambda taking two parameters, and so forth.

In contrast, the lambdas for Spark GraphX are instances of scala.Function1, scala.Function2, and so on. If you look at the Javadocs (as opposed to the regular ScalaDocs) for GraphX, you'll see these in the signatures of functions like Graph.mapVertices(). But instantiating Function1, Function2, and so forth directly in Java is next to impossible due to the dozens of functions (most of which contain a $ sign somewhere in the name) you'd be required to override. That's why the Scala library provides scala.runtime.AbstractFunction1, scala.runtime.Abstract-Function2, and so forth for the convenience of Java programmers. With these, you only have to override the apply() function you're interested in. But wait, even that's not good enough for our needs, because Spark is not only functional, it's also distributed. Lambdas for Spark also need to be serializable, which AbstractFunction1, AbstractFunction2, and so on are not. We define SerializableFunction1 and SerializableFunction2 toward the top of the following listing and use those throughout instead of AbstractFunction1, AbstractFunction2, and so forth.

Listing 10.2   EdgeCount.java

```java
import java.io.Serializable;
import java.util.Arrays;
import java.util.List;

import scala.Tuple2;
import scala.reflect.ClassTag;
import scala.reflect.ClassTag$;
import scala.runtime.AbstractFunction1;
import scala.runtime.AbstractFunction2;
import scala.runtime.BoxedUnit;

import org.apache.spark.SparkConf;
import org.apache.spark.api.java.*;
import org.apache.spark.api.java.function.Function;
import org.apache.spark.api.java.function.Function2;
import org.apache.spark.api.java.function.PairFunction;
import org.apache.spark.graphx.*;
import org.apache.spark.rdd.RDD;
import org.apache.spark.storage.StorageLevel;

public class EdgeCount {
  // sendMsg and mergeMsg supplied to aggregateMessages()need to be
  // both Scala (for GraphX API) and Serializable (for Spark)
  static abstract class SerializableFunction1<T1,R>
    extends AbstractFunction1<T1,R> implements Serializable {}

  static abstract class SerializableFunction2<T1,T2,R>
    extends AbstractFunction2<T1,T2,R> implements Serializable {}

  public static void main(String[] args) {
    JavaSparkContext sc = new JavaSparkContext(
      new SparkConf().setMaster("local").setAppName("EdgeCount"));

    JavaRDD<Tuple2<Object, String>> myVertices =
      sc.parallelize(Arrays.asList(new Tuple2<Object,String>(1L, "Ann"),
        new Tuple2<Object,String>(2L, "Bill"),
```

```
          new Tuple2<Object,String>(3L, "Charles"),
          new Tuple2<Object,String>(4L, "Diane"),
          new Tuple2<Object,String>(5L, "Went to gym this morning"))));

  JavaRDD<Edge<String>> myEdges = sc.parallelize(Arrays.asList(
    new Edge<String>(1L, 2L, "is-friends-with"),
    new Edge<String>(2L, 3L, "is-friends-with"),
    new Edge<String>(3L, 4L, "is-friends-with"),
    new Edge<String>(4L, 5L, "Likes-status"),
    new Edge<String>(3L, 5L, "Wrote-status"))));

  Graph<String,String> myGraph = Graph.apply(myVertices.rdd(),
    myEdges.rdd(), "", StorageLevel.MEMORY_ONLY(),
    StorageLevel.MEMORY_ONLY(), tagString, tagString);

  Graph<Integer,String> initialGraph = myGraph.mapVertices(
    new SerializableFunction2<Object,String,Integer>() {
      public Integer apply(Object o, String s) { return 0; }
    },
    tagInteger, null);

  List<Tuple2<Object,Integer>> ls = toJavaPairRDD(
    propagateEdgeCount(initialGraph).vertices(), tagInteger).collect();

  for (Tuple2<Object,Integer> t : ls)
    System.out.print(t + " ** ");

  System.out.println();

  sc.stop();
}

// Must explicitly provide for implicit Scala parameters in various
// function calls
private static final ClassTag<Integer> tagInteger =
  ClassTag$.MODULE$.apply(Integer.class);
private static final ClassTag<String> tagString =
  ClassTag$.MODULE$.apply(String.class);
private static final ClassTag<Object> tagObject =
  ClassTag$.MODULE$.apply(Object.class);

// sendMsg
private static final SerializableFunction1<
    EdgeContext<Integer, String, Integer>, BoxedUnit> sendMsg =
  new SerializableFunction1<
      EdgeContext<Integer, String, Integer>, BoxedUnit>() {
    public BoxedUnit apply(EdgeContext<Integer, String, Integer> ec) {
      ec.sendToDst(ec.srcAttr()+1);
      return BoxedUnit.UNIT;
    }
  };

// mergeMsg
private static final SerializableFunction2<Integer, Integer, Integer>
  mergeMsg = new SerializableFunction2<Integer, Integer, Integer>() {
    public Integer apply(Integer a, Integer b) {
      return Math.max(a,b);
    }
  };
```

```
    private static <T> JavaPairRDD<Object,T>
        toJavaPairRDD(VertexRDD<T> v, ClassTag<T> tagT) {
      return new JavaPairRDD<Object,T>((RDD<Tuple2<Object,T>>)v,
                                        tagObject, tagT);
    }

    private static Graph<Integer,String> propagateEdgeCount(
        Graph<Integer,String> g) {
      VertexRDD<Integer> verts = g.aggregateMessages(
        sendMsg, mergeMsg, TripletFields.All, tagInteger);
      Graph<Integer,String> g2 = Graph.apply(verts, g.edges(), 0,
        StorageLevel.MEMORY_ONLY(), StorageLevel.MEMORY_ONLY(),
        tagInteger, tagString);
      int check = toJavaPairRDD(g2.vertices(), tagInteger)
        .join(toJavaPairRDD(g.vertices(), tagInteger))
        .map(new Function<Tuple2<Object,Tuple2<Integer,Integer>>,
                          Integer>() {
          public Integer call(Tuple2<Object,Tuple2<Integer,Integer>> t) {
            return t._2._1 - t._2._2;
          }
        })
        .reduce(new Function2<Integer, Integer, Integer>() {
          public Integer call(Integer a, Integer b) {return a+b;}
        });
      if (check > 0)
        return propagateEdgeCount(g2);
      else
        return g;
    }
  }
```

There are other API changes to note:

- `JavaSparkContext` instead of `SparkContext`.
- `Object` instead of `VertexId`. If you need to compare the values, you'll have to cast the `Object` to `Long` at those places you need to.
- `parallelize()` instead of `makeRDD()`.
- `parallelize()` only works on `Lists` and not `Arrays`.

Due to lambdas always needing to return a value and the lack of `Unit` in Java, Scala provides the singleton `scala.runtime.BoxedUnit.UNIT` for that purpose.

A lot of Scala niceties aren't available in Java. One that's quickly missed is default parameters. Every single parameter has to be supplied in calling the GraphX Java APIs. For example, the call to `Graph.apply()` to create the graph takes seven parameters instead of two as in Scala. To fill all these parameters, it's often necessary to consult with the ScalaDocs to see what the defaults were.

Some of those default parameters are the implicit `ClassTags` that Scala automatically supplies. In Java, you have to compute and supply them manually every time.

Also missed are the automatic conversions between `RDD` and `PairRDD` (or in the case of Java, between `JavaRDD` and `JavaPairRDD`). That's why we wrote a helper function `toJavaPairRDD()` to force that conversion where we needed it.

10.1.2 *Using GraphX with Java 8*

Many think of Java 8 as introducing elements of Scala-like functional programming to Java. But Java 8 lambdas only help with the Spark Core, and in listing 10.2 the only Spark Core lambdas were the `map()` and `reduce()` used to compute the variable check. The next listing shows the computation of check using Java 8 lambdas.

> **Listing 10.3   EdgeCount.java fragment converted to Java 8 lambdas**

```
int check = toJavaPairRDD(g2.vertices(), tagInteger)
    .join(toJavaPairRDD(g.vertices(), tagInteger))
    .map(t -> t._2._1 - t._2._2)
    .reduce((a,b) -> a+b);
```

10.1.3 *Whether GraphX may gain Python or R bindings in the future*

Python bindings to GraphX are the subject of Jira ticket SPARK-3789, which as of the Spark 1.6 release has not been targeted for a particular Spark release. As for R bindings, an AMPLab developer suggested on the Apache Spark User mailing list on August 6, 2015 that although it might make sense to expose to R programmers interfaces to high-level algorithms like PageRank, it might not make sense to expose the entire GraphX API. GraphFrames, covered in section 10.4, do offer Python bindings.

10.2 *Another visualization tool: Apache Zeppelin plus d3.js*

Instead of having a separate Spark REPL and Gephi to visualize graphs, the combination of Apache Zeppelin and d3.js can give you the powerful capability of visualizing graphs inline in a REPL-like notebook. The only downside is that tweaking the visualizations requires some knowledge of d3.js and JavaScript, which are outside the scope of this book. But we provide you with some code here to get you started. The visualizations this starting point gives you may be good enough as quick visualizations, and you can use Gephi if you need something more sophisticated.

The notebook concept is a powerful one started by Mathematica and later imitated by IPython Notebook, which is now known as Jupyter. Zeppelin is a variation on the theme, except that it comes with Spark built in, making it trivial to download and be productive immediately. Figure 10.1 shows how the notebook concept allows you to interleave Spark commands with visualizations.

To get started, download Zeppelin from https://zeppelin.apache.org and then perform the following steps at the Linux command line (you may need to change the version numbers):

```
tar -xzvf zeppelin-0.5.6-incubating-bin-all.tgz
./zeppelin-0.5.6-incubating-bin-all/bin/zeppelin-daemon.sh start
xdg-open http://localhost:8080
```

This last step opens up a web browser to port 8080. From the browser page, click "Create new note."

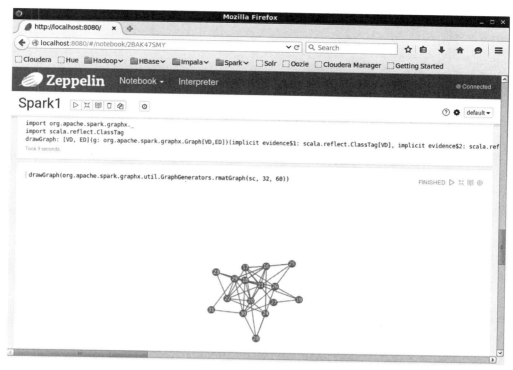

Figure 10.1   Zeppelin is like the Spark REPL except that visualizations can be displayed inline.

Like most other modern notebook software, Zeppelin supports inline JavaScript, and that means it can use the d3.js visualization library for JavaScript. Listing 10.4 shows how to do some basic visualization, the results of which are shown in figure 10.1. To customize it further (such as by adding edge labels, positioning the vertex labels, or adding arrowheads for directed graphs), you'll need to customize the JavaScript code. The book *D3.js in Action* by Elijah Meeks (Manning, 2015) may be of some help.

Listing 10.4   `drawGraph` in d3.js JavaScript and Scala

```
import org.apache.spark.graphx._
import scala.reflect.ClassTag
def drawGraph[VD:ClassTag,ED:ClassTag](g:Graph[VD,ED]) = {
val u = java.util.UUID.randomUUID
val v = g.vertices.collect.map(_._1)
println("""%html
<div id='a""" + u + """' style='width:960px; height:500px'></div>
<style>
.node circle { fill: gray; }
.node text { font: 10px sans-serif;
             text-anchor: middle;
             fill: white; }
line.link { stroke: gray;
            stroke-width: 1.5px; }
```

```
</style>
<script src="//d3js.org/d3.v3.min.js"></script>
<script>
var width = 960, height = 500;

var svg = d3.select("#a""" + u + """").append("svg")
    .attr("width", width).attr("height", height);

var nodes = [""" + v.map("{id:" + _ + "}").mkString(",") + """];
var links = [""" + g.edges.collect.map(
  e => "{source:nodes[" + v.indexWhere(_ == e.srcId) + "],target:nodes[" +
      v.indexWhere(_ == e.dstId) + "]}").mkString(",") + """];

var link = svg.selectAll(".link").data(links);
link.enter().insert("line", ".node").attr("class", "link");

var node = svg.selectAll(".node").data(nodes);
var nodeEnter = node.enter().append("g").attr("class", "node")

nodeEnter.append("circle").attr("r", 8);

nodeEnter.append("text").attr("dy", "0.35em")
        .text(function(d) { return d.id; });

d3.layout.force().linkDistance(50).charge(-200).chargeDistance(300)
    .friction(0.95).linkStrength(0.5).size([width, height])
    .on("tick", function() {
        link.attr("x1", function(d) { return d.source.x; })
            .attr("y1", function(d) { return d.source.y; })
            .attr("x2", function(d) { return d.target.x; })
            .attr("y2", function(d) { return d.target.y; });
        node.attr("transform", function(d) {
          return "translate(" + d.x + "," + d.y + ")";
        });
    }).nodes(nodes).links(links).start();
</script>
""")
}
```

If you paste the code from the listing into a Zeppelin cell, you can test it out in another cell with something like this:

```
drawGraph(org.apache.spark.graphx.util.GraphGenerators.rmatGraph(sc,32,60))
```

The code from listing 10.4 is a mix of Scala and JavaScript, and in order to inject the vertex and edge data into the JavaScript, in the Scala code it does a bit of code generation of JavaScript. To fine-tune the layouts, you can play with the parameters set following the `d3.layout.force()`, documented at https://github.com/mbostock/d3/wiki/Force-Layout. It doesn't require a great deal of JavaScript knowledge to tweak the colors and canvas size, but label positioning, arrowheads, and so on are probably going to require d3.js expertise.

10.3 *Almost a database: Spark Job Server*

The entirety of this book has been about how GraphX is a graph processing system rather than a database. It does processing in batch (as a "job") on graph data and spits out a result at the end.

Well, given the hammer of Spark that a growing number of developers and enterprises have in their toolbox, it's possible to fashion something that slightly resembles a database using GraphX. It won't have anything like transactions or locking, but it may be good enough for your purposes.

In early 2014, the streaming video technology company Ooyala started a GitHub project called Spark Job Server for the purpose of sharing RDDs. Spark Job Server deserves its own chapter, if not its own book, but in this section we'll show a quick example of using it with GraphX.

For the reason behind why Spark Job Server was created, consider developers new to Spark. They often say to themselves: Well, I've got all this great data stored in RDDs—how can I share it among multiple applications? You can't, because an RDD is tied to a `SparkContext`, and the `SparkContext` is tied to a particular JVM application. You can't share RDDs unless you're using Spark Job Server (for now—at least until long-standing Jira ticket SPARK-2389 gets resolved). Figure 10.2 shows how Spark Job Server maintains the single `SparkContext` and allows incoming REST calls to use that sole `SparkContext`.

With a GraphX graph loaded into Spark Job Server, multiple applications can "query" this common graph. That can be useful even for a single application if the Spark cluster is a being used in cluster mode rather than client mode. Cluster versus client mode is out of scope for this book, but suffice it to say that in cluster mode the application doesn't maintain hold of the `SparkContext`, so for a cluster used in cluster mode, Spark Job Server can allow a single application to reuse an RDD (or `Graph`) over and over again without having to submit a new Spark job and reload the data from distributed storage.

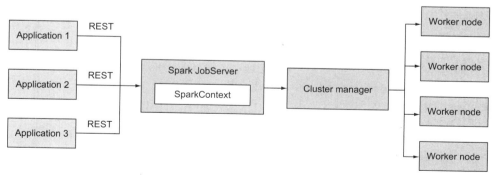

Figure 10.2 Spark Job Server maintains the `SparkContext`, which in turn has its associated RDD references and allows multiple applications to share the same `SparkContext` and share the same RDDs. A graph of reference data can be loaded up into a Spark Job Server job, and multiple applications can "query" this reference graph. Even providing a way to update the graph is not out of the question.

10.3.1 *Example: Query Slashdot friends degree of separation*

In this example of using Spark Job Server to provide a static set of graph data that can be queried, we show how to install and launch Spark Job Server, how to build a .jar that can be loaded in Spark Job Server, and how to issue REST calls against it. We use the same dataset from SNAP as in section 5.2.2—the Slashdot friends and foes dataset—and we provide the ability to query, given two Slashdot user ID numbers, the degrees of separation (as in Kevin Bacon) between those two users.

INSTALL AND LAUNCH SPARK JOB SERVER

First, make sure there isn't a Spark Job Server already running. With old versions of the Cloudera QuickStart VM, you might find an obsolete Spark Job Server running. You can kill that with the following:

```
sudo pkill -f spark-jobserver
sudo rm -r /tmp/spark-jobserver
```

Next we'll clone the Spark Job Server GitHub repository and choose the branch that corresponds to Spark 1.4.1. At the time of this writing, that's the most recently named branch. You may want to use the master branch instead if you can ascertain which version of Spark it's targeting.

```
git clone https://github.com/spark-jobserver/spark-jobserver.git
cd spark-jobserver
git checkout jobserver-0.6.0-spark-1.4.1
sed -i '/spark-core/a "org.apache.spark" %% "spark-graphx" % sparkVersion,'
➥ project/Dependencies.scala
sbt
reStart
```

DOWNLOAD THE SLASHDOT DATA

Next, get the Slashdot data and put it in our home directory:

```
cd ~
wget http://snap.stanford.edu/data/soc-Slashdot0811.txt.gz
gzip -d ~/soc-Slashdot0811.txt.gz
```

BUILD THE CUSTOM JOB SERVER JOB JAR

To build the custom job jar, we use sbt, as shown in listing 10.5. As with other sbt-based projects like those in this book, the .scala file in listing 10.6 goes into the src/main/scala directory. Ensure that the Spark version numbers and the Spark Job Server version number match the version numbers in the Spark Job Server branch name selected earlier.

> **Listing 10.5 sjsslashdot.sbt**

```
scalaVersion := "2.10.4"
resolvers += "Job Server Bintray" at
➥ "https://dl.bintray.com/spark-jobserver/maven"
libraryDependencies += "org.apache.spark" %% "spark-core" % "1.4.1"
```

```
libraryDependencies += "org.apache.spark" %% "spark-graphx" % "1.4.1"
libraryDependencies += "spark.jobserver" %% "job-server-api" % "0.6.0" %
➡ "provided"
```

Listing 10.6   sjsslashdot.scala

```
import org.apache.spark.SparkContext
import org.apache.spark.graphx._
import org.apache.spark.graphx.lib.ShortestPaths

import com.typesafe.config.Config

import spark.jobserver._

object Degrees extends SparkJob {
  val filename = System.getProperty("user.home") + "/soc-Slashdot0811.txt"
  var g:Option[Graph[Int,Int]] = None

  override def runJob(sc:SparkContext, config:Config) = {
    if (!g.isDefined)
      g = Some(GraphLoader.edgeListFile(sc, filename).cache)

    val src = config.getString("src").toInt

    if (g.get.vertices.filter(_._1 == src).isEmpty)
      -1
    else {
      val r = ShortestPaths.run(g.get, Array(src))
                           .vertices
                           .filter(_._1 == config.getString("dst").toInt)
      if (r.isEmpty || r.first._2.toList.isEmpty) -1
      else r.first._2.toList.head._2
    }
  }

  override def validate(sc:SparkContext, config:Config) = SparkJobValid
}
```

Then it's simple to build:

```
sbt package
```

LOAD JOB JAR

To interface with Spark Job Server requires making REST calls. Here you'll use curl to make REST calls, but normally you would do this under control of, for example, a Java or Scala program.

The following code submits the job jar to Spark Job Server and gives it the label sd. Then it asks Spark Job Server to create a SparkContext called sdcontext:

```
curl --data-binary @/home/cloudera/sjsslashdot/target/
➡ scala-2.10/sjsslashdot_2.10-0.1-SNAPSHOT.jar localhost:8090/jars/sd
curl -d "" 'localhost:8090/contexts/sdcontext'
```

SOME EXAMPLE QUERIES

Interrogating our "database" involves more REST queries. The code in sjsslashdot
.scala is set up to tell us the degrees of separation between any two given users. In the
next bit of code we find out that Slashdot users 0 and 1000 are separated by two
degrees of separation. Note that we're throwing a couple of Spark Job Server flags
into the REST parameters that you normally wouldn't use in production. First, we set
sync=true for a synchronous call; normally in the REST world for a long-executing
function, you would make an asynchronous call and poll for its completion. Second,
along with that, we specify a longish timeout of 100 milliseconds:

```
curl -d '{"src":0, "dst":1000}' 'localhost:8090/jobs?appName=sd
➥ &classPath=Degrees&context=sdcontext&sync=true&timeout=100'
{
  "result": 2
}
```

As expected, a user to himself/herself is zero degrees of separation:

```
curl -d '{"src":1000, "dst":1000}' 'localhost:8090/jobs?appName=sd
➥ &classPath=Degrees&context=sdcontext&sync=true&timeout=100'
{
  "result": 0
}
```

Sometimes the chains can be quite long:

```
curl -d '{"src":77182, "dst":77359}' 'localhost:8090/jobs?appName=sd
➥ &classPath=Degrees&context=sdcontext&sync=true&timeout=100'
{
  "result": 10
}
```

10.3.2 *More on using Spark Job Server*

We could say much more about Spark Job Server. For example, Spark Job Server represents a single point of failure. It has no redundancy built in. You could try running a
Spark Job Server on two machines with a load balancer in front, but you'd need to
ensure all your jobs were completely stateless. All of the state operated on by your job
would have to be derived from a combination of distributed storage (HDFS) files and
data/state sent as part of the REST request.

Spark Job Server provides a facility for creating "named RDDs" that we didn't use
earlier—we kept the RDD in a Scala var, which is simpler if you don't need the named
RDD facility.

Finally, there's the override validate() that we stubbed out above. This can be
used, for example, to determine whether your job is ready to accept requests before
issuing a long-running request.

The example laid out in this section is a read-only example. If you want to provide
an updatable graph, you would have to roll your own synchronization/locking mecha-
nism. But using Spark Job Server with GraphX is a way of avoiding (if you want to)
standing up another cluster such as Neo4j.

10.4   Using SQL with Spark graphs with GraphFrames

Looking ahead to the future of graphs on Spark, a new graphing library called Graph-Frames, which is not part of Spark as of Spark 1.6, promises better performance and easier querying. It provides a lot of the same functionality as GraphX, but adds the ability to query using a combination of the languages Cypher (from Neo4j) and SQL. In this section we show basic usage, look at performance, and expand chapter 8's poor-man's graph isomorphisms into something a little more complex.

GraphFrames makes use of the Spark SQL component of Spark and its DataFrames API. DataFrames offers much better performance than the RDDs that GraphX uses because of two optimization layers that Spark SQL provides, known as Catalyst and Tungsten. Catalyst is the original AMPLab name of Spark SQL, but now refers to the database-style query plan optimizer part of Spark SQL. Tungsten is another, newer layer introduced in Spark 1.4 that speeds up memory access by doing direct C++ style memory access using the direct memory API that bypasses the JVM, known as `sun.misc.unsafe`.

For a deeper dive into Spark SQL, see *Spark in Action* by Petar Zečević and Marko Bonaći (Manning, 2016). For those familiar with Python, GraphFrames exposes a Python API right from the beginning, but as with using Python Spark SQL, knowing SQL is still required.

In this version of GraphFrames, for Map/Reduce type operations there's an `AggregateMessagesBuilder` class, which serves a similar purpose to GraphX's `aggregateMessages()`, but there's no Pregel API. GraphFrames's strength is in querying graphs rather than the massively parallel algorithms that are GraphX's forte, but it would require benchmarking to determine which is faster for which application. GraphX has the optimization of maintaining routing tables internally between vertices and edges so that it can form triplets quickly. But GraphFrames has the Catalyst and Tungsten performance layers that GraphX doesn't have.

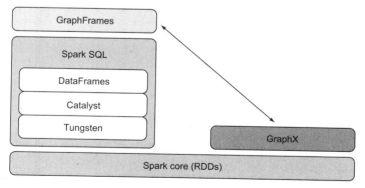

Figure 10.3   Because GraphFrames is based on DataFrames rather than RDDs, it's much faster than GraphX due to the Catalyst and Tungsten performance layers built into Spark SQL. Catalyst, the query optimizer, and Tungsten, the direct memory manager that bypasses the JVM, can be considered turbo-charger add-ons. GraphX has no way to optimize `join()`s, for example, and must go through the JVM for all memory operations.

10.4.1 *Getting GraphFrames, plus GraphX interoperability*

As of Spark 1.6, GraphFrames is out on GitHub. In later versions, GraphFrames may be available on spark-packages.org (see appendix C) or as part of the Apache Spark distribution itself. To download and build the precise version used in this book, execute the following commands (for more information about Git, see *Git in Practice* by Mike McQuaid [Manning, 2014]):

```
cd ~
git clone https://github.com/graphframes/graphframes.git
cd graphframes
git checkout b9f3a30
sbt package
```

Then, to launch the Spark REPL with the GraphFrames jar:

```
./spark-shell --jars ~/graphframes/target/scala-2.10/graphframes_2.10-0.0.1-
    SNAPSHOT.jar
```

The fundamental graph type in GraphFrames is the `GraphFrame`. A `GraphFrame` contains two `DataFrame`s from Spark SQL (see figure 10.4), where `vertices` is expected to have a data column called `id` and `edges` is expected to have data columns called `src` and `dst`. Additional user columns for vertex and edge properties can be added.

The GraphFrames API provides functions to convert `GraphFrame`s to and from GraphX `Graph`s. For example, assuming myGraph has been defined in the Spark Shell as from listing 4.1

```
import org.graphframes._
val gf = GraphFrame.fromGraphX(myGraph)
val g = gf.toGraphX
```

Note, though, that when converting back into GraphX, the parameterized `VertexRDD` and `EdgeRDD` are based on `Row` from Spark SQL rather than on any user-defined type-safe data type.

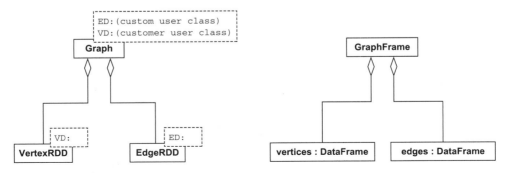

Figure 10.4 Whereas the fundamental graph type in GraphX is `Graph`, in GraphFrames it's `GraphFrame`. The parameterized type system isn't used in GraphFrames—rather there's a convention (enforced at runtime) where columns in the `DataFrames` are expected to have particular names.

EXAMPLE: TRIANGLE COUNT

Although GraphFrames is generally much faster than GraphX, the exceptions, at least as of this version of GraphFrames, are the built-in algorithms. That's because this version of GraphFrames converts the GraphFrame to a GraphX Graph and forwards the call to GraphX. Assuming the graph g2 is defined as from listing 5.2, the next listing shows the performance difference in the Triangle Count algorithm between Graph-Frames and GraphX.

Listing 10.7 Benchmarking Triangle Count in GraphFrames

```
import org.graphframes._
val gf = GraphFrame.fromGraphX(g2)
def time[A](f: => A) = {
  val s = System.nanoTime
  val ret = f
  println("time: " + (System.nanoTime-s)/1e9 + "sec")
  ret
}

time { g2.triangleCount.vertices.map(_._2).reduce(_ + _) }
time: 3.562754321sec
     res0: Int = 2592813

time { gf.triangleCount.run.vertices.groupBy().sum("count")
        .collect()(0)(0).asInstanceOf[Long] }
time: 6.493085995sec

res1: Long = 2592813
```

This code uses the DataFrame functions groupBy() and sum() to do the aggregation, but in the next subsection you'll see how to use SQL.

10.4.2 Using SQL for convenience and performance

In this section, we'll see how implementing functions in GraphFrames is not merely convenient due to SQL but also results in faster execution times. In section 8.5, we tackled reading RDF files, a standard file format for graph "triplets." From a GraphX perspective (and GraphFrames, as well), the challenge is assigning vertex IDs and matching vertex names with the made-up vertex IDs—because RDF files have no vertex IDs in them, only vertex labels. To accomplish this, the readRdf() from listing 8.5 has lots of complicated join()s and remappings. When implemented in Graph-Frames, the code is not only simpler and easier, but the performance is also improved by a factor of eight, as shown in the next listing.

Listing 10.8 readRdf() rewritten in GraphFrames

```
import org.apache.spark.sql.Row
import org.apache.spark.sql.types._
def readRdfDf(sc:org.apache.spark.SparkContext, filename:String) = {
  val r = sc.textFile(filename).map(_.split("\t"))
  val v = r.map(_(1)).union(r.map(_(3))).distinct.zipWithIndex.map(
```

```
                          x => Row(x._2,x._1))
// We must have an "id" column in the vertices DataFrame;
// everything else is just properties we assign to the vertices
val stv = StructType(StructField("id",LongType) ::
                     StructField("attr",StringType) :: Nil)
val sqlContext = new org.apache.spark.sql.SQLContext(sc)
val vdf = sqlContext.createDataFrame(v,stv)
vdf.registerTempTable("v")
val str = StructType(StructField("rdfId",StringType) ::
                     StructField("subject",StringType) ::
                     StructField("predicate",StringType) ::
                     StructField("object",StringType) :: Nil)
sqlContext.createDataFrame(r.map(Row.fromSeq(_)),str)
        .registerTempTable("r")
// We must have an "src" and "dst" columns in the edges DataFrame;
// everything else is just properties we assign to the edges
val edf = sqlContext.sql("SELECT vsubject.id AS src," +
                         "       vobject.id AS dst," +
                         "       predicate AS attr " +
                         "FROM   r " +
                         "JOIN   v AS vsubject" +
                         "  ON   subject=vsubject.attr " +
                         "JOIN   v AS vobject" +
                         "  ON   object=vobject.attr")
  GraphFrame(vdf,edf)
}
```

In this listing there is still some use of RDDs. This is because as of Spark 1.6, Data-Frames don't have `zip()` or `zipWithIndex()` and trying to convert back and forth between RDDs and `DataFrames` would result in slower performance. Adding `zip()` to `DataFrame` is the subject of Jira ticket SPARK-7460.

10.4.3 *Searching for vertices with the Cypher subset*

In section 3.3.4 you saw how much easier it is to use the Cypher query language from the Neo4j graph database technology to answer the question "Show me the friends of the friends of Ann" (for example, in the graph that's repeated in figure 10.5). To attempt the query in GraphX required several lines of dense code, whereas in query languages such as Cypher, it only required one or two lines of simple query code.

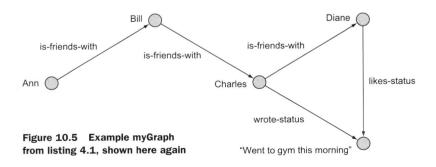

Figure 10.5 Example myGraph from listing 4.1, shown here again

QUERYING MYGRAPH FROM LISTING 4.1

GraphFrames supports a limited subset of Cypher that makes such queries easy. The subset of Cypher that GraphFrames supports doesn't allow vertex or edge names to be matched; it only allows the miniature graph structures to be queried. Querying on vertex and edge names has to be a second step using standard Spark SQL-querying facilities.

Then, assuming myGraph from listing 4.1 has been loaded into the Spark REPL, the following listing finds the friends of the friends of Ann.

Listing 10.9 Finding the friends of the friends of Ann using the Cypher subset

```
val gf = GraphFrame.fromGraphX(myGraph)
gf.find("(u)-[e1]->(v); (v)-[e2]->(w)")
  .filter("e1.attr = 'is-friends-with' AND " +
          "e2.attr = 'is-friends-with' AND " +
          "u.attr='Ann'")
  .select("w.attr")
  .collect
  .map(_(0).toString)
res2: Array[String] = Array(Charles)
```

The ()-[]->() syntax is intended to invoke a graph diagram, where the () are supposed to represent vertices and the edge label is contained with the []. Putting a variable placeholder name inside the () or [] is optional, but if you do, it gives you the option to query against it in a subsequent Spark SQL query. Also, variable placeholder names that are repeated in () for vertices refer to same vertex, creating a graph structure. An example of this is shown in figure 10.6.

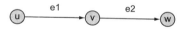

Figure 10.6 The graph fragment represented by the Cypher syntax (u)-[e1]->(v); (v)-[e2]->w. This will find all graph fragments that match this structure—specifically, where the destination vertex of the first edge matches the source vertex of the second edge.

This code is much simpler than trying to use aggregateMessages() from GraphX, which is intended for massively parallel graph computation, not for finding particular graph vertices or graph fragments.

DIFFERENCES IN TRIPLETS() BETWEEN GRAPHFRAMES AND GRAPHX

GraphFrames does provide a triplets() function, but as you might assume, it returns a DataFrame rather than an RDD. The implementation behind Graph-Frames.triplets is surprisingly simple. With the string constants expanded out, and assuming gf is a GraphFrame, the implementation is the following aesthetically pleasing Cypher code:

```
gf.find("(src)-[edge]->(dst)")
```

Now if you execute `triplets()` from the Spark REPL on `gf` (derived from `myGraph`) from the previous subsection, you get something that seems a little complicated:

```
scala> gf.triplets.show
+--------------------+-----------+--------------------+
|                edge|        src|                 dst|
+--------------------+-----------+--------------------+
|[1,2,is-friends-w...|    [1,Ann]|            [2,Bill]|
|[2,3,is-friends-w...|   [2,Bill]|         [3,Charles]|
|[3,4,is-friends-w...|[3,Charles]|           [4,Diane]|
|   [3,5,Wrote-status]|[3,Charles]|[5,Went to gym th...|
|   [4,5,Likes-status]|   [4,Diane]|[5,Went to gym th...|
+--------------------+-----------+--------------------+
```

Each column in the resulting DataFrame is a structure (struct). Structures were introduced in SQL:1999, which in the world of SQL means it's a "new" feature, relative to the better-known parts of SQL. Spark SQL DataFrames do handle structures, but—as of Spark 1.6—not always in a friendly way. For example, to retrieve the edge attribute, you have to know it's called `attr` and is of type `String`. You have to explicitly reference it by name and explicitly cast it to its type:

```
scala> gf.triplets.select("edge.attr").map(_(0).toString).collect
res3: Array[String] = Array(is-friends-with, is-friends-with,
is-friends-with, Wrote-status, Likes-status)
```

There's no way to convert the `edge` struct into a `List` of attributes, for example, or into a Scala Tuple or Map.

10.4.4 *Slightly more complex isomorphic searching on YAGO*

In section 8.3, we identified information potentially missing from Wikipedia by plugging a set of edges from the YAGO graph into the recommender algorithm SVD++. We saw, based on pairs of (country, exported item) pairs extracted from the larger YAGO graph, that Canada should probably be associated with exporting electronics.

With the power of the Cypher subset language, we can search not for only pairs of vertices but also for triangles. Specifically, we can search for triangles with a missing edge, as shown in figure 10.7.

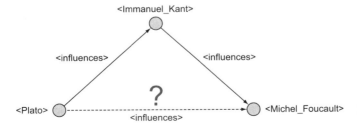

Figure 10.7   A potentially missing edge from Wikipedia, found using Cypher

In this example, we again use the file yagoFacts.tsv, but consider people (philosophers, poets, artists, and so on) who influence one another, as indicated by the edge "<influences>." We look for highly influential people like Plato who statistically influence directly those who are influenced indirectly. In listing 10.10, absent (aliased as table a) is a DataFrame containing all the triangles with the missing third edge, and **present** (aliased as table p) is a DataFrame containing all the triangles with all three edges. The code to compute absent introduces the Cypher operator ! (exclamation point), which looks for missing edges.

Prior to executing the next listing, first pare down the size of the yagoFacts.tsv file by using grep to retain only the lines containing "<influences>":

```
grep "<influences>" yagoFacts.tsv >yagoFactsInfluences.tsv
```

Listing 10.10 Using Cypher and graph isomorphisms to find missing Wikipedia info

```
val in = readRdfDf(sc, "yagoFactsInfluences.tsv")

in.edges.registerTempTable("e")
in.vertices.registerTempTable("v")

val in2 = GraphFrame(in.vertices.sqlContext.sql(
                "SELECT v.id," +
                "       FIRST(v.attr) AS attr," +
                "       COUNT(*) AS outdegree " +
                "FROM   v " +
                "JOIN   e " +
                "  ON   v.id=e.src " +
                "GROUP BY v.id").cache,
              in.edges)

val absent = in2.find("(v1)-[]->(v2); (v2)-[]->(v3); !(v1)-[]->(v3)")
absent.registerTempTable("a")

val present = in2.find("(v1)-[]->(v2); (v2)-[]->(v3); (v1)-[]->(v3)")
present.registerTempTable("p")

absent.sqlContext.sql(
  "SELECT v1 an," +
  "       SUM(v1.outdegree * v2.outdegree * v3.outdegree) AS ac " +
  "FROM   a " +
  "GROUP BY v1").registerTempTable("aa")

present.sqlContext.sql(
  "SELECT v1 pn," +
  "       SUM(v1.outdegree * v2.outdegree * v3.outdegree) AS pc " +
  "FROM   p " +
  "GROUP BY v1").registerTempTable("pa")

absent.sqlContext.sql("SELECT an," +
                "       ac * pc/(ac+pc) AS score " +
                "FROM   aa " +
                "JOIN   pa" +
                "  ON   an=pn " +
                "ORDER BY score DESC").show
```

The results to this last query, shown next, show that Plato is the most influential in terms of also directly influencing everyone he indirectly (by two degrees of separation) influences. In the computation, we used a scoring formula. The core of that scoring formula, `pc/(ac+pc)`, is a straight percentage of complete triangles divided by total number of (both complete and incomplete) triangles. Then we threw in a multiplication by ac. This is a heuristic we made up to give favor to well-known people.

```
+--------------------+--------------------+
|                  an|               score|
+--------------------+--------------------+
|   [7662,<Plato>,102]|  3.822406412297308E7|
|[10648,<Aristotle...|3.2961326121938106E7|
|[4959,<Immanuel_K...|2.6445857520978764E7|
|[2961,<Georg_Wilh...|2.1092802441273782E7|
|[9304,<Baruch_Spi...|1.4513392385496272E7|
|[12217,<René_Desc...|1.2407118036818413E7|
|[12660,<Johann_Wo...|1.0109121178397963E7|
|[11895,<Jean-Jacq...|   9081581.748842742|
|[11615,<Gottfried...|   7146037.710399863|
|[2025,<Friedrich_...|  6897244.1896990575|
|[1082,<William_Sh...|   4168778.144288711|
|[11034,<Adam_Smit...|  4100936.5022027283|
|[1121,<John_Locke...|   3868447.819527024|
|[1566,<Heraclitus...|  3616900.3025887734|
|[3746,<Karl_Marx>...|   3575419.671920321|
|[10954,<Søren_Kie...|  3143375.914849735|
|[7322,<David_Hume...|  3122089.3473657905|
|[8540,<Arthur_Sch...|   2978239.727690162|
|[3186,<Ibn_Tufail...|  2234249.031615453|
|[8267,<Epicurus>,24]|  1812594.4073720106|
+--------------------+--------------------+
only showing top 20 rows
```

In the final query, we restrict it to Plato (identified by vertex ID 7662 as reported in the preceding results) and find people from the "absent" table (which represents triangles with the third leg absent). Again, we strive to prefer well-known people by preferring all three vertices in the triangle to have high degree. Notice how easy it is in SQL to calculate the vertex degree. In considering this final query's results for potentially missing edges emanating from Plato, the top two candidates are Marx and Sartre. But these two intentionally took stances opposite to Plato's, so it's not consistent with Wikipedia's usage of "influences" to say they were influenced by him. The third person on the list, Foucault, spoke favorably of Plato's Letters, but more from the standpoint of an analysis, given his own already-decided philosophy. It's questionable whether it's appropriate to apply the "<influences>" edge in this case:

```
absent.sqlContext.sql(
  "SELECT v1.attr, " +
  "       v3.attr, " +
  "       SUM(v1.outdegree * v2.outdegree * v3.outdegree) AS score " +
  "FROM   a " +
```

```
            "WHERE  v1.id=7662 " +
            "GROUP BY v1.attr, v3.attr " +
            "ORDER BY score DESC").collect
res24: Array[org.apache.spark.sql.Row] = Array([<Plato>,<Karl_Marx>,7139388],
[<Plato>,<Jean-Paul_Sartre>,3143640], [<Plato>,<Michel_Foucault>,2871606],
[<Plato>,<Gilles_Deleuze>,2689128], [<Plato>,<Henri_Bergson>,2179128],
      [<Plato>,<Maurice_Merleau-Ponty>,2088450]...
```

A possible improvement to the scoring system might be to penalize the search whenever the birth dates are vastly different. After all, is it fair to say a philosopher from the ancient world can directly "influence" someone who has already adopted a modernist philosophy? Doing such a search would involve bringing in the YAGO file yagoDate-Facts.tsv and merging it with the yagoFacts graph, and then searching for more complex graph fragments that also involve the edge type "<wasBornOnDate>."

10.5 Summary

- Scala is the native language of Spark and GraphX.
- Using GraphX from Java 7 is complex and requires ten times as much code as Scala.
- Using GraphX from Java 8 requires only slightly less code than from Java 7 because Java 8 lambdas can only be used straightaway in a couple of places.
- It is unknown as of Spark 1.6 whether and when GraphX will support R and Python, the other two languages Spark supports.
- The combination of Zeppelin and d3.js provides a powerful notebook capability that's the equivalent of the REPL but with inline graph visualization.
- Further tweaking of graph visualization requires knowledge of d3.js or falling back to using Gephi.
- Spark Job Server adds a REST interface to Spark, which means that when used with GraphX, graph data can be kept around in RDDs, and an almost-database can be cobbled together.
- GraphFrames is a new library that makes it easier to query graphs for particular vertices or graph fragments using a combination of SQL and a subset of Cypher.
- GraphFrames, because it is built on Spark SQL, performs well due to the optimization layers, known as Catalyst and Tungsten, that are built into Spark SQL.

appendix A
Installing Spark

This appendix covers
- The quickest ways to get started in Spark
- Using virtual machines (VMs) to run Spark
- Using Amazon Web Services / Elastic Map/Reduce to run Spark

Using Spark typically means first having 1) Hadoop installed and 2) a cluster of machines to run them on. The simplest scenario is if you're doing GraphX work for your job and your job already has a Hadoop/Spark cluster set up that you can use. If that's not the case, this appendix is for you. It describes various options where you don't necessarily need either Hadoop or a cluster of machines.

The three options described in this appendix are as follows:

1 *On a local virtual machine*—Cloudera QuickStart VM (with Hadoop and Spark preinstalled and ready to use).
2 *On your Linux or OS X laptop, desktop, or VM*—Hadoop is not necessary.
3 *In the cloud*—Amazon Web Services.

A few developers prefer to do all development on virtual machines, and this appendix reflects that not-too-common bias. (In this context, we mean VMs hosted on one's laptop using VMWare Player or VirtualBox, not VMs in the cloud.) Multiple VMs allow one to easily work on multiple projects, each with their own environments, versions of Java, versions of Scala, OS versions, and so on. And VMs are easy to hand over to colleagues and team members. As a final benefit, VMs allow one to copy and paste to/from the host OS where email client, familiar tools, and data files reside.

Using Spark directly on Windows is strongly discouraged, even by the Spark team, although it is supposed to be possible using Cygwin. Using Spark directly on Mac OS X is much better, of course, due to OS X having ancestry in BSD UNIX. Still, our preference is to run Spark in a VM running CentOS, which is a "community" clone of Red Hat Enterprise that in 2014 gained support from Red Hat itself. Red Hat and derivatives/clones such as CentOS and Oracle Linux are used in many enterprises, so developing in Spark on CentOS ensures an environment close to what many organizations are doing in production.

A.1   *On a local virtual machine: CDH QuickStart VM*

The option that (usually) requires minimum effort is to download the Cloudera QuickStart VM. It's available for three different VM host software packages: VMWare, VirtualBox, and KVM. Each sports different features and different licensing. We use VirtualBox the most because it's GPL and can be used for free, even for commercial purposes. We haven't used KVM because it requires Linux to be the host OS, and our host OS is usually Windows or OS X.

By using the Cloudera QuickStart VM, you get Cloudera's Hadoop package (called CDH) preinstalled, which automatically starts when the VM starts. Because CDH has included Spark and GraphX, you get GraphX as part of this VM.

To use this VM, you'll need the following:

- At least 8 GB of physical RAM because the VM requires 4 GB
- A fast enough Internet connection (or enough patience) to download the 3 GB compressed (.7z) file
- Your BIOS configured to allow hosting of 64-bit guest VMs

This last one is tricky. For security reasons, many if not most computers have disabled by default the capability to host 64-bit guest VMs, even though they are 64-bit computers and are able to run 64-bit base operating systems. First, if you don't know how to enter the BIOS settings screen for your computer, you may need to Google that for your particular laptop or desktop computer. Second, if you're unable to find the option to allow hosting of 64-bit guest VMs once you're in the BIOIS settings screen, you may need to Google the keywords "BIOS VT-x" (for Intel processors) or "BIOS AMD-V" (for AMD processors) in conjunction with the model name of your computer.

Once you've launched the Cloudera QuickStart VM, to log in, use the following credentials:

Username: cloudera
Password: cloudera

A major downside of the Cloudera QuickStart VM is that because it brings up all the Hadoop services automatically, you're left with only 800 MB of free memory in the default 4 GB configuration of the VM. This is limiting due to the manner of immutable data in which Spark works in general, and GraphX in particular; the largest practical dataset you can use is about 30 MB. Another disadvantage, compared to using AWS or a physical cluster of multiple machines, is that you'll see limited parallelism, the hallmark of Spark. Spark will parallelize over the multiple cores of a single-CPU computer, but you won't see the massive speedup for extremely large datasets that Spark is famous for.

A.1.1   VirtualBox tweaks

If you're opting for the VirtualBox version of the Cloudera QuickStart VM, here are some tips and tweaks:

- Use "Import" rather than "New" or "Open" to initially load the VM into Virtual-Box after you download and uncompress it. This can be confusing to those who are used to VMWare.
- Within the VirtualBox Manager window, you can set various settings for the VM:
- The QuickStart VM defaults to one core. Because today's computers have 4, 8, or even more cores, increase this via System > Processor > Processors.
- If your computer has more than 8 GB of RAM, increase the memory allotted to the VM via System > Motherboard > Base Memory. A good guideline is to subtract 4 GB from your physical RAM (for example, if your computer has 16 GB of physical RAM, set the VM to use 12 GB).
- Copying and pasting between the VM and your host OS is extremely useful, yet it's disabled by default. Change it to "Bidirectional" via General > Advanced > Shared Clipboard.
- Sharing files is also useful. Add a shared directory via Shared Folders. Click the folder icon with the plus sign to create a new shared directory. For Windows, for example, you can use "C:\" for "Folder Path" and "c" (lowercase) for "Folder Name." Then, once you've launched the VM, from a terminal shell you would do the following:

```
sudo mkdir /c
sudo mount -t vboxsf c /c
```

A.2   Onto your laptop and Hadoopless: Linux or OS X

The dirty secret is that you don't really need Hadoop to run Spark. Let us qualify that: if your "cluster" consists of a single node, you definitely don't need Hadoop. The only thing Spark uses Hadoop for is reading and writing files, and if all the Spark processes have access to a common file system (namely, your plain old local file system), then there's no need for a distributed store like HDFS, Cassandra, or Amazon S3.

As a matter of simplicity, if your main goal is to become familiar with the GraphX API and not necessarily to operate on huge datasets and performance-tune them, then installing Spark by itself onto a UNIX-like operating system (Linux or OS X) is perfectly acceptable.

The scenarios where this would be applicable are as follows:

- Your laptop or desktop has Linux as its base OS.
- Your laptop or desktop is set up to dual-boot (for example, using Grub or BootIt Bare Metal) into different operating systems, one of which is Linux.

- Your laptop or desktop has OS X as its base OS.
- You've created a custom VM with Linux as the VM's OS (see next section).
- You're using a VM in the cloud—for example, Amazon AWS, Azure, or even a web-hosting company VM.

You can download "pre-built" versions of Spark from the Apache website, pre-built for various versions of Hadoop (Hadoop 1.x, Hadoop 2.x, MapR, and so forth). Because in this option we won't use Hadoop at all, it doesn't matter which one you pick. As long as you don't try to read or write HDFS files, you'll be fine.

Download the Spark tgz file, uncompress it, and you're ready to go. To use only the Spark Shell, you don't even need Scala installed, just Java. To build Spark programs in Scala, though, you'll need to install Scala.

A.2.1 *On a custom local virtual machine*

Combining the preceding two ideas—to be both Hadoopless and on a virtual machine—is another convenient option, with the following advantages:

- Without HDFS and other Hadoop services running, you gain an extra gigabyte or two compared to using the pre-built Cloudera QuickStart VM.
- Compared to the option of installing Spark as your computer's (or VM in the cloud's) base OS, a VM has the benefits described at the beginning of this appendix.

Creating a VM from scratch is non-trivial. It's a lot of steps—selecting the right options, tweaking a lot of things—that are out of the scope of this book but that you can Google. Or you can try to find a pre-built VM for the virtual machine host software of your choice and for the Linux flavor of your preference and download that.

A.3 *In the cloud: Amazon Web Services*

Amazon Web Services provides dozens of different cloud services, the most well-known of which are S3 for storage and EC2 for elastic compute. For the purposes of Hadoop and Spark, Amazon offers Elastic MapReduce (EMR). EMR allows you to manage S3 and EC2 resources to bring up an entire Hadoop cluster (with or without Spark).

The advantage of AWS EMR over the options described previously is that you can actually run on a cluster, realize the benefit of parallelization, handle large datasets, and become familiar with developing Spark applications for YARN and submitting Spark applications to a YARN-powered cluster.

The obvious downside is that AWS isn't free. The other downside is that if you use the AWS automatic Spark cluster, there's no way to pause it. It has to be completely destroyed every time you would otherwise want to walk away and pause it. There's no way as of the time of writing to pause an AWS Spark cluster to prevent billing. That means you have to be conscientious and save your work on S3. But there's no way, for example, to leave data stored in the REPL and come back to it later.

appendix B
Gephi visualization software

Chapter 4 contains code to generate .gexf files, the native file format of Gephi. Downloading and installing Gephi from http://gephi.github.io is straightforward (it's available for OS X, Windows, and Linux), but its user interface can be intimidating at first. This appendix points you to the most important UI elements—enough to get you started—and you can then explore the remaining rich set of features on your own.

B.1 Laying out your environment

Gephi has dockable windows, much like an IDE. Figure B.1 is how we used Gephi when generating some of the diagrams in this book. The three dockable windows to choose from the Window drop-down menu are shown in figure B.2. Once they're displayed, drag and drop them to the arrangement shown in figure B.1.

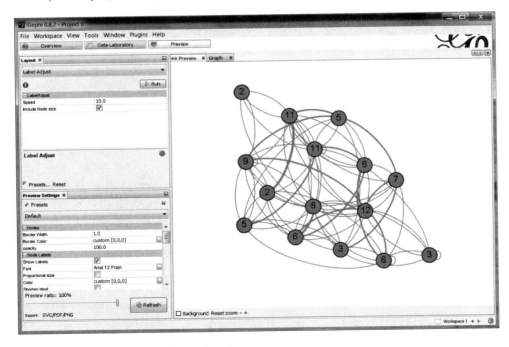

Figure B.1   Gephi's dockable window layout

You'll notice the Graph tab, which, given its position and name, seems like an important tab, but it's for doing processing on the graph. Because we're typically doing graph processing in GraphX and are interested in Gephi for its visualization capability, you should ignore the Graph tab at first.

Figure B.2 The three windows to choose from the Window drop-down menu

B.2 Basic recipe

Here's the basic loop of steps you'll typically do to visualize:

1 Adjust something in the Layout or Preview Settings window.
2 Click the Refresh button in the Preview Settings window.
3 Pan the Preview window via right-click-drag and adjust zoom via the buttons at the bottom of the Preview window.

B.3 Key settings

Gephi has a lot of options. This section covers some of the more useful ones.

B.3.1 Layout window

Here you can choose a layout algorithm and its parameters. Some layout algorithms are incremental (they tweak what has already been laid out) and some start from scratch. You'll want to choose a "start from scratch" algorithm first and then tweak it with an "incremental" algorithm only if necessary. The available algorithms are shown in figure B.3. Usually, Force Atlas is a good starting point because it reliably produces reasonable results.

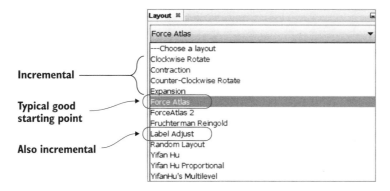

Figure B.3 Available layout algorithms from the drop-down list inside the Layout window. The ones we haven't labeled as `Incremental` are all first-class layout algorithms that perform a complete layout from scratch. The incremental ones nudge around an already-laid-out graph.

For small graphs, you may need to first adjust "Repulsion strength" (or "Optimal distance" in other algorithms) to a much larger number, as highlighted in figure B.4. Gephi is designed to handle very large graphs with hundreds or thousands of vertices, and its default settings provide for very short edges. For graphs with a dozen or a few dozen vertices, you'll want to make the edges longer by increasing "Repulsion strength" or "Optimal distance."

May need to vastly increase Repulsion Strength (or Optimal Distance in other algorithms) for smaller graphs

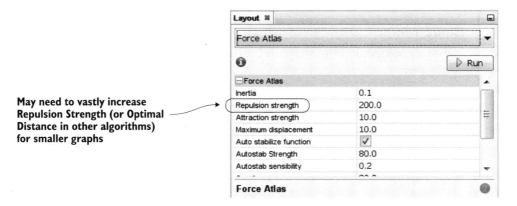

Figure B.4   Key adjustment so that small graphs don't end up as a tiny, scrunched-up bunch

After making any setting adjustment in the Layout window, click the Run button (seen in figure B.4) and then click the Refresh button in the Preview Settings window.

B.3.2   *Preview Settings window*

Important settings in the Preview Settings window are highlighted in figure B.5.

> **NOTE**   Gephi uses the term *nodes* to mean vertices. In this book, we've used *nodes* to mean computers participating in a cluster for cluster computing.

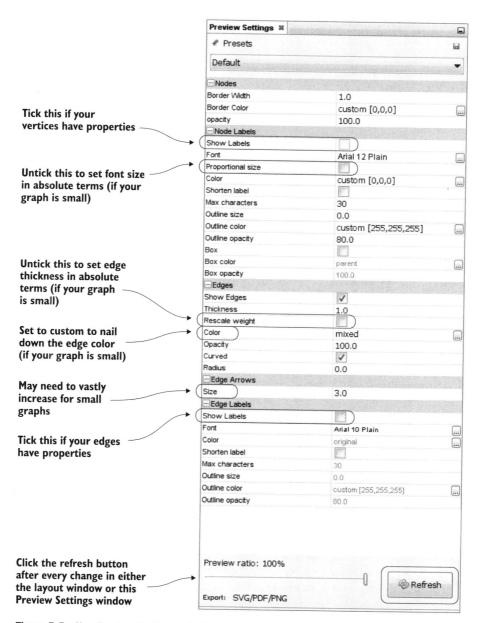

Tick this if your vertices have properties

Untick this to set font size in absolute terms (if your graph is small)

Untick this to set edge thickness in absolute terms (if your graph is small)

Set to custom to nail down the edge color (if your graph is small)

May need to vastly increase for small graphs

Tick this if your edges have properties

Click the refresh button after every change in either the layout window or this Preview Settings window

Figure B.5   Key Preview Settings window settings

appendix C
Resources:
where to go for more

C.1 Spark

The number of books on Spark finally started growing in 2015—six years after Spark development first began. But Spark development is still moving fast, and the best resources are online.

Apache mailing lists

As with any open source project, especially one from Apache, the mailing lists are the best sources of information, and subscribing to them—and asking questions when you can't find answers on the web—should be considered the minimum you have to do. The mailing lists are known as user@spark.apache.org and dev@spark.apache.org. You can subscribe to them from https://spark.apache.org/community.html.

Databricks forums

Databricks is the commercialization of Spark that offers a commercial product of a Spark notebook in the cloud. But the forums on www.databricks.com aren't limited to only the commercial product. As a large percentage of the commits to Apache Spark come from Databricks, the Databricks forums also contain a lot of general-purpose information about Spark, including future plans that pertain to the open source Apache Spark as well as the commercial Databricks product.

Conference and meetup videos

There are four major sources of Spark videos. None should be overlooked; they are all outstanding. Spark is moving fast, and watching these videos on your smartphone while on the treadmill or as a bedtime story is sometimes the only way to keep up:

1. Spark Summit (West, East, and Europe)
2. AMPLab AMPCamp
3. Bay Area Spark Meetup
4. O'Reilly Strata Conference (West and East)

Jira

If staying current with Spark is important to you, there's no substitute to following the Spark Jira. Create an Apache Jira account if you don't already have one, list all the issues every day in reverse chronological order, and click Watch for the issues that are important to you. That way you can know what new features, bug fixes, performance improvements, architectural changes, and support for third-party systems (file systems, cluster managers, database connectors, compression formats, serialization schemes, and so on) are coming down the way—and, more importantly, which versions they're being targeted for.

There are some long-standing gems of planned features buried within Jira from the early days that are still being worked on or planned for, so, as painful and time-consuming as it may sound, the first time you list Spark Jira tickets, it's probably worth your while to go through *all* of those that are still open.

Twitter

If you think Twitter is just about celebrities and that nothing useful could possibly be expressed in 140 characters, you're in for a surprise.

There's a lot on Twitter in terms of Big Data, data science, and machine learning. You can regard Twitter as a link aggregator to hot or important blog posts, news stories, or Git repositories.

spark-packages.org

Because the developers of Apache Spark are reluctant to overload the official distribution with too many features and sub-packages, they set up the website spark-packages .org. Available add-on packages are broken up into categories such as machine learning, graphs, Python, and so on.

AMPLab

Spark came out of AMPLab, and AMPLab continues to develop new modules that work with Spark, as well as some other brand-new technologies unrelated to Spark. Modules that come out of AMPLab have a tendency to either be incorporated directly into the Apache Spark distribution (such as GraphX, Catalyst, which became Spark SQL, and SparkR) or at least semi-officially supported, such as Tachyon.

Google Scholar Alerts

You're likely familiar with Google Alerts, which sends you an email whenever a page is updated. But there's something completely different called Google Scholar Alerts, part of scholar.google.com, which sends an email whenever a new paper is published that cites a paper you're tracking.

If you set Google Scholar Alerts on some of the seminal Spark papers, such as Matei Zaharia's "Resilient Distributed Datasets: A Fault-Tolerant Abstraction for In-Memory Cluster Computing" or Gonzalez et al's "GraphX: Graph Processing in a Distributed

Dataflow Framework," you can keep track of the latest advances in academia before they become commercialized.

Author blogs

If you do all that we've suggested so far, you won't need to read these blogs. But if you want to save time and read only a distilled version of what's coming in the future for Spark, Big Data, data science, and machine learning—at least through Michael Malak's personal crystal ball—then his blogs are good resources:

- http://technicaltidbit.com
- http://datascienceassn.org/blogs/michaelmalak

C.2   Scala

The best Scala resources are books. Some Scala books are quite long. But because Scala has so many tricks, an alternative is to get the ones that are encyclopedias of tricks:

- *Scala Cookbook* by Alvin Alexander (O'Reilly, 2013)
- *Scala Puzzlers* by Andrew Phillips (Artima, 2014)

C.3   Graphs

There are tons of books on graph theory, many of them highly theoretical, either for use as college textbooks or for use by researchers. Practitioners, however, may find the following useful:

- *Graph-Based Natural Language Processing and Information Retrieval* by Rada Mihalcea and Dragomir Radev (Cambridge University Press, 2011)
- *Graph Databases* by Ian Robinson et al (O'Reilly, 2015)

This book is not intended to teach you Scala, but rather provides Scala tips along the way to help you along, under the assumptions that Scala may not be your first and most familiar language and that you may not have seen all the requisite Scala tricks before. For books on learning Scala, see appendix C.

Below is a list of the Scala tips sprinkled throughout the book:

index